EYE OF THE CHILD

ONWARDS, A FULFILLED LIFE

21st Nov. 2019

For Phil.

May your wheels keep turning as we embrace the mysteries of life. Travel well with that smile in your heart.

Walt

First published in October 2017 by Wayan Lengar
Second impression - January 2019
Copyright © Walter John Thornhill
www.walter-thornhill.com

Cover design courtesy of The Brooklyn Brothers
Layout and typesetting courtesy of Izak Janse van Rensburg
Set in 10.5 pt on 14pt Minion Pro

Printed and bound by Novus Print Solutions
The paper used is Holmen Cream, which is FSC certified.

Certain names of relatives changed to avoid unnecessary anguish.

A CIP catalogue record for this title is available from the British Library.

ISBN 978-1-9998642-0-0

To You

and to that place,
in all of us,
that grows from healing . . .

CONTENTS

FOREWORD

BY WILLIAM AYOT

On the surface, this is the memoir of a successful banker, business consultant and corporate finance director, the kind of prosperous insider you might meet at a London cocktail party, or a week-end country house party. More than that, it is the story of a sportsman, someone who knows the loneliness of endurance training, the reality of breaking through the cyclist's wall of pain, and the elation of bursting from the pack to win the stage in that final, wild sprint for the line. Most importantly it is the tale of a lost and often neglected little boy, shunted from pillar to post and hurt in ways that no youngster should be hurt. This is a tale of survival.

I first met Walter Thornhill through what was rather grandly called the men's movement, a random gathering of teachers, poets, shamans and everyday men who met at workshops and conferences, back in the nineteen nineties, to explore the deeper issues of masculinity. By delving into the underworld of myths and wonder tales, we were able to explore our naivety, our shadowy behaviours, and our emotional incompetence. By talking-out the pain that lays beneath the surface in most men's lives, we found ourselves cleansing the often-overlooked, and rarely-healed wounding that is the male lot.

Over the years Walter and I kept in touch, in that desultory way that men do when they have profound experiences and unfinished business in common. We would talk through the odd local difficulty or share our occasional ups and downs, doing each other favours as we could and generally maintaining a kind of friendship through a sense of fellow-feeling and a typically male distance. It was therefore no surprise, after writing and publishing my own story of survival, denial and growth, to discover that Walter was doing much the same sort of thing over the same period of time.

Walter Thornhill is an adult child. That is to say, he is a fully-grown survivor of alcoholic parenting. Growing up with a father, and particularly with a mother who drank to excess, he had visited upon him many of the hurts and traumas experienced by any boy or girl when the primary focus of a parent's life is the bottle and not their child. While he never resorts to such an easy label, his book is infused with the bewilderment, shock and inescapable diminishment of the adult child. It is also filled with the self-determination and tenacity of the child who seeks out love wherever he can find it; who finds a place of belonging when no such thing is on offer at home. This book is a testament to Walter Thornhill's resolve to travel beyond mere witness and return with the gold of healing and understanding.

As an adult child myself, and a frequent flyer down the routes that he travels in this book, I was profoundly moved by young Walter's loyalty to his mother and yearning for his absent father. I was also touched by his bafflement, his constant ability to bounce back, and his life-preserving ability to dip into and out of denial. Truth in alcoholic homes is known to be a delicate and perishable thing, often bent out of shape by drunken cruelties and the shame of waking to the carnage of the night before. What we often overlook in such circumstances, is the need we have as children to maintain the fiction that all is well and that our carers – no matter how lost – remain reliable sources of solidity and safety. Following Walter's slow dawning around his mother's helpless slide into alcoholic viciousness brought it home to me, once again, how the growing human mind has the most extraordinary ability to unpick its denial systems as the ability to 'handle the truth' develops with age.

To survive in such difficult formative circumstances, one needs more than the random kindness and generosity of 'onlookers' caught so well in the pages of this book; one needs a focus and a passion, a kind of saving obsession. The great mythologist and men's work leader Michael Meade, once said that to thrive in the wide world, a boy needs a cosmology and a skill. In Walter's case, he found his skill, which he terms his 'anchor', in sport, specifically in road and track cycling. We follow his development from schoolboy tyro to Springbok status, to representing his country, and becoming a sporting celebrity in his chosen field.

Like many of their alcoholic parents, adult children are invariably both sensitive and gifted. The discovery and development of their gift – and the necessary drive that accompanies it – is what can turn a shambolic start in life, into concrete achievement and ultimately self-realisation. Walter's cycling career is just such a triumph. Having come from a similar background, where encouragement and support were rarely given in the home, I was right there with Walter, at the road side in Mozambique as the peloton pelted through, cheering him on as he found meaning and self-respect on the track, and finally applauding as he crossed the finishing line, a fully-fledged champion – and alive.

As for a cosmology – by which I mean a map of our surroundings, their cultural history, mythic topography, and belief systems – *Eye of the Child* is set in the polyglot, many cultured suburbs of South Africa from the nineteen fifties through to the sixties and seventies. In suburbs and villages with reassuringly English names, we meet a broad mix of Afrikaner, Dutch, and Greek friends and family members, their distinctive voices and stories weaving into and around Walter's own as he moves from school to school and neighbourhood to neighbourhood. Furthermore, the whole is played out before the vast rotting edifice of the already crumbling apartheid system, with its atrocities, betrayals, cruelties and petty indignities. Piquant stories of friends and family are added into the mix, balancing the hidden and traumatic events of suburban family life with the ever-expanding trauma of post-colonial South Africa. Thus, the traumas of hearth and home are paralleled by the ever-present, and equally worsening viciousness of the apartheid regime.

A journey through shame then, and humiliation – private, public, cultural and personal. We follow Walter as he grows and learns – arriving at the thresholds of manhood, military service and marriage only part-formed and yet fully independent; naïve in many ways yet street-wise and savvy; full of hope yet depressive and despairing – the eternal paradox of the adult child.

It's important to say that this is not a 'victim book'. It takes pains to point out the vulnerabilities and 'backstories' of all the major players, as well as the other kids and adults that surrounded, and inevitably influenced, the life-hungry and observant young Walter. We don't get the endless litany of accusations and self-justifications we might expect in such a book. We find a tightly observed and often amusingly detailed accretion of experiences, the laying-down of a life, and the alternate, sediment-like seams of wounding and hidden potential that go into the making of a man. We also find that it is written with a great deal of love.

A word of warning. Don't read this book if you are looking for a well-wrought treatise on the incidence of alcoholism in middle-class white families in post-colonial Cape Town, or a literary masterpiece about the history of cycling in South Africa. This is neither an academic text, a sporting history of the sixties and seventies, nor a platitudinous new age self-help book. It is infinitely more urgent, more raw, and more demanding than that. In fact, Walter Thornhill's words and images tumble out in such a stream-of-consciousness rush that (despite a clear explanation for this in the text) a reader can find themselves momentarily disorientated or confused by both the use of language and the intensity of Walter's *need to tell.* This is a deliberate choice on the author's part, a way of dropping us into the perplexities, upheavals and gradual clearings of his path. It's well-worth staying with this, as the raw unfiltered nature of the telling adds to the depth and quality of the read. All in all, this rousing and engaging book bears all the authentic hallmarks of one man's unique and often fascinating experience, delivered in the first full rush of heartfelt and occasionally visceral recall. I hope you enjoy the ride!

William Ayot
Author of *"Re-enchanting the Forest:*
Meaningful Ritual in a Secular World"
Vinalhaven, Maine.
August 2017

CHAPTER 1
SURRENDER

London - December 2003

The results had been mislaid; it had been over three weeks since the scan. That morning, I contacted the cardiologist's practice. A few hours later the phone rang, "The Doctor will see you at five this evening at Saint Mary's, after surgery."

Routine I thought, *more of the same*, but with hardly a greeting, and devoid of any bedside manner, he blurted: "You are a walking time bomb and can die at any moment."

My anger rose, I was furious, "But . . . you said everything was OK. What's changed?"

Three weeks earlier, after the angiogram, he discovered that my left and right coronary arteries lay next to each other, unusual in itself.

"It's the MRI . . . you have a malignant variant of an anomaly that leads to sudden death. Your left coronary artery traverses over the top of your heart between the aorta and the pulmonary artery. Only a dozen or so cases exist in the world; the longest known survivor died at the age of twenty-eight, the others in their teens – it's Sudden Death Syndrome!"

I was stunned, in shock and vaguely heard, "We can operate in the New Year. Unfortunately, the surgeons are away now for their Christmas break."

Perfunctorily I enquired, "Can I still go skiing? I don't want to disappoint my son." We were to leave two days later.

"I'll speak to the surgeon and let you know tomorrow."

I was fifty, more or less single parenting my fourteen-year-old son, Stefan. It was a dark, wet, winter Friday evening – the 19th December, a year after my divorce. Dismally I sat in the car, watching the rain pounding the windscreen, as I reflected numbly . . . feeling overwhelmingly alone, I called my friend Benji, who lives in South Africa, and burst into tears – the world seemed pretty grim and frightening at that moment.

Forbidden to ski, I accompanied Stefan and rewrote my will while he enjoyed the slopes. Each morning, upon awakening, I would smile – grateful to see him and be alive.

Introspectively, I accepted my fate. I had lived a rich, full life and was unafraid of death. My biggest concern was for Stefan – close friends were asked more than they realised – *in the event of my death, would they please remember to call him every three months or so to enquire about his well-being.* What I really wanted was for them to hold him in community, to acknowledge him and in so doing, provide him with a sense of belonging – something indigenous tribes do so naturally.

A Peruvian shaman I knew, who in an altered state of consciousness looked at my heart, confirmed that there was nothing untoward. A clairvoyant also specifically warned against the surgery. My anger rose – how could they be so authoritative at such a life-threatening moment? In my shocked state, I had surrendered to Western Medicine, turning my back on the alternative paths I had walked.

In January, my sister Gayle, eight years younger than me and Piet, my childhood neighbour and friend, travelled to London from South Africa to be by my side during the operation. That month, I cancelled two open heart surgeries, for distinct reasons. The second time, it was the night before my pre-med when my friend, Dr Peter Stubbs, a cardiologist, called.

"What's up? Apologies for not calling sooner."

I explained my heart predicament as best I could.

"Fax me the various reports now. I'm at the hospital."

Two hours later: "Cancel the operation – implanting the left coronary directly into the aorta is flawed says Amrani. He is the world's leading coronary expert and has just taken over from Professor Magdi Yacoub. Amrani knows someone in Sweden. Give us a week and we'll get back to you."

Feeling despondent, I feebly asked, "What do I say?"

"Tell them you are going away for a week on holiday and that you'll let them know thereafter."

Disempowered, I made the call – the cardiologist's secretary a bully. "Mr Thornhill, this is the second heart surgery you've cancelled. They are professional men you know. You can't just keep cancelling." I retreated further into my shell.

The one week became two – it seemed an eternity. The Swedish lead proved ineffective. For the next three months, I lived in limbo with the inevitability of not knowing exactly what the future held as Peter continued his research, and Stefan, living with me, accompanied the journey . . .

Was this incident a manifestation of my emotional heart, bruised in childhood; and what drove me onwards through my youth?

CHAPTER 2
FLASHBACKS

Bali - 10 years later

While on a sabbatical in Bali, unexpectedly, I had a flashback – the presence and love of Aunty Ronnie permeated my consciousness – and I wondered what it was all about. Astounded and overwhelmed, but in the next instant, let it go, attaching no further importance to it.

Days rolled by . . . surrounded by the lush tropical vegetation, I felt so at home there. The thatched roof bungalow and the soft cooing of the doves emphasised my memories of a distant time growing up in South Africa. It took me back to Aunty's country retreat in Athol, a few kilometres north of her city flat in Johannesburg.

My mother and I would spend the weekends out there – enjoying the most delightful gardens imaginable, all set on an acre of rolling land, and tended with love and care by Aunty and her gardener. I busied myself exploring the garden shed and vegetable patches, only to laze away on the long garden swing, returning for a welcome lunch under the evocative smell of the thatch bungalow.

It took forever to get there in her old-fashioned, round-backed Chevrolet, which I did not mind. The smell of the leather seats was so luxurious. At times the excitement of riding up front, the sudden braking and Aunty's natural reflex as her protective outstretched arm braced my forward movement, long before seat belts were invented, was marred only by my unspoken irritation as I grew older. Could she not see I was robust enough to protect myself? Those moments with Aunty Ronnie were special.

In the early Balinese mornings, I would often hear the clatter of plates in the open kitchen, a thief perhaps? No, only a little rascal who true to her shy nature would swiftly dash off. I was lucky once to spot her, a wader, with her two chicks in tow as she tentatively walked by. I revered her presence and did not flinch a muscle lest she saw me. She had a small white patch on her breast, a hint of russet colouring under her tail, which she would flick to alert her brood of impending danger, while the rest of her body was black. That black-white ratio was roughly similar to the ethnicity in South Africa during the apartheid era, where I lived for my first thirty-three years before moving to London for business reasons.

On one of those balmy Balinese nights, I awoke from a dream, drifting . . . and could retrace my steps with absolute clarity through the haven of Aunty Ronnie and Uncle Jack's simple one-bedroom flat: 54 Constantia Court, Koch Street, Joubert Park, Johannesburg. I was four or five years old. It seemed so large then and had everything I could ever wish for, even a balcony where on occasion tiny origami paper water bombs were prepared and lobbed upon unsuspecting pedestrians below. Of course, the fun was in the preparation and the anticipation of the outcome, but I was never actually brave enough to watch the point of impact; justifying it would give my strategic fifth-floor position away and then I might really be in trouble. The intended victims would have heard my innocent, uncontrollable laughter from behind my lofty barricaded vantage point. It was delightful growing up there, a week a lifetime, and being mischievous was the sensible way, checked by the occasional reprimand.

Looking out from the balcony, the railway station terminus was on the left and Joubert Park on the right. The flats had a resident caretaker, who lived on the ground floor – it seemed so posh – while my mother and I lived across the road in a very simple flat. Aunty would sometimes send me on errands to the caretaker. I was rather scared of him. He seemed all-powerful and appeared to have the answers to many things way beyond my comprehension.

There was a small swimming pool on the top of the building, the ninth floor. The water was always cold and peppered with soot. At the neighbour's cocktail parties, I would hear them whisper about the crack in the pool, which fuelled my fear that it might leak and flood the flats below. Its brilliant blue colour was the only agreeable thing about it.

I was never allowed to be there alone, yet going to the park on my own was fine. There was an art gallery, a botanical garden and an open area which became my playground, seemingly so enormous but it was not really. I doubt parents would allow it today but I enjoyed that freedom. Yes, there were moments when I could sense danger and learned to rapidly move away.

Sometimes, instead of going to the park, I took the small street, out of curiosity, that ran towards the station. I was the only white boy there – it was strange and I felt apprehensive being there alone. The park was preferable.

All races inhabited it, but there were strange signs on the benches saying WHITES ONLY or *NET BLANKES*, the Afrikaans equivalent.

My mom and I moved to our flat across the road from Aunty Ronnie, upon my parents' divorce – I was four years old. Not that I understood it, other than that my Dad had to live at the coast for his heart, nor do I recall him visiting us while we lived there.

My father, Walter Albert Thornhill, had been a successful businessman. The financing of Tropic Airline, a charter airline, was one venture too many. Seven months after I was born – he was declared insolvent – remaining so for the next ten years, a broken man and an alcoholic. Measured by his own standards, he never really recovered from his perceived fall from grace, dying from a heart attack at the age of sixty-four – I was nineteen.

I held on to the last of his infrequent, short father-son letters, like a talisman for my fabricated emotional solace. It attempted to assuage his sense of guilt for a lack of proper parenting – *Maybe now I can finally give you something that I could not previously do.* This was his last venture, an aluminium utensil manufacturing company that was to be his panacea – it never was. This I knew, trying to run the business at the age of nineteen. But really what I wanted, and was silently screaming for, was emotional support, love and above all, a sense of belonging.

After turning eight I visited my Dad annually in Cape Town for three weeks; our December summer holiday. I always looked forward to my time there, and by fifteen, the competitive cycling arena allowed more trips – an absolute bonus.

My mother, Desiree Thearle Ridewood, and George Lostrom, my stepfather of Greek descent, married when I was seven, and my sister Gayle was born a year later. George was a jovial sort with thickset spectacles that could light a fire.

Life was confusing and complicated in my early years. Initially, I felt safe and loved by my mother and Aunty Ronnie – mischievously lost in my world of paper bombs and detective games, like thumbing through Aunty's cheque stubs, while never forgetting the adventures in Athol. Then, the emotional fallout from our puzzling family was fuelled by the damaging aspects of my father's and mother's alcohol addiction – my comprehensible recollection of this was from the age of eight onwards for my father, while for my mother, a few years later. Clearly, my father had this affliction since my birth.

The Lord created the World in six days and rested on the Sabbath. My mother's strewn path of ignited nocturnal havoc only abated on the seventh; her day of rest and refrain from *drinking*.

Not surprisingly, cycling became my way of being and its fraternity my greater family; a substitute for our peculiar home dynamics both in Johannesburg and Cape Town. Of course, there were reprieves and delightful anecdotes, sprinkled with dashes of humour, along the way.

Good therapists know the issues are rooted far deeper within the family constellation. Some kids turn to drugs and alcohol, their cry for help. That was not my route, a sort of irony really, as the competitive cycling arena has been known for performance enhancing drug abuse. Initially, I was unaware of its use in South Africa and always wished to believe the best of my fellow cyclists. I did, of course, try stimulants like tea, coffee and a delectable exotic Italian recovery elixir.

Cycling saved me and was my escape. My achievements were never the cure-all, but unknowingly an enormous help from the earlier trauma, which surprisingly and unconsciously lived with me way into my adult life, affecting close relationships and other social interactions. Its hand showed in many ways.

My vivid recall of indelible moments, as will be retold, were imprinted on my psyche by my reactions to the extremes experienced on either side of the emotional spectrum – from hurt and distress to sheer joy.

. . . and, in my early fifties upon visiting my Aunt Beth, my father's youngest sister, I realised that I was unwittingly abandoned by both my father and mother, though differently . . . and it was in Bali that I decided to write and see where it might lead to . . .

CHAPTER 3

RITES OF PASSAGE

A STORM BREWS

How stupid I thought adults were, continually spewing their hypocrisy, an insult to those forced by circumstances to grow up sooner than expected – and by thirteen, I had discovered cycling.

My classmate challenged, "You've had your racing bike for over six months and haven't even raced?"

"Where can you race?" not knowing that there was such a sport.

"In Fontainebleau!"

Not the French one, but a northern suburb of Johannesburg some fifteen kilometres from Kensington, where I lived. It was my second year at Jeppe High School for Boys, a government school, which served me well, particularly after my schooling when society attempted to pigeonhole me. Jeppe, being the oldest school in Johannesburg, was recognised alongside other private schools; its reputation better than in reality.

Were they ideal years? Not really, but they were filled with all sorts of adventures requiring me to be street-smart and most importantly, to *hang on to my sandwiches*.

The Bezvalley cycling gang, as I dubbed them, would bunk, our colloquial term for absenteeism, during the winter months on Wednesdays, figuring it would have the least impact on our academic studies, as it was the shortest school day. I became an honorary member – the acceptance hinged on a willingness to do long training rides to Bapsfontein, some hundred and sixty kilometres there and back. We set out first thing on those frosty winter mornings.

Allan de Roche, Gavin Beetge and I were the core trio: Allan was the eldest, tall slim and wiser; Gavin, thick-set and strong, while as the youngest, I held on to their slipstream for dear life – a few years made an enormous difference.

Forty years later while travelling nostalgically down memory lane, Allan's home telephone number traced, I merely said, "This is your old Bapsfontein cycling buddy."

An immediate warm response followed, "Wally!", as I was affectionately known.

Allan came from a poor family, where other prevalent qualities so often shine through, like an immense richness and generosity of spirit with life lived in the *now*. My soul was crying for that type of nourishment and continued to do so, as I went about slowly but surely healing my spirit.

Every Sunday, we somehow managed to load the bicycles and all the gear into and onto their dilapidated family car, which steadfastly undertook the journey to Fontainebleau. There was a pecking order, Gavin, living closest, had the first preference and if a family member stayed behind I could tag along. Otherwise, I rode the 15 kilometres there, the 25 kilometre time trial race and home again; a distance of 55 kilometres. Johannesburg, deceptively hilly, made this quite an ordeal. I would arrive home, exhausted.

One of our Bapsfontein rides had an inauspicious start. Could the metaphorical *school gods* be punishing us for bunking? The outward journey had us riding into a strong headwind. We arrived hungry and spent of energy. We had no option other than to rest a while and replenish our food supplies from the local street vendors. The mouth-watering pineapples were washed down with thirst-quenching gulps of milk. We did not realise the combination was lethal. Our stomachs did, churning, while we slowly battled our way home, and a mighty battle it was.

The gods unleashed their wrath – lightning, thunder and relentless hailstones pelting our bodies. We were caught amid an afternoon thunderstorm, unusual for that time of year, in the middle of open farmlands with nowhere to take shelter. It was reminiscent of a typical Highveld summer afternoon's electrical storm that terrified me at the age of five, while on occasion staying on my own, when my mother was at work. Daylight darkened as the storm encroached; even the light bulbs made no difference. The repeated lightning flashes and deafening thunderclaps terrified me. At times they were so close together that it appeared as if the lightning had struck and an evil brooding force had entered our flat. Petrified, with nowhere to hide, I imagined being devoured and that I would surely die – the sanctity of Aunty Ronnie's home, so close, seemed distant and far away.

We grinned and bore the excruciating pain of the hailstones, ripping like bullets at our bodies, while the rain and wind lashed our faces. Our gear was rudimentary: no helmets, fancy UV protective sunglasses, lightweight rain jackets, nor mudguards. What we had was spirit, plenty of it, and our immediate concern was to make it home. We mustered our inner strength, kept our heads down and in a slow rhythmic delirium, clawed our way back.

It was a trade-off between avoiding the relentless and irritating splashes of the dirty tarmac water that shot straight into our eyes from the wheel of the rider ahead, while still trying to gain the advantage and protection from the slipstream. Energy was rapidly depleting and the looming onset of extreme fatigue and the dreaded *bonk*, a hypoglycaemic state, was to be avoided.

The battle was disheartening – would this seemingly endless journey never end? The storm broke, abruptly abating. My palpable concentration relaxed momentarily, but the daunting distance still to be covered, remained. Slowly, silently and monotonously, each rider took his turn at the front, carrying thoughts so far and no further. We were driven, believing *those long rides were essential to becoming a truly great cyclist* – that was my dream.

Deep down I knew the gods were not really vengeful but rather secretly smiling. They watched and admired our tenacity. That day, we unknowingly participated in our own rite of passage, something I would learn about later in life, while spending time with traditional indigenous tribes in Peru.

Yet, as a white child growing up in apartheid South Africa, I never had the opportunity to explore other local racial group's cultures and traditions – instead, indoctrinated by the pervasive thought *indigenous people were inferior* – but I never succumbed. The last vestiges of the colonial mindset disparagingly remained, like a broken timepiece, *they just don't understand the importance of time.*

THE DREADED KISS

Aunty Ronnie, my mother's older sister by seventeen years, took on the role of her surrogate mother. Towards the end of my mother's life we finally uncovered the reason for her perpetuated adult love-hate relationship with Aunty Ronnie. Similarly, in Aunty's latter years we found out that she had had an early hysterectomy – just nineteen – it must have been incredibly traumatic.

Uncle Jack, eight years older than Aunty, loved her dearly, and sadly died, aged sixty-four, of an untreatable heart condition. I was thirteen years old. Aunty nursed him at home during the last three years of his life – bedridden and continually on oxygen.

She often spoke of her loss, remained heartbroken and never remarried, nor did she accept the advances of some very interesting suitors. Her true love and soul companion – loved more than was imaginable and missed until her dying day.

Thinking back, Uncle Jack and Aunty Ronnie's marriage was an early example of what healthy relationships looked and felt like. This stood in stark contrast to my own family.

I liked Uncle Jack. He was tall, slim and dapper and always had a twinkle in his eye. He treated me like an adult, even when I was only seven or eight, and introduced me to a little frivolity – *talent scouting* – our Saturday morning ritual at his club, The Wanderers. While having our tea and sworn to secrecy, he would give me a running commentary about each blonde or brunette, as they graced the terrace. I never broke our bond and was enriched by new big words like brunette. Of course, I would far rather have been doing things boys of my age did, rather than his silly pastime.

A few years before he died, I remember his sage advice to my insurmountable problem – *exercising choice*. I loved and wished to play all sporting activities, but timetables clashed – it was very disappointing, as if my world would end. Calmly and skilfully, Uncle Jack guided me suggesting, *as tough as it was, I couldn't do everything*. So unfair I thought, but it forced me to make my first difficult decision.

What was it that made me feel so safe in their home? Was it the sense of empowerment knowing every nook and cranny or that I had surreptitiously opened Aunty's desk drawers and curiously thumbed through her diaries? Or was it my fascination watching her put on her tummy-tucking rubber corset, powder dusted, and extracted from a cylindrical cardboard container?

There were awkward moments like when my mom and I left, and I had to face that dreaded farewell compulsory parting kiss. Aunty was a big woman and her red lipstick lips would pout ready for the attack. That, and the smell of her breath like the dying of the species, made me do everything in my power to avoid the onslaught. At best, I would escape into the elevator where she could only plant a big friendly kiss onto the glass panel of the outside door. As the elevator descended, I breathed a sigh of relief until the next bout.

There was another, of a different type – custody. My aunt Selina, my father's elder sister and Adrian, her husband of Belgian origin, a psychiatrist whose bulbous eyes always seemed to be able to look right through me, were the culprits. They too, like Aunty Ronnie and Uncle Jack, could not have children and wanted to adopt me after my parent's divorce.

A feud ensued. Aunty Ronnie victoriously intervened ensuring I stayed with my mother, so the story goes. It was never spoken about other than in a fit of rage when my mother dropped her guard. But the die was cast, indeed set, leading to a roller coaster emotional ride that I would encounter in the years to come.

SACRED HEART

I had spent my first term of school at a state school in Johannesburg – I was six years old. Next stop was the Convent of the Sacred Heart in Potchefstroom, where I boarded for almost two years. No explanation was given for this change. Perhaps it allowed George and my mom to explore their early courtship, not that I realised it was happening.

Like Harry Potter, I would mostly travel by train – the eighty kilometres from Koch Street station close by to Aunty Ronnie's home. Preferable was the trip in George's old black Citroën with my mom, but alas it didn't happen again as we broke down causing George some dismay.

There was another convent, when I was three or four, albeit for a brief period, a time before Koch Street. I never knew why. A recent perchance conversation with Gayle, my sister, clarified – *I had to prove to the state that I could look after Walter when he was put in a convent,* our mother had shared with Gayle, who had assumed it was the Sacred Heart.

At the first convent, our dormitory was mixed. When the lights were turned off, sometimes, a few boys crept across to the girl's side; a simple herd instinct was to follow. There were no recriminations, merely a reminder to stay in our own beds.

Daily morning routine, under the watchful eyes of the stern nuns, was a quick brushing of our teeth, a basin face-wash, followed by a quick dash through the cold showers. Once a week, we had a hot bath. A lathering, then a quick jump into the warm water to rinse off. Pleasant you may think but alas, dreaded. Getting as close to the front of the naked queue of boys – a survival tactic – for the unchanged water soon became murky brown and awash with the slime of floating dead cells. I imagined being contaminated, and questioned emerging alive?

Then, enduring the inescapable gauntlet of inspection – *the thumb-rub* – a solid handgrip and any remaining dirt behind my ears dispersed with a friction burn. We never complained or even spoke about it, and maybe it was on those days we found our way into the other beds.

Sacred Heart was different – a kaleidoscope of experiences. The first day, I was accompanied to my classroom and introduced to the teacher. The class was already underway. While standing there and wondering what to do with myself, for some unbeknown reason, I looked at the board and started to read out aloud. It was something about *a boy flying a kite.* Encouraged to continue, I did, but my pronunciation of some words never seen before, impeded me.

Suddenly, I felt awkward and was grateful when instructed to take my seat.

I discovered new playmates and a general sense of ease and enjoyment during the first few weeks in that class. Arithmetic seemed particularly easy and I was chuffed to be able to spell it using the silly phrase, *a Red Indian thought he might eat tobacco in church.* There was an exactness – right or wrong, no shades of grey; unlike languages.

Then, unexpectedly, a few weeks later, I was moved to another class. The arithmetic was harder and the kids were stronger than me. It was more of a struggle and an emotional loss of my former classroom friends. I did not like it, nor was I sure what was going on – a lot of the fun had now disappeared. Unknowingly, I had been advanced into my second year, to grade two. I persevered, passed into standard one and, clearly, *playtimes were far preferable to lessons.*

There was a simultaneous religious immersion into the Sacred Heart. It was as if the strength and rigidity of the Irish nuns' white habits would elevate them to a status that allowed them to flow like apparitions carrying the authority of this almighty God, our father, the one we could not see and certainly never understood. The whiteness of the headpiece tightly tucked covering their hair and only showing their faces from the eyebrow line, seemed to confirm their pureness – some faces showed otherwise.

We quickly sussed them out – tough as old boots or of a friendlier disposition, softer and angelic. It seems there was so much I never knew or understood about this strange new world, and with mild dyslexia, it is not surprising I thought *sacred* was *scared*.

Like most kids, I accepted the instructions given and did the best I could. Every morning at some God-awful hour, the incessant ringing of the bell awoke us; our cue to leave the land of slumber to attend catechism and prayers – that, before breakfast.

The repetition in sequence of the *Our Fathers* and *Hail Marys* or the learning about original sin was watched over by the angelic beings hanging on the walls, captured in paintings and always present, lest we forget. Their omnipotence, enhanced by haloes and individual streams of light, gave them their supernatural powers of all understanding, which I thought must be real.

I loved the variety of rosaries with their different coloured beads, the purple so alluring. Then God spilled the beans – *although my mother was Roman Catholic, I was of my father's faith, an Anglican.* His almighty powers were such that he must have instructed the nuns to remove me immediately from those early morning teachings. It too was never explained, but I was most grateful – an extra half-hour's sleep – being Anglican had its advantageous.

Tuck-boxes filled with all sorts of goodies would arrive for the other kids.

Maybe my mom never knew about those things? Anyway, at the end of the week, we could buy sweets from the tuck shop. I was very aware that there was a pecking order: my allowance was at the bottom end of the scale, a tickey (3 pence), while some kids could spend a sixpence or even a massive shilling (12 pence).

But with a bit of prudence, it was easy to work out how to get the most value for your money – the gobstoppers filled that slot perfectly. They lasted forever, determinedly rolled and sucked. They were removed only to check the changing of the colours. At times, my salivary glands, intoxicated by the thought of a delicious liquorice black sticky toffee, commanded that the additional cost had to be endured.

The school grounds, fronted by pine trees, were generous, and allowed much exploration and introspection. We fashioned tiny toy boats by rubbing and smoothing pieces of the thick scaly bark against a concrete slab. One rub too many exposed the brittleness, and the boat would break. Some of the kids were superb at this craft. How did they know when to stop rubbing or for that matter fishermen know when to strike? These skills escaped me, but I was learning.

Cupping my hand and using the lower bit of my palm as a scraper, I fashioned a waterway in the loose red sand – the patterns were elaborate and hours were passed in bliss. Yet, at times I was a solitary skipper and quite lonely.

There were other crazes like making surfboards from the end of an old plastic toothbrush – talented kids made exquisite boards with thin and curvaceous fins, while mine broke frequently – the finishing touch, a sandpapering and a *Brasso* polish.

Next were *scooby doobies* made from telephone wires; the endless permutations pushed boundaries: bog standard four strand overlays were superseded by more, while using different combinations of shapes, twists and colour – there was no stopping a boy's creativity and ingenuity.

The choice of our three games, *Bok-bok*, (buck-buck), *Kennetjie* and one using a penknife, was influenced by the whim of a charismatic boy. The first, muscular strength was helpful, while a good batting eye and a skilful throw was desirable for the others.

The posture of a buck was made by a team member bent from the waist at right angles with their arms interlocked around the boy in front. The opposing players, in turn, would take a running leap onto the back of the buck, and hang on for dear life. The object was to collapse the buck's back with rules learned and made up on the hop, often at the fancy of the team seeking advantage and rebuffed by those disadvantaged. Perhaps that is how all games develop until a consensus is reached?

Mostly, I would ignore the war cries of two self-appointed captains summoning this game and about to do territorial battle – being puny, that dreaded sense of ranking – my selection way down. Injuries happened; why play such a game, my least favourite.

Kennetjie was a batting and striking game, much like a game of cricket with the wickets a scraped-out hollow on the ground. The bat, a fifteen-inch baton, and the ball, a smaller stick – if caught or landed in the hollow dugout, then the striker was out. Points scored were never challenged unless the accumulative tally became crucial when our animated spirits could be heard with cries of indignation.

It happened – less protected parts of the anatomy were hit; reinforcing the nuns' decree: *the game was forbidden.* Our special warning code allowed us to innocently abandon the game – *chips, chips, chips* – called in rapid succession. It was delivered with a tonal sense of urgency and handed down from one generation to another, indeed, we were mimicking nature's alarm calls.

Of course, our penknives were used to develop our throwing skills, either into a tree or the ground. A game developed – we faced each other a safe distance apart, feet together. The knife was aimed at an appropriate stretch-length from the opponent's foot and with a skilful flick of the wrists, released. The blade had to lodge firmly in the ground. The opponent then moved his foot to that point; throws alternated. When the opponent could stretch no further, the game was won.

I admired the boys displaying adept qualities, being more of a bystander and always observing. It was as if an ancient, deep-rooted hunter instinct encouraged my learning for survival.

Playtime was broken by that infernal bell that the nuns seemed to relish ringing. Although, by meal times our rumbling stomachs were already calling us. Strange how the sound of that same bell at the end of the school day was a delight; not so the meals.

We were instructed, under the careful pacing of the nuns monitoring our moves, *to eat all our food.* It was near impossible to stomach quartered red beetroot helped only by the brainwashing, *it is good for you and will thicken your blood.* Worst of all was the repulsive smelling spoiled cabbage – if eaten, I would have surely retched.

The nuns' eyes were everywhere, their tongues lashing and reinforcing the indoctrination that God saw all. Nervously, copying the swift and cunning actions of the older boys saved the day – a sudden nifty flick of the fork and the limp cabbage was under the table. There was never a scolding. Perhaps the more compassionate nuns swept it under the metaphorical carpet.

The first break was the exact opposite, a daily treat – a cold pint of unpasteurised full cream milk; every sip savoured trying to make the thick cream on top last forever. On occasions, we sneaked another bottle, but mostly the nuns were too smart. Removing the silver foil cap, with a continual turning and a gentle upward pressure so that there would be no crease, was a prize possession, and won the admiration of the other kids.

The winter mornings were bracing when temperatures would fall below freezing. We dashed to the outside loos, tasting the biting cold, for the necessary *number twos*. The chilling winds crept through the cracks of the corrugated iron shacks and under the toilet seats.

There was an interesting library consisting of strips of newspaper, pierced and held on a bent hook; our toilet paper. To bide the time, I would rip a sheet and read the latest news on the right-hand side of the front page, STOP PRESS – clearly important and always in *red*.

There were countless times I heard, but never understood the humour of the schoolboy joke, *what is black white and red all over . . . a newspaper.* It was only upon the subsequent explanation by my son that the *play* was on the word, *read*, that my slowness could finally be forgiven.

Anyhow, excellent engineering skills were needed to mould the recycled *read newspaper*. It was unpleasant and ineffective; my father's square wax papers were to come a close second.

By ten in the morning, the African winter sun had warmed the day. During the first break, I attempted my skyward jump from the surrounding wall of the still partially frozen fish pond; influenced by a real treat of watching a black and white movie shown by the nuns. Television was still sixteen years away.

The amazing ability of the basketball players to control both their speed of ascent and descent, gracefully and skilfully, mesmerised me. Defeating gravity and perfecting their technique was worthy of practice. I tried, and despondently gave up – the ribbing of the other kids ringing in my ears . . . *you'll never be able to do that*!

The best were the visits by my mom, few, but treasured; the picnic most memorable. My friend Roger joined us on our outing – a freedom escaping the confines of the convent, not that I would ever try it on my own. The whispers of expulsion and the nuns warned, *God would know*!

We went to a pleasure resort close by: verdant grass surrounded by beautiful shady trees of every description, and a stream that meandered through the grounds of our temporary sanctuary. My mom's picnic basket was a godsend – we frolicked and had such fun. Roger's athletic physique struck me, a natural six pack. I pondered, if I had muscles like that might I be able to achieve the feats of the basketball players. Years later, I realised the basketball scene was a slow-motion replay.

Somewhere between the dawn toilet rush, and my insistent *jumping practice*, I contracted double pneumonia. I must have been quite delirious that morning, not hearing the typical raucous preparation. The dormitory was deserted except for the white hooded apparitions floating around, muttering under their breath. My reflexive thought was of concern: *punishment for not being up and ready*. Instead, I was transferred to the infirmary.

I did not know how long I was there, and the visit by my mother, although welcomed, remained a blur. It was a mystery – she arrived and was gone again. Apparently, I spent two weeks recuperating, the days meandering into one another, but with scant recall.

Dormitories were segregated, playtimes not. Inevitably, early sexual inquisitiveness followed. Once, the older boys excitedly whispered, *quickly, we are going to see a girl's thing*. The forbidden fruit loomed.

The game was to suggest to the willing participants that we knew what their private parts looked like – the girls, quizzically took the bait and asked, *how? Just bend your arm as tight as you can* – dutifully they did what they were told. Such excitement, the revelation unfolded before my eyes. The boys, using their forefinger and thumb, would press the flesh of the upper and forearm together at the elbow crease line. Suggestively, various shaped vulvas emerged. The girls, naturally giggled, feigned indifference and rebuked us.

The boys' audacity amazed me, continuing with an even more daring twist, where the power of the tuck shop delights knew no bounds. Once the negotiations were agreed, the sweets were handed over – an inducement to show us their private parts. Our eyes froze with a fixated stare of excitement.

Had the girls played the game before? A quick flash – their dexterity and cunning invoked the cries of our indignation reverberating down the corridors of time, *that's unfair*! Our duping was only drowned by the girl's sniggering, ensuring the show was over before it had even begun. They disappeared with their bounty, and we never played that game again.

My periods of introspection occurred while playing on my own under the pine trees, making sand waterways and roads into time. Pangs of loneliness abounded, broken only by the call of the other boys to join their games or the summoning sound of the school bell.

The pine tree branches were Nature's protective arms, my extended family, where I experienced a similar comfortable feeling to that at Aunty Ronnie's plot in Athol. These were moments where thoughts could wander unimpeded by the expectations and controls of society and, quietly incubate.

My radar was always scanning. Even then, littering, by way of example, pained me. Was I weird, or did no one care? This exacerbated my loneliness.

Yet, other seeds were already sown, like my early love of nature: the trees, the smells, the wetness and sparkle of the dew, the colour of the red sand below the pine trees and the rich brown fertile soil on Aunty's plot. Nature was my home, and I took solace there. It was restorative and with renewed vigour, I enthusiastically embraced every aspect of life.

In my mid-adult life, I sensed and vocalised: *all the answers we ever need are staring at us if we only know how to look and read Nature properly*; axiomatic, I know.

Perhaps my son Stefan, at the age of seven, had more insight, writing: *You know some people believe that God made the world, well it isn't true because nature made the world and nature made the universe. But nobody knows who made nature, maybe God made nature, who knows, not even God.*

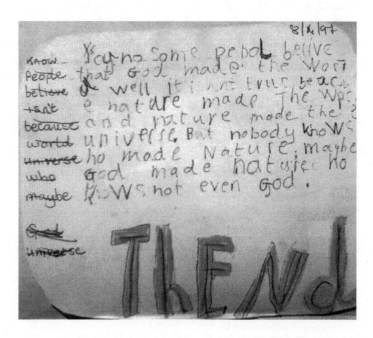

Stefan's writing and his mom's corrections

No, not the end . . . unlike the Mayan calendar in 2012 . . . perhaps, this subsequent period will be like a Darwinian evolution into a new form of consciousness, assisted by the lightning exchange of information through the World Wide Web.

I am ahead of myself. It was Sister Deocara's benevolent disposition, support and kindness as my teacher in standard one that gave me a fillip for my journey ahead.

It was the annual prize giving and the last day of my second school year, not that I was aware that it was the end of my time at the convent. Possibly, this was her way of wishing me bon voyage, and planting a seed of encouragement – it worked.

The previous year, in Grade 2, I never received a prize, understandable as cramming two years into one was quite a stretch. However, the principal's remark on my report card was kind; *Walter did very well in the short time he was here*. Notwithstanding, my envy followed the other boys and girls as they walked up onto the stage – they had distinguished themselves, were recognised, honoured and special. The ambience was grand. A sense of unknown, exciting and full of expectations; much bigger than my experiences at that age.

I looked forward to the next year, hopeful that I might achieve an accolade but I was not sure how to go about it. I remained attentive during class but otherwise did the bare minimum. Playtimes were naturally more fun, and I soon forgot about my momentary need to achieve an award.

Prizes were awarded, and my name was not amongst them – disappointment – then, my name, a citation, *diligence*. Thrilled, I shook hands. It was the only *weird award* that evening, so it probably had some significance, but I had no clue what it meant.

As soon as the proceedings were over the reunited happy families left. Loneliness crept up on me, I was upset . . . we stuck out like sore thumbs, five young boys bravely showing faces of bravado and trying not to be sissies.

I felt abandoned, although I never understood it as such. It was a rather rapid change from the excitement of the evening. That night I remained alone with my thoughts in the gloomy dormitory – *my mom never came*. Deep inside I hurt. I wanted my mother to be there. Did she no longer love me? Could I not at least be part of a family, like other children?

My last image of the convent the next morning was a veiled nun waving goodbye as I took the train unaccompanied for Johannesburg, assured that my mother would be waiting at the other side. The luscious green corn fields flashed by but they remained bleak. Rather, I was entrapped by the stifling December summer heat of an airless carriage; a journey that took forever.

The train arrived. My momentary anxiousness evaporated as we rushed into each other's arms – my mother looked so elegant and beautiful.

Years later I confronted her. She claimed not to have known about the prize, otherwise, she would have been there – I was never sure.

ROBBEN ISLAND

My annual visits to my father were infused with childhood confusions. Mostly, I stayed with him in his shoebox sized bachelor flat in Mouille Point. We would visit Adrian and Selina, the wealthy ones, either at their flat in Green Point, Cape Town, around the corner from my father's or on weekends at their farm, Sunshine, near Malmesbury, a small town where my father was born.

Adrian van Bergen had two medical government posts of note: Valkenberg, the psychiatric hospital for the Western Cape, and the notorious Robben Island where Nelson Mandela spent eighteen of his twenty-seven-year prison sentence.

As a kid, I involuntarily and intermittently rolled my eyes, a touch of Saint Vitus Dance. On one of my visits to my father, it was decided that I would stay with Adrian and Selina on the Island so he could observe my disorder. I was nine or ten years old. His penetrating gaze, seemingly like a hypnotist, left me with no place to hide.

There were many memories, one related to a reprimand, *forbidden to take any more photos*. My Brownie camera's two-inch square black-and-white photographs captured the prisoners marching with wheelbarrows, picks and shovels en route to mindless hard labour – yet, in my play world, they were soldiers on an intriguing special mission. Adrian revealed that the island was a penal colony – my folly was trivial, while the political prisoners' intent would change the destiny of South Africa.

Good inmates were allowed privileges to serve as *house servants*. Whenever there was an *incident*, these were suspended, seemingly causing more stress to the residents who now had to do their own chores. Their mutters and grunts echoed across the Island, *how long before the Governor restores our privileges?*

Then there were the nocturnal rabbit hunts from the back of a vehicle – the work of men. The burly prison guards revelled in this joy as they shot rabbits, frozen by the menacing headlights of the vehicles. My stomach churned, finding it abhorrent. I kept a brave face, the kind that pretends, *it's OK*, for fear I never become a man.

Later, in my mid-forties, I was exposed to the question, *what is it to be a man?* This happened while attending my first *men's work retreat* in England during the late-nineties. My curiosity was stirred when I first heard the attributed Native American phrase, *You can't give a man a weapon until he can dance with a feather.* Jungians espouse a similar virtue: *the male must discover the feminine within.* The implication being, *a proper man must be in touch with his feminine side, and only then would he know when to use a weapon wisely.*

We met as men, with a common purpose, to truly come to know what it is to be a man. The gathering's heartbeat was contained by the men drumming, while the facilitators shared mythological stories and poetry. It culminated in an enactment of a ritual – connecting to the feminine within and to the healing of the soul.

Robert Bly, the outstanding American poet and translator of Rumi's work, author of Iron John and many other books, spearheaded this movement. He had an uncanny way of seeing *beyond*, unleashing a pertinent snippet in conversation that, with the passing of time, proved to be deadly accurate. At book signing ceremonies he would never hurry with his dedications. What he penned came from elsewhere: a doodle of a butterfly, a heartfelt message of intent or an encouragement for the road ahead. He was a role model, intolerant of meaningless trivia and a child of alcoholic parents.

But back under the moonlit nights of Robben Island's quayside, I tried fishing with some of the fishermen. They had a natural bent, read the weather conditions and knew which bait to use. Most impressive was knowing when to strike and to successfully reel the fish in – that knack, eluded me.

How calm the waters were in the harbour, a refuge for the boats from the tempestuous nature of the sea. Quite unlike the rougher crossings experienced in the Diaz, the ferryboat, between Cape Town and Robben Island. Each relentless pounding, a moment to brace myself as the metal hull crashed into the bowels of the rough rolling waves; the shudder reverberating through me. Then, a subtle easing and a hint that the storm may soon be over.

The captain's stories were mesmerizing like the time the Diaz lost engine power in a violent storm – a cork tossed – at the mercy of the mighty colliding force of the Atlantic and Indian Oceans crashing off the elongated tip of Southern Africa. Fearfully, they awaited the rescue of the tugboat and witnessed the dangerous attaching of the tow rope.

At times, the weather was so severe that the ferry could not operate, and Adrian would be transported by helicopter. This only added to my sense of island adventure and, as his nephew, a minuscule amount of his importance rubbed off and belonged to me.

Conversely, and notwithstanding Uncle Jack was a naval officer and that Aunty Ronnie's love and admiration gleamed, while looking at his portrait saying, "He is so handsome in his uniform", I knew the diesel fumes from those rough ferry crossings had already told me, *you don't have the stomach of a sailor.*

The ANC was outlawed in 1960, a month after the state massacre of sixty-nine people in the Sharpeville crisis with many more injuries. The subsequent sporadic sabotage attacks on the country's infrastructure, which lead to the 1964 Rivonia treason trial, were designed to be disruptive and to instil fear into the heart of the nation – it did. Finally, the global economic sanctions applied during the mid-eighties brought the South African government to the negotiating tables – the rest is history.

In "Memories of Mandela" at the British Museum on Friday the 13th January 2017, Lord Joffe shared his account of Mandela's most celebrated speech during the trial.

"In consultation with Mandela and the other accused on the proposed speech, we the defence lawyers, pointed out that it could be taken by the Judge as an invitation to sentence him to death and we tried to persuade him to leave it out. However, he was not willing to do this so the speech was handed back to me to be finally re-typed to take account of a few minor amendments.

I could not bear the thought of Mandela being hanged and decided that on the re-typed version I would leave out the prepared to die sentence and handed the re-typed speech back to Mandela.

The next day I received a handwritten note from Mandela asking for the sentence I had omitted to be put back with the addition of the words 'IF NEEDS BE, it is an ideal for which I am prepared to die.'

On Monday 23 April 1964, Bram Fischer opening for the defence outlined the defence case and ended 'The defence case my Lord, will commence with the statement from the dock by Nelson Mandela who personally took part in the establishment of Umkhonto, and who will be able to inform the Court of the beginning of that organisation and of its history up to August 1962 when he was arrested.'

The Courtroom was packed, divided into two sections – one for whites, the other for blacks. Armed police stood at every door. Outside the Court in the Square the police dogs bayed and solid lines of policemen scowled at the crowd of singing ANC supporters.

Impeccably dressed in an elegant suit, tall and powerful, looking every bit the leader that he was. Nelson Mandela began very slowly and very quietly to read the statement which he had prepared in a flat even voice. At no stage did he raise his voice very much, or change from the slow, measured speech with which he had started. Gradually as he spoke, the silence became more and more profound until it seemed that no one in the Court dared move or breathe.

After two and a half hours, he ended: 'Our struggle is a truly national one. It is a struggle of the African people, inspired by their own suffering and their own experience, it is a struggle for the right to live. During my lifetime, I dedicated myself to the struggle of the African people. I fought against white domination and I fought against black domination. I have cherished the ideal of a democratic and free society in which all persons live together in harmony and with equal opportunities.'

At this moment, he paused, a long pause, in which one could hear a pin drop in the Court, and then looking squarely at the Judge, he finished, 'It is an ideal which I hope to live for and to achieve', and then dropping his voice very low, he added, 'But if needs be, it is an ideal for which I am prepared to die.'

Lord Joffe continued, "I also have the notes in his own handwriting of what he would have said to the Judge if sentenced to death. They read: 'I meant everything I said. The blood of many patriots in this country has been shed for democracy in conformity with civilized standards. If I must die, I declare to all that I will meet my fate like a man.'"

Mandela's time on the Island may have been a period of adaptation and formulation, which allowed him to emerge as a great statesman and subsequent Nobel Peace Prize winner.

Adrian was well placed, and I remember a conversation in my early teens, when he was talking about the government attempt to subvert the course of justice in what probably was the same trial.

The idea was to encourage a plea of insanity, which would be corroborated thus allowing the case to be expediently removed from the public eye – insanity cannot be prosecuted. Indelibly imprinted were Adrian's words, "They looked at me directly and unflinchingly said, *it does not matter what you want to say or do, Doctor, we know what we did and why*" and in that same breath Adrian whispered, "Things will change in this country, the whites will not rule forever." Adrian knew what the state was after and as he said, "My conscience would not allow that deception", and I was proud of him.

In a similar vein, my uncle practised medicine and always transferred prisoners to the mainland for appropriate medical attention, irrespective whether it was a ruse, despite the Governor's protests. Prisoners did purposefully injure themselves and attempt escapes from the mainland. The seven kilometres to swim in the cold strong currents of the shark infested Atlantic was impossible. Any temptation to escape the confines of Robben Island, a sort of Alcatraz, must have been overwhelming and mentally torturous, compounded by the breath-taking view of the awe-inspiring Table Mountain.

MALMESBURY, MELONS AND CYCLOPS

My paternal grandfather, another Walter Thornhill, a Scouse, was born on the 31st August 1878 and came to South Africa as a Private in the British Army, to fight in the Anglo-Boer War (1899 – 1902). Afterwards, he remained in search of a better existence, fell in love, and married Elizabeth Rachel Everson, my grandmother, a Dutch woman. Her family had emigrated from Holland in the 1800's.

During that war, the dreadful concentration camps interned many a belligerent Afrikaner, mostly from upcountry Orange Free State and Transvaal. My grandmother's family were from the Cape where the Afrikaners were generally more supportive of British rule and hence remained free.

My grandfather was short and thick-set with a scar on his left cheek, noted in an old passport as a *distinctive mark*. His hard face looked as though it had seen a round or two in the boxing ring, and during the First World War he enlisted again, this time fighting for South Africa. I never knew him and vaguely recall my grandmother, barrelled from the short stock farm vintage – a friendly face and a jovial disposition.

Somehow, they found their way to the sleepy quaint farming village of Malmesbury that hugs the west coast, some sixty-five kilometres north of Cape Town. These days it is fancifully known as the Tuscany of Africa, and famous for its easily identifiable *Malmesbury Brei*, a gutturally rolling of the letter R in a colourful depiction of the Afrikaans language.

My father was born there on 25th October 1908. Later, when he was a young man, the family moved to Cape Town as though that place carried a mystery, forsaken and casually referred to as a mere reference point. Was there a family secret, an embarrassment of sorts that needed to be hidden – *we are much better than that place* – an upward move disguising their roots? I do not know, but despite our numerous car journeys together, whenever I spotted a Malmesbury road sign, excitedly I hollowed, "Hey dad, that's where you were born" – but we never took the detour.

Some thirty-three years later, I did – a veteran's cycle race took me there. Standing on the soil of my ancestors, my awareness was tweaked by the veneration bestowed on ancestors by certain indigenous cultures that I have known, like the Peruvian Quechua, Balinese and Zulus.

The Quechua rest their ancestors' skulls on the mantelpiece as an imbuing of their presence. The Balinese, by contrast, cremate and after elaborate rituals and the dispersing of the ashes out to sea do the ancestral spirits finally return to the family temple. The veneration of the temple with its ancestral history ensures that a Balinese home is never sold, only the outlying paddy fields. In these cultures, consciously or unconsciously, the ever-present ancestral spirits are drawn upon, thus ensuring the emotional and psychological well-being of the families. Our family was bereft of such a comforting state.

My dad and I, and sometimes Joyce, his girlfriend, would often visit Adrian and Selina in their beachfront two-bedroom flat, which had a large open plan sitting and dining room with spectacular sea views. It took the full brunt of the afternoon summer sun, only cooling into those endless Cape evenings where natures enigmatic opera emerges – churning waves repetitively crashing to their thunderous clap against a backdrop of constantly changing cloud formations and colour tints – I could watch forever.

Mid-summer, the setting sun way after nine o'clock – the beauty of each was enhanced by atmospheric conditions and has never ceased to amaze me. The Brazilians face the last disappearing sliver, while standing on the beach, and applaud the moment it disappears. Other cultures honour the cyclical rebirth every morning.

Cape summers were always fun, with days distinctly longer than the Transvaal Highveld's. I hankered after those endless days, but not so the distinctive smell of *over-ripened yellow melons* in their flat. Every time we left, Adrian's habitual offering from the *fruit basket* so proudly displayed in the corner of the sitting room seemed to compound the effect of the invasive smell.

Mostly he chose an over-ripened fruit – "It's good for you." I resisted, as best I could. Occasionally, under duress of his continual harassment, I accepted. My thoughts were contaminated as if by that pervading melon smell, or was it a sense of my disappointment of things to come?

My father's flat was equidistant to theirs and the Mouille Point lighthouse. On fog-bound, gloomy, wet winter days, the deep penetrating blast of the foghorn would continually reverberate through my bones and dislodge my very being. Like Siren, the foghorn called continually in a lonely, melancholic way, perhaps already knowing of the impending fate of the ships and sailors at sea.

Awakening in the early dark hours of a cold misty morning, I would listen to her plaintive cry, already filling me with a foreboding. But, I fell asleep again to her deceptive soothing lullaby. Could her voice or the light of her swirling Cyclops eye really penetrate the fog? Or was it merely illuminating the ghosts of my mind?

Which is more than I can say for the countless nights of having to be my Dad's drinking companion – regaled with repetitive stories of his grandeur – deep into the early hours of the morning, when even match sticks would have struggled to keep my eyes open.

Stories about how he broke the shipping strike amongst the local Coloureds, another of the previously displaced groups in South Africa. It only made me shudder and was more about his macho ego.

In reality, he was an insolvent broken man, the one lost, talking to his captive audience. I knew only too well the dreaded familiar sound, the unscrewing of the bottle top, turn by turn, with a euphemistic, *one for the road*. It was as if it excused it all – I never knew when it was finally the last.

My body was screaming for sleep in between the bouts of my wavering closing eyes trying to remain as attentive as I could. I never told him the extent of my tiredness, feeling it might be misconstrued as a lack of love for him.

My father never spoke about how he acquired his gammy left leg – it was shorter than the other and mangled. He was probably embarrassed, but my mother told the story. *He was seventeen, a legal article clerk – while out walking one day a truck hit a lamp post which fell across his leg, but not before he managed to push two young children to safety. Hospitalised for months and the leg very nearly amputated, he lost his will to continue studying and, instead, joined a shipping forwarding and clearing agency.*

Maybe, he too had to grow up quicker than normal, learning the tricks of that business. By the time of the Second World War, in his early thirties, he understood the value of the right types of import permits and the trading thereof, often it seems in the corridors of corruption. My father's affluence was often mentioned by my mother, Jimmy Shephard my cousin, and my father's second wife.

Jimmy, with a roguish twinkle, added more colour. He initiated me into the clandestine stories, as if we were ancient marauding pirates. Embellished, perhaps – it had to do with the theft of the Oppenheimer jewels. Hearsay was they left the country, embedded in a tube of toothpaste, on my father's airline.

Stories of aggrandizement, together with my father's inflated ego, while drinking way into the night, were all unnecessary for my love. I loved him unconditionally as most little boys and girls love their parents.

HALCYON DAYS

I liked Joyce. She was kind, gentle and understanding, and loved my father dearly. She lived in Fish Hoek, with her aged father, Fatty Whitehead as he was affectionately known, in a cottage overlooking the sea, where the railway line hugs the coast all the way to Simonstown. The beach was on their doorstep, a mere hundred yards away, with access via the short pedestrian tunnel below the railway track. Our routine weekend sleepovers there were so exciting.

No malice was attached to his nickname, a big man, rather than fat – he knew about fishing – to catch, fillet, cook, and most importantly, how to avoid the fish bones while eating. A special relationship existed with the local coloured fishermen, who always kept a few fish aside for him. Best of all, he could lie on his back floating forever; never sinking.

Up at sunrise, he had to pass my sleeping area on the veranda, the only way in or out of the cottage. I was disappointed if the sleep gods kept me asleep while Fatty went on his adventures and always so grateful when he could not escape my lair. Some mornings we would help the fishermen to pull their catch in; men working side by side. The air was bracing, early morning pangs of hunger present, yet as men we would all take our places, pulling the ropes in unison with our feet slipping in the sea sand. The rope and sand were cold to the touch whilst we gripped the slippery wet rope, anchoring ourselves as best we could with a heave-ho. There was a rhythm to this ancient work of men. Slowly but surely the net would draw closer to be beached. The excitement mounted, the size of the catch sensed by the weightiness of the effort, confirmed by the bulging pulsating net as the fish instinctively pushed for their freedom. There was a sense of pride, of being useful, and a primal innate sense of belonging.

A successful catch needed the eagle vision of the lookout fishermen, perched on the mountain overlooking the bay, to spot the shoals. There were no mobile phones – communication was by prearranged hand and flag signals. The boats were launched from the beach and the nets dropped in the most beneficial places in the long sickle bay of Fish Hoek. The battle commenced – man versus nature – respect and a harmony between the elements and the sea ensued: what was needed taken and indeed given. The salt of the earth fishermen – knew everything: their boats, the types of nets, the currents, the varieties of fish that could be caught in different seasons or weather conditions – my heroes.

There were many adventures walking along the promenade nestled between the railway line and the strong rocks that held back the sea as if it could go no further. When the sea was really angry, the waves would pound the rocks and the spray would engulf both the walkway and the railway track. Sometimes, when travelling home with Joyce by train from the city centre, it happened. It was so exciting, yet a part of me was anxious lest we were washed away; my imagination rampant and unchecked.

Then there were the anglers trying to recover their hand lines entangled on the rocks, the loss of hooks and sinkers, and the mutterings under their breath. At times, I could approach them, at others the visceral sign blinked, *do not disturb,* and I would move on. I was always distressed when the fish were caught. The hook extracted, then tossed into a small rock pool vainly flapping, knowing the end was near; even worse, the immediate fatal clubbing. Humaneness, the natural order of things and an understanding of the food chain were slowly developing, while my immediate reactions were still emotional. Some comfort was taken in being told *fish are cold blooded and do not feel any pain,* but I was unsure if that was true.

Snorkelling in the pools revealed the treasures of that magnified world; some kids were naturally talented. They knew where to look and how to find an octopus. More importantly, how to catch these quick creatures, masters of disguise and once caught, how to immobilise them by turning their head inside out, to avoid a nasty nip of the beak. I valued being part of their entourage, their adeptness, ever hopeful to capture one, but it was not to be. In truth, I was a tad scared of the octopuses' agility, speed and movement of their tentacles; the exaggeration of comic book stories captured and coloured my thoughts.

The highlight of one particular holiday was to discover the mountain tunnels and cave system from the Clovelly side of Fish Hoek bay through to Kalk Bay. Rumours abounded: they were used by pirates in the old days, who could suddenly vanish into thin air; all of which I am sure was unfounded, but it was so real and heightened our sense of daring and adventure. Essential equipment consisted of a bathing costume, a T-shirt, a flashlight and a pair of *tackies.*

Thinking back, this too was another early rite of passage. We knew the objective was to get through the mountain to the other side, only we had no idea what the journey entailed. There was a natural degree of apprehension, tinged with the excitement of the unknown – the collective spirit of the other fifteen or so young boys, all in the same boat. Fortunately, an elder's supervision at the tiller.

We climbed the mountain and entered the mouth of the cave. It took a while for our eyes to adjust, as new smells, like dampness, filled the air. We progressed slowly as the passageway became impeded. Water dripped from above, rugged jutting rocks clawed at our bodies whilst crawling through tight crevices and along chest-high underground water streams. At a point, we were instructed to turn our flashlights off. Immersed in total pitch-black darkness, the imagined *what ifs* heightened our senses further. It was an uncanny moment, unnerving as my sense of fear rose, restricting my throat. Then magically, a calm pervaded as I adjusted to and felt the spirit of the mountain – how long were we in that space, when a minute or two can feel like an eternity.

The reverie only interrupted by the switching on of a flashlight. Then needed less and less as we finally emerged into brilliant sunlight overlooking a completely different bay. It was as though, suddenly, I had grown immensely and had an unusual perspective, having glimpsed a little of the mountain's mystery. What else was out there, I pondered?

Falling asleep on the open veranda was blissful – I relived all the day's adventures accompanied by the strong smells of the night air infused with the spray of the warm, rolling Indian Ocean; only the mosquitoes were a real pest.

I always looked forward to holiday times spent in Fish Hoek from the age of eight onwards, but it ended abruptly when my father died.

There was something in the way my mother took the telephone call in her bedroom. She walked over, "There is something I need to tell you."
I retorted with a sense of finality, "I know."
She looked on, astonished, "How?"
Who knows, an inner sense.

Those halcyon days would not have been possible if it were not for Joyce or her father. On reflection, he was my first exposure to and an admiration for a grandfather, as I knew neither of mine. Oblivious to this, he merely followed his dawn routine of swimming in the bracing morning waters of the warm Indian Ocean.

THE CAPE DOCTOR'S MEDICINE

Those early cycling days as a thirteen-year-old were challenging in competing against the *Juniors* (under nineteen) on a borrowed club track bike, a few sizes too big. The beginning of the race was fine – a comical stick-like-insect, atop a frame with large wheels, desperately trying to propel it forward – but once the pace increased, deflated, I watched the older boys accelerate away.

Basil Cohen's enthusiastic voice, blaring over the public-address system, did its best to encourage and lift my spirits. "Here comes little Walter Thornhill, let's give him a huge round of applause and bring him home." That, finishing a lap or more behind was my lot.

Holding on, I never let anyone know that cycling was my refuge from the concealed drama in my family life; my mother causing much of the heartache.

Cycling as a sport is a continual compromise between equipment, aerodynamics, different riding positions and styles, physical ability and, most importantly, a psychological understanding of oneself to sustain performance.

Instinctively, endless strategies and changing tactics are deployed, poker faced. Paramount is the reigning in of youthful testosterone exuberance, while evaluating the opponents' use of theirs. Skills are honed in the hard knocks of competition. The determination needed is time honoured and, the *coup de grâce* becomes an art form in its execution.

Yet underpinning all of this is the basic ability to spin gears rather than to push them. This helps in slowing the rapid accumulation of lactic acid that leads to unbearable leg ache and the ensuing tell-tale fatigue.

Gotty Hansen was a key protagonist for the 1968 first ever Tour de Jugend cycle race in South Africa held in and around Bellville, a suburb of Cape Town, and modelled on its European equivalent. It gave *Juniors* a taste of competing in a mini type of Tour de France four-day stage race. Its tenet was to prevent unnecessary psychological and muscular damage – essentially *spinning* – achieved by restricting the maximum gear ratio allowed. Fifteen years old, delighted to be competing expenses paid, our team finished ninth.

All weather conditions were experienced from intense heat to heavy rains. Unexpectedly, a visit from the infamous South Easterly wind, *The Cape Doctor*, the cleanser of the polluted air trapped between the city and Table Mountain. Fortunately, we only had to endure it for a stage – our limit. We were young and inexperienced, and struggled to hold onto our buffeted bikes, while precariously leaning into the crosswind. Finally, when her belching bellows ceased, an absolute calm prevailed – Capetonians know it well.

Our initiation into the raw nakedness of nature's strength – physical, mental and technically demanding – like early pioneers, and survivors of this gruelling, yet exciting event. Those Bapsfontein rides facing nature's unleashed power certainly helped.

Cyclists seldom talk about the amount of pain experienced. Perhaps, coupled with self-belief, it is an innate quality necessary for survival. Somewhere in the recesses of my mind was a seed of hope that maybe one day I might ride the greatest Tour – the Tour de France.

Our score was settled on the last day of racing, twiddling in the sweltering heat. Our tired, yet satisfied aching legs followed the celebrations attended by the mayor and an entourage. My ears tried to listen to the speeches but my eyes wavered – delicious food adorned the tables – tummy rumbling, and my salivary glands agreed.

Our dehydrated bodies could not get enough of the delicious thirst quenching watermelon, most suitable for a pip fight – missiles deftly squeezed between thumb and forefinger – even the mayor was fair game. The frivolity ended only when our bloated tummies exclaimed, *enough*!

It was like that with cyclists – strict training and racing disciplines, fastidious attention to detail in everything you ate, drank or did, except for the exuberant excesses after major events.

The participation and exposure were a veritable gift outside of home life. Yet, I felt a deep sense of loneliness after the celebrations, for my father, even though he lived in Cape Town, was not there.

My mother, father and me

Photo sent as an Xmas present
to my father – age 7

Robben Island - my play world of soldiers
- taken with my Brownie camera

Pure bliss, my mom and me

Aunty Ronnie

Uncle Jack

CHAPTER 4
THE HAWKER

AL CAPONE

Valentines, located in Bree Street in the heart of Cape Town, was a wholesale stationery and import-export company. Aunty Selina, the third eldest of the seven Thornhill siblings, inherited it from her first husband. She was nepotistic – initially, Grace, the eldest worked there, next Pam, the second eldest, and Johnny, two years younger than my dad – he became their general manager.

Valentines was well known and profitable. Johnny also understood the value of trading valuable import permits, except he had a ruse and misappropriated funds. The giveaway was lifestyle: a new home in a fashionable suburb and a farm, neighbouring Adrian and Selina's. Settling this *family incident,* the farm was consequently transferred to them – Johnny became their pariah.

Long after my dad's insolvency and his foray into other business ventures, he too, joined Valentines as their commercial salesman. The business had by then morphed into a generalist wholesale stockist, and his business card – General Manager – seemed pretentious.

Every time we visited Johnny's family the cloak of secrecy was drawn – *now don't forget we can't tell Selina and Adrian we were here,* my father reminded me. The fun of these visits was in huge contrast to the staidness of the Van Bergen home, built on the edifice of middle-class expectations and the pervasive smell of overripe melons. It was confusing as Johnny showed no animosity and often asked after them – embarrassed, I answered perfunctorily.

Johnny and Doreen were an incongruous couple. He, thin as a rake with a pugnacious clown-like red nose and a twinkle in his eyes. She, rather large, carefree and of a pleasant disposition. My initial repulsion to her flabby arms which I was told related to a medical condition, was softened by witnessing her overwhelming love and compassion for her family. Johnny was funny and had an inimitable knack of making us roar with laughter. A grimace of his face or a witty comment of sorts would do. It was good to be there, enveloped by my bloodline – a special sense of belonging.

My favourite cousin was Joan, the middle sibling of the three sisters. Marilyn was the eldest and Charmaine the youngest. Joan was exactly eleven months younger than me. I adored the way she moved, her infectious smile and long blonde hair.

My adolescent infatuation grappled for her attention, while she feigned indifference with a playful indignation. A quick tug of her hair or stepping onto the back of her flip-flops. The last resort was to tickle her hips. This caused her to laugh uncontrollably, sometimes to the point of wetting herself. It became the show stopper, never won any favours, and certainly put the kibosh on any further ideas; not that I needed the constant reminder, *you can't marry your cousin, you know.*

Joan and Charmaine had their own special language, developed by adding *very* onto randomly selected words, spoken rapidly. We, the cognoscenti, were in a world of our own with local shopkeepers and customers looking on in astonishment, no doubt playing along. Peripherally, I was part of their gang.

On one occasion they returned home, shaken, and explained how their secret language was successfully used to escape the clutches of a paedophile.

Marylyn refused to wear shoes, much to the consternation of her parents but her defiance had our stamp of approval. She was pleasant enough but the age gap made her seemingly boring, so we simply ignored her, as she probably did us.

Aunty Grace, the matriarch amongst the Thornhill siblings was married to Clifford Shephard, the owner of Devine Gates, a shipping, forwarding and customs clearing agent. He worked his way up as a young man, and upon the death of Mr Gates and finally Colonel Devine, was bequeathed the business for a nominal amount. I could imagine Clifford answering the phone, "Devine Gates, good morning, Shephard here" and anyone that did not know the company may well have thought they had dialled the Pearly Gates.

Grace and Clifford's manner was contained, like *old money*, with nothing to prove and in my eyes like the lords and ladies of society. It was as if Grace had the qualities true to her name, and it was not surprising Clifford chose her for his bride. I loved visiting them, the serenity of their home, the smell of antique furniture, their calmness, their intellectual gentle questioning, tempered with compassion, and best of all were family celebrations.

Aunty Grace always had a little something for me. Discreetly, she would hand me an envelope with my name on it, beautifully wrapped and sealed, almost with Japanese attention to the detail of presentation, rather than the present itself. The card had a handwritten heartfelt message and a generous amount of money, by my standards. Mostly it was her dulcet tone and pronunciation that I loved listening to, while observing the gracious way she conducted herself. It infused me with a feeling of well-being.

Their two children, Jimmy, the diamond-story raconteur and his elder sister, Val, were much older than me by twenty plus years, and it was only much later in adulthood that I got to know them better.

Born from my father's third marriage and my mother's second, I met my dad's second wife Joyce, another Joyce, sanguine and friendly. My mother always said, "She enjoyed the good life with your dad, money no object. He had race horses, a garage and fingers in many pies. I warned him about the pilfering, but he never listened, only telling me to stop interfering in his business affairs."

It seems in part my mother was correct, but his real downfall was the insolvency of the airline. The times my mom spoke nostalgically about their happier moments together were the vignettes that I would cling to and treasure, as I created my universe of them.

Joyce subsequently married Desmond, a window dresser of a departmental store. He had strong feminine qualities, and compared to my father seemed an inconsequential partner, was mostly inebriated and ignored by the other adults. A strange couple – I could not imagine them in bed and pondered whether their marriage was of convenience.

Yet, he had other qualities and that is what she must have seen in him. While the other adults were busy doing *adult things*, like lip service regurgitated, he had a flair of recognising that the child in me was alone and would gently enquire – how are you? – and I felt seen.

They also lived in Mouille Point, and even closer to the lighthouse. One afternoon a plane flew overhead between their flat and Table Mountain; an unusual flight path. In my excitement, I hastily dashed through the closed glass door crashing onto their fifth-floor balcony. The shattering sound of the shards changed the atmosphere. I feared the worst – I was in for it. However, their concern was only for my well-being, and to my relief, I came away unscathed on both accounts.

Joyce, in her relaxed carefree way, would at times casually speak about those balmy *shipping days* during and after the Second World War. My father would arrive home a little inebriated, bearing gifts, like a fur coat, or unexpectedly, with a cadre of poker playing men in toe, drinking into the early hours of the morning. Was it my imagination or an inference that the fur coat and other goods were purloined; a box cut for customs inspection?

Thus, it was, my dad, Al Capone and his cronies. I kept a lid on this with no need to wave the flag any further – unimpressed and embarrassed, it was not the way I would lead my life.

There was another poignant moment when Desmond, at my father's funeral, was more reassuring and sensitive to my emotions than anyone else, except for the other Joyce, my father's girlfriend.

My relatives were of scant support.

We walked by and paid our last respects. I stopped and looked at my father laying in his coffin – unconsciously, touched the cold pallid lifeless skin of his right hand resting on his chest. My defences fell for the first time, a tiny tear welled . . . and the enormity struck me . . . my father was dead.

"It's OK Walter, it's OK", as Desmond's comforting hand gave my shoulder a squeeze. I was grateful for this simple gesture – consoling, despite his alcoholic breath.

That emotional bond, forged by Desmond's awareness of the child-in-me growing up, suspended my judgement of him. If not, I would have missed his gift of kindness and compassion that I so needed and have since reflected upon. Judgements strangle and prevent the best from being seen in each other.

ROAD TRIPS

My dad had a Morris Minor station wagon, old-fashioned even then. Whenever we visited his friends living high on the mountainside, I was concerned whether the car had sufficient power. My latent fear was exacerbated when the engine was about to stall with a hint of a shudder. Could the brakes hold the car on such a steep incline?

Was it my dad's game? A challenge between the steepness of the mountain and the car's capacity in a particular gear, or was he merely too lazy to change down? The stall-shudder always worried me; was he testing my bravery? I did not understand much about the mechanics of it all and out of a false bravado, I never revealed my fear and remained uncomfortable.

Maybe it was the memory of a reprimand by my mother's boyfriend when I was about five that kept me silent. We were returning from a country picnic, when I noticed from my rudimentary knowledge of the dials, thanks to lessons from Aunty Ronnie on those countless trips to her plot, that the needle of the fuel gauge was dropping.

I questioned my mom's friend as to whether we had enough petrol to make it home. Initially, he was polite, but as the journey progressed with the needle falling further, my relentless pestering continued thinking that I was being helpful. It reached an explosion point, "If that annoying kid of yours does not shut up, I'll stop the car and belt him one." Silently my anxieties were held, while still peeking at the gauge that flirted with the reserve line.

I loved the sense of freedom and bonding my father and I shared while driving along the Cape Peninsula coast to visit his customers. The windows wound down and the wind blowing through our hair to the mesmeric sound of the tyres on the tarmac – a doorway for meaningful storytelling before the dreaded lunch time pub stops.

Some road trips were tedious because of the long distance travelled in the heat of the day – unreachable mirages of lakes on the horizon. Magically, the tedium was broken by the charm of my father singing his favourite songs – *When Irish eyes are smiling*, and *I wonder who's kissing her now*. My heart could only but smile.

Yet, he changed part of the lyrics in the latter song from *breathing sighs* to *scheming schemes*, which did make me question the keys to unlock certain mysteries of romance.

The car rumbled along, and my dad sang – caught up in my own thoughts – *he was travelling down the road of nostalgia, reliving times,* ". . . and it was only with your mother I decided to have you." I felt special and our relationship was complete, becoming our unspoken secret.

Nowadays, whenever I hear these songs, spontaneously, I sing along and am transported back to those relatively carefree trips, reliving memories and bathing in his warmth and the love known.

~

My parents were married on the 28th December 1951 – an eighteen year age difference – my mother twenty-five and my father forty-three. Their marriage had its early cracks, possibly exacerbated by the insolvency – divorce was rare in those days with just a hint of stigma – they tried a reconciliation. My mother and I went to visit my father in Cape Town when I was about four or five. I am not sure if we stayed with him but I do remember something happened while we were all together in his flat. Exactly what I do not recall; there was an inkling of an argument. What is crystal clear is our trip was curtailed having barely arrived, and as my mother softly breathed, *it just didn't work out*. I felt the overhanging sadness of her disappointment.

~

The insolvency happened seven months after my birth. On one of our many car trips, my dad shared a story about a rich woman, years later, blatantly offering to maintain him, provided they were seen to be in a meaningful relationship. This would have resolved his financial struggle. Significant and honest conversations like that occurred in between the singing, and I was glad my dad, now the commercial salesman, never compromised himself. The car journeys became our unconscious metaphor, sharing the roads my father had travelled.

Our next stop was to procure an order from his seaside customers – those multipurpose beach shops selling an eclectic array of seasonal goods. Some dangled precariously from the shop awnings, like unreachable prizes at fun fairs, and seemed equally tricky for the shopkeeper to retrieve with his long pole.

I soon learned which products earned the better margins or what constituted a meaningful order. My dad's relaxed and friendly smile said it all when he returned to the car. Treasured moments – his successes were mine.

Before being taken under the protective wing of his sisters at Valentines and while still an insolvent, he tried his hand in many endeavours. Initially, an old-fashioned *smous* (hawker), an armature winding business and then a laundrette.

My cousin Val, whom I mentioned having only recently met, recalls, "During your father's insolvency, his *smous* period was the most colourful. A vehicle packed to the brim with all sorts of merchandise for the farmers in the outlying areas. He also arranged marriages you know."

It was fascinating and made perfect sense being in a privileged position of knowing who the eligible candidates were. I have scant recall of that period, but this revelation fed my admiration for his strength of character and sheer determination to find a way to survive.

The armatures business – copper wires tightly coiled – was beyond my grasp; the laundrette on the other hand, with my Dad as the middle man, was more obvious. Escaping intoxicating chemical smells from the thin protective plastic covers were quite pleasant, but not the goodwill pay-out to a disgruntled customer for a ruined article of clothing.

More than anything else, I could feel my father's spirit ebbing away, as he tried to find a way to sustain himself, while rebuilding his self-confidence and respect. We never had a chance to have those conversations, although upon his rehabilitation from insolvency, we had others about the refinancing of Norden Industries, an aluminium utensil manufacturing company that he had acquired two years before his death.

RITUALS

Fascinated, I loved watching my father's morning rituals as he prepared himself for the day. The lathering of the badger brush was time honoured. A carefully selected new blade, screwed down into the razor, deftly removed his Santa Claus mask as his face slowly emerged. The skin expertly tugged to allow the closest shave with a studied reflective look in the mirror – a confirmation that the sculpting was impeccable. A splash of after-shave lotion embraced his naked skin; the scent of fresh beginnings and an absolution from the drinking of the night before.

He had strange habits. A clearing of his throat always followed the brushing of his teeth – did it have to do with the smoking of unfiltered cigarettes, the type men would rhythmically tap? His middle and forefinger, just below and between the tips, had yellow nicotine stains. The entire ritual was enjoyable: the opening of, and removal from, the ornate, colourful cardboard boxes of that time; the tap and portrayal as if a sense of irreverence – that space preceding the sharing of vital information or indeed a secret. It was manly and worldly and somehow his smoke never bothered me, but my mother's always did.

Then the greasing and the meticulous combing of his hair, ensuring the hair purposely grown longer on the sides could be safely cemented from side to side to hide his baldness. It looked glaringly obvious and was ridiculous . . . as were those small square individual waxed sheets used for our ablutions. They were an improvement on the strips of newspaper used at the convent. Often, the call of nature was delayed if I knew we were visiting elsewhere – the luxury of softer toilet paper, treasured.

My Dad was embarrassed about his left leg – it was shorter with a severe loss of muscle into the top part of the calf because of *the accident*. Without trousers, it was unpleasant to look at, quite deformed and responsible for his noticeable limp, but he was my dad and I loved him dearly.

Then there was that strange unspoken subject, copulation. Do parents think we do not know? I mean, after all, the school playground is a font of entertaining erroneous information and, nature, although explicit, often confuses matters. I am not referring to the many elaborate and beautiful mating rituals but rather that fleeting split second sexual contact by birds. What do they think about during the momentary balancing act?

Maybe, like most kids, my curiosity was awakened ever since I realised we had different anatomical parts and that the one seemed to fit into the other.

Initially, my father and I shared his bedroom, while Joyce slept on a single bed that doubled as a sofa, in the front room . . . one evening a most intriguing thing happened. I must have been about ten or eleven years old. The lights were out and the room was dark, but I had not yet fallen asleep. Quite unusual, for normally as soon as the back of my neck nestled in the comfort of a pillow, I would drift off.

That night was different – the excitement I was going to experience had already rooted itself in my father. He surprised me by going to Joyce's sleeping area. Of course, pretending to be asleep I never blinked an eye nor moved a muscle, although my alert ears, like a radar screen, relayed these new unexplored signals to my brain. My senses tweaked, an excitement stirred deep within my loins. There was a daring in the air – could I get up without the mattress creaking, tip toe the eight feet to the hallway and watch the act?

I wanted to witness this, a need from deep within but then other rational thoughts crept in – *Would I be embarrassed if I were caught*? *What were the repercussions and would my father be angry*?

My fear prevailed. Laying riveted and breathless, lest my breathing gave me away, I listened to the entire symphonic movement, including Joyce's unexpected grunts and words of encouragement; my dad was quite a lion. I saw them in an entirely new light, would never have guessed, and certainly never let on.

There was a peculiar irony; whenever we went to her father's place in Fish Hoek, they naturally slept together in her room, while I slept outside on the porch. One year it finally changed. Upon my arrival in Cape Town they suggested, *it would be better if you sleep in the front room and we share the bedroom* – so it was.

~

Sexual arousal and the comfort of bodily touch are often confused and even denied, yet seemingly easier for primitive and indigenous cultures – women too, touch more easily than men. My provenance was mixed – our family's blurred emotional fingerprint and the collective cultural memory of the English stiff upper lip, although unspoken, permeated the air. By contrast, I would find out about the natural Afrikaner family warmth and become more appreciative of their cultural ways.

After an enjoyable Fish Hoek weekend, we would travel the thirty-six kilometres back to my dad's flat. It always seemed like an eternity in the lateness of the hour, particularly after an exhilarating and enjoyable weekend of frolicking by the seaside. Joyce, a grandmother of three, spotted my tiredness and her natural instincts came to the fore. "Walter, why don't you put your head on my lap and go to sleep? I'll wake you when we get home."

I was always another pair of eyes when we drove alone – trying to be a man, to warn of road dangers ahead, out of necessity. My father was mostly in an inebriated state.

"The curb dad . . . red traffic lights," and so on. Sometimes he would nod off for a second or two and I would immediately force conversation, shaking him from his stupor. Thoughts swirled – what if we crashed and were all killed? The press was always full of those horror stories.

Joyce's kindness allowed me to succumb that evening as my rigid internal facade melted into her femininity. Enveloped by feelings of longing and a need to be loved – it swept through my body now no longer on road-watch. I fell contentedly to sleep, except I never allowed it to happen again despite her numerous subsequent offers. Something inside prevented me – was it that I was not deserving of her generous gift of touch and consolation or was it merely a fear it would soon disappear and was only ever part of the Cape Town holiday magic?

PUNISHMENT

It happened a year after the Tour de Jugend – December holiday time – coinciding with my riding in the prestigious Cape December track events. Rather than staying with my father, as was our custom over the past eight years, I declared, "I will be staying with my cycling friends". My cruel dagger pierced his heart. We never spent much time together that holiday – emotionally difficult and guilt-ridden – not the terrain for a sixteen-year-old. Many years later, Selina confirmed that he had been hurt, and upon hearing this, nonchalantly, I shrugged it off – my father never knew my true motivation.

It had to do with my perception, as portrayed by my mother, of his wrongdoing relating to infrequent monthly maintenance payments of R20. I believed the stress it caused her was an attributable cause for her nocturnal drinking habits and behaviour that marred our family life. My vision was blurred and the amount inconsequential when compared to my stepfather's earnings of R1,000 per month.

"Your father doesn't even pay the maintenance and he is in arrears again. Perhaps I should have him locked up as I did before", spewed with vitriolic anger. My heart sank, my father in prison? I did not have the wherewithal to ask her whether it had happened, but rather buried it deep into my subconscious. But I did wish to put an end to her continual disagreeable outbursts.

For my dad's part, was he genuinely unable to pay? Was it a *power* game, a psychological denial of his responsibility, or some other unresolved matter like finding his dignity, that perhaps broke the camel's back? I never uncovered any further clues but what was clear is *they never communicated effectively*.

Unbeknown to me, my punishment of my imagined hero, my dad, was an imploring to show insight and tease out the true nature of my hurt. A soft enquiry like *what is this really about, or how can I help,* may have resolved and restored the father-son bond I so desperately yearned for. It never happened that way.

It was not only about the *maintenance*. I was also fed up having to amuse myself either waiting in the car or playing on my own near the pub, while my dad had a *quick one* at lunch time. His peace offering, a passion-fruit-and-lemonade, or a kola-tonic-and-soda-water, both my favourites. The *quick one* always became *another*. The justification was always the same: *they wouldn't let me go and bought me another round, then it was my turn to reciprocate; it's important for business you know*. It may well have been but the three weeks we had together were precious. I tried to discourage the lunch time drinking habit, but mostly to no avail.

Time slipped away to the dreaded devil of the bottle. His alcoholic breath greeted me upon returning to the car with a guilt-ridden feigned smile. He tried to resume conversation from before, except it was not easy for me. Still smarting from his deceit of *just fifteen minutes,* which always stretched to *an hour plus,* I remained disappointed and lonely, but again. Even now, the acrid smell of alcohol on anyone's breath still haunts me.

When my dad was flush, he drank his preferred drink, whisky, otherwise, brandy; it was cheaper. The nonsense of *money is tight* did not fool me. There was always enough for another bottle to feed his habit, while he remained oblivious to my emotional needs – then, addiction, dependency, or denial was not understood by me.

Saddened by his deception, the amount spent on that bottle could have fed us for a few days with a home-cooked meal of bangers, mash and a tomato-and-onion salad. Notwithstanding, whenever he prepared that simple enjoyable meal, I always felt an overwhelming sense of love and completeness.

My father relaxing at Sunshine farm

Tumeric - my father's race horse

My father on the right - The docks with Table Mountain in the background

CHAPTER 5
SECRETS

The Valentines I knew while growing up was a smaller business; only Pam, Selina and my father were involved then. The evocative smells of the stationery, packed high on the shelves and the polished wooden floors of those old Cape Dutch buildings, created a pleasant, serene atmosphere, of something older; antiquity.

The sisters' regular inquisition shattered it, mostly during tea times. Two wicked witches, huddled like conspiratorial gossips, would interrogate me as if schooling me in the ways of their world, but only when my father was not present. *Now don't you grow up drinking like your father . . . did he drink yesterday when you were on the road? . . . you know he is very conscious about his gammy leg.*

The pronouncements uttered were pointed and unhelpful, mostly because they, as busy bodies, never invited candid, compassionate conversation. Instinctively, I remained guarded and would never respond meaningfully. Of the two, Selina was the most devious and talkative, while Pam silently nodded, kowtowing to the boss. On her own, she was more likeable, but at work, she played second-fiddle to Selina, the dictator.

~

Some forty years later, dark stuff that had been swept under the carpet, surfaced. It related to Pam's husband Damien. It was Beth's story, the youngest of my father's siblings, then in her eighties and the only one still alive. I was staying with her while competing in the 2006 World Masters Cycling Championship in Manchester, England, the main reason for being there – not so, it turned out.

While Selina was alive, her relationship with Beth had already soured and was exacerbated upon Selina whimsically changing her will excluding her overseas relatives. Many years after Adrian's death, when I was in my late thirties and living in London, Selina, then in her late seventies, travelled down memory lane visiting her roots – she stayed with Beth. While there, she suggested spending a few days with my family – hardly my favourite aunt and having already distanced myself from her, I made a feeble excuse . . . but alas, her feisty fortitude and persistence could not be refused – "I can sleep on the floor."

She had a strong constitution, sheer guts, and plenty of it, living way into her nineties after having had part of her cancerous bowel removed in her early seventies. Her post-operative recovery was slow, unlike her determination to live. Her initial daily short walks progressed to longer ones. This passion developed once Adrian had died. She was a stoic survivor and had a pleasant enough superficial disposition.

My distancing, unlike Beth's, had to do with freeing myself from Selina's controlling manner and feigned generosity. There was a clincher – it happened on one of my many visits back to South Africa, where I would visit relatives to nurture our family bonds.

While sipping our rooibos tea, many years after her successful operation, we politely danced around stilted conversation. Her usual questioning prevailed, utterly meaningless within the context, *do you have a respectable job*? . . . *is she a decent sort*? . . . and so on, then veering to my father. Pompously, she extolled their virtues – always protective of blood ties – taking me back to those conspiratorial conversations, deceptively out of her husband's ear shot.

I remained patient up to a point, experiencing my inner child reliving the perpetual untruths uttered by her. My head shook in disbelief, and my irritation grew. Our roles had not changed. The boy in me felt increasingly suffocated, a reminder of the overripe smelling melons in her flat. Selina, cocooned in her world, was oblivious to my reaction – her denial had to be challenged and stopped.

My experience of *men's work* helped. Surprisingly, my newfound calm *adult voice* came to the fore, "It's not true, my father was an alcoholic!" It was the first-time stated, matter of fact – this confrontation simultaneously overcame my denial. Prior to, and particularly with friends, I kept up an illusionary relationship regarding my father – necessary for my survival, and partly influenced by hovering adult indoctrination, *never speak badly about the dead*!

Selina, hardly taken aback, dug her heels in, "He wasn't an alcoholic, he used to serve the drinks at our annual Christmas party and would only ever have *a drink* when he came to us for dinner."

I was incensed – "Really, do you recall those dinners at your home? Well, he had already slipped *one or two* in beforehand and upon returning to our flat, the drinking spree continued . . . often into the early hours of the morning."

"He had a problem once, but Adrian sorted it out," Selina clumsily blurted. In her mind that was the end of the matter; denial is, after all, denial.

There was a funny side to the Christmas party: the guests, mostly doctors and psychiatrists, rivalled the imagined baseball game in *One Flew Over the Cuckoo's Nest*. Bulbous-eyed Adrian and Dr John, sporting an impish twinkle, were the main characters, while the rest of the wacky cast wore an array of bow ties that complimented their unkempt eccentric hair. The more they drank, the funnier they became. They told the same annual joke, laughing as though they had heard it for the first time. After that, Dr John's famous choo-choo train ensued. The merry band, clasping onto each other's waists, held on as best they could and flapped their arms like a parade of ducks off to the market with an occasional lift of the leg to some sort of rhythm. The inebriated room was slowly circled.

My dad, Joyce and I would share a knowing smile. He, a brilliant master of ceremonies and raconteur, had predicted their capers. Joyce was elegant, far more real and refined than the rest of the bored wives who appeared to trail in the shadows of their husbands. And in that moment, our world was complete and full of fun.

My father made a superb barman, never having a glass of his own in his hand. Of course, he would have a *quick one*, in between serving the guests, undetected. I noticed, and in his superb guise, he fooled them.

~

Perhaps Selina and Adrian were from the same cast, or through marriage had become like one another. Adrian's direct bribe of offering to pay for my university education never sat well with me. It was the proviso – I had to study medicine. During my early teens, his glaring eyes would continually prompt me to be grateful for their largesse and generosity.

An onlooker may be fooled into believing he had only my best interests at heart. It was the way Adrian did it. He let me know it takes seven years to qualify, rather than three for a basic degree. Therefore, the paying of the fees was exceptionally generous – Selina's silence indicated her concurrence.

My armour was thin and without a shield of confidence, I never challenged him. I could have said *if you really wish to be supportive of me then perhaps you may consider paying for my university education, irrespective of the chosen faculty?* This would have flushed out his real intent, rather than my perception of control and yet more inter-family manipulation.

Was it a self-centred gesture for their aggrandizement, as if a vindication for the adoption battle lost? Was it to show that on balance, they had my very best interests at heart? Maybe I am too harsh, for they had other redeeming qualities, but that is how it felt.

In their adaptive roles, they were ostensibly content, civil and good companions. Selina was the boss at work during the day and the sweet deferring wife at home. It may seem like a contradiction but, in a strange sort of way, I liked them as a couple.

Old *bulbous eyes*, interested in my cycling achievements, could be very amusing and had an endearing way of telling stories. Mostly, he treated me like an adult but, in another vein, that ever-present *bribe* was lurking just below the surface – it kept me on my guard. Somehow, I remained polite and thanked them for their offer, but inwardly I was appalled and forlorn.

If the truth be known, I did want to study medicine, but my pride intervened – my soul could not be sold to the devil, nor did I intend to empower the skewed family dynamics and the tug of war between Cape Town and Johannesburg.

The scales tipped to another uninformed decision to study for a Bachelor of Commerce degree instead – my perceived optics of wealth guided my illusion that the road to riches would lead me out of my emotional morass. My mother's boss, a Chartered Accountant, who lived in the affluent neighbouring suburb of Bedfordview, would often give her a lift home; he drove a white Mercedes Benz, was polite and refined. It seemed natural to emulate him, even though I had not the faintest idea as to what accountants did.

My mom worked as a freelance comptometer operator for auditing practices. She had an elegance, sat upright, and I was proud of her. Without looking, her fingers glided seamlessly across the protruding keys on an abacus type machine, skilfully depressed in a sequence and, as if by magic, the answer automatically appeared in the lower transparent window.

Desiree had a fortuitous windfall, a rare luxury in our family, from an investment recommended by one of her auditing bosses. Generously, when I was sixteen years old and in my final year of school, she gave me a thousand rands – sufficient for a couple of years of university education. At that time, she was convinced that she would die of throat cancer, and at least I would have some money towards my education. She never died that way, and no doubt the sore throat was from her habitual smoking.

~

Many families have fallouts over bequests; Selina's was no different. Beth took umbrage, more so when it finally transpired that all relatives were excluded, except Charmaine, Johnny's daughter, who became the sole beneficiary. Most peculiar – remember, I was forbidden to mention to Selina or Adrian that we had visited Johnny's family – what had changed?

Time moved on . . . Johnny had died, and I had lost contact with Selina.

Meanwhile, a surprising co-dependent relationship developed between Selina and Charmaine. It was insidious by nature – a cruise holiday entourage accompanied her after Adrian's death: Doreen, Charmaine and Charmaine's children.

It proceeded from there – Charmaine convinced her to sell the Green Point flat and to move in with them as a paying boarder. Initially, mutually beneficial, until Selina's frail care needs became more demanding. Next stop, a nursing home that Monty, my eight year older cousin on my father's side and son of Pam and Damien, dubbed, *death-ville*. He watched these happenings and interceded, moving her to more suitable accommodation.

If anyone should have felt aggrieved by exclusion from Selina's Will, it was Monty, not Beth for he had done much for Selina after Adrian's death. Was it appropriate that Selina's remaining assets went to Charmaine or was it an appeasement for the *Johnny incident*?

Who knows – what struck me most was the irony.

~

During the Manchester Championships, Beth casually mentioned that she had been in therapy for help with a family matter. Unexpectedly, it became the trigger to enable her to air *her secret* – never spoken about until into her eighties.

Julia, her daughter, and I attentively sat around the dinner table – the environment beckoned.

Beth's mother had arranged for her to live with Damien and Pam shortly after their marriage because of my grandfather's alcoholism and its consequences. She was still a teenager.

"A lifetime . . . It took me a lifetime to have the courage to talk about it!"

I shuffled forward on my seat . . . lest a snippet was missed . . . her words hung – Damien, her brother-in-law had sexually violated her.

Her modulation lowered, "It affected my marriage as well."

There was silence . . . I was flabbergasted, broken only by Beth's sigh, "Something in Sarah's voice (Monty's sister) made me feel it had happened to her as well."

"Did you ask her", I feebly asked.

"No, it was just in her voice."

Normally, this inference would seem bizarre, but another lateral happening made it plausible. A family friend, who had been abused as a child, and I had witnessed a healing modality for a dying man. Quite distressingly the healer accused him of having committed various abuses, which surprisingly he admitted. Perhaps with death imminent, further deception is forgone as the soul dictates the need for forgiveness.

The family friend said, "I knew before he was even accused. Whenever I'm in the presence of an abuser, my energetic body feels uncomfortable."

Beth continued, "Damien said it was our special secret – he was preparing me for marriage so that I would know what to do." The prevalent abuser's tentacles of purported kindness manipulated Beth who was dependent on their sanctuary. She, like so many other young people abused, do not know where or whom to turn to.

"I thought of telling my sister, but I was afraid she would not believe me, and that it would probably create a disastrous fallout."

During *men's work events*, I often heard similar stories relating to abuse. The misplaced sexual arousal further complicated the confused thinking, which only made the abused feel guiltier about their complicit conduct.

Somehow, she meandered through the haze of it all to meet and marry Vernon, a professor of Sociology. On their wedding day, she dutifully walked down the aisle clutching Damien's arm; he *gave her away*.

It got worse – Beth nearly fainted. The knot in the pit of her churning stomach was not from the bridal jitters but rather Damien's inappropriate wedding speech. *The beautiful blossoming rose, so carefully nourished, and looked after by us, awaited Vernon to arrive and take his beauty away*, Beth recalled. Barely overcoming her nausea, she stifled back her tears and her involuntary need to retch. The rest of his words drifted aimlessly over her numbness, frozen in stunned disbelief.

Vernon, for his part, did – in time, they went to the Belgian Congo. Their fresh start from distasteful memories, not that he knew, was soon interrupted as they fled with their two children during the Congolese conflict in the 60's, returning to England. Ultimately they divorced, while she remained on in Manchester returning to her ancestral Liverpudlian roots.

I have been unable to discuss *Beth's secret* with Monty, nor the implications relating to Sarah. Perhaps the darkness of his letter about his sister's suicide at the age of sixty-seven had contributed. For him it may have been a simple sharing to lighten his load or an unconscious cry for help, but it was the way he blamed her for her bipolar condition and the bizarre things she did in her puberty.

Upon each rereading of the letter, a repugnant energy descended – I meant to reply, but could not – ultimately, it was crunched and thrown away; but had that freed me of a responsibility to respond?

On some level as the last in the Thornhill male bloodline, but for my son, Beth needed me to know, as if by osmosis, her, and her family's healing would be assured. We discussed how the Quechua in Peru seek guidance from shamans journeying in altered states, identifying past and present ancestral traumas, and healing them. Ritual and ceremony is used to resolve any further emotional harassment – ignored, it will flare again.

Meal times, normally an enrichment of spirit, a time of emotional bonding, a sharing of our stories and our dreams of the future. At Beth's table that evening I was captive and would absorb more unexpected psychological fodder.

The river had burst its banks – the twirling flotsam and debris trapped in the tributaries of Beth's soul needed an escape. In full flow, Beth spoke unabatedly, as if the outcome might be one act of absolution for all, except I was oblivious to its direction. The intensity increased and became overpowering.

Julia chidingly interjected, "Mom, you simply cannot talk to Walter like that!"

Vaguely, as if in a trance, I recall donning my mask but again, the one worn most of my life that hid my emotional hurt. With a misplaced sense of responsibility, as if Beth's hurt was more important than mine, I feebly mumbled, "It's OK."

Beth continued with conviction and a dismissive ease, "We had family meetings and thought it was hopeless. What chance did you have? An insolvent father . . . and a drunk like my dad. We thought the worst, shrugged our shoulders and simply moved on!"

The impact was enormous – bare, vulnerable and thunderstruck – a trapped animal. A sense of abandonment welled and an emotional flurry of chemicals rapidly spread throughout my body – shutting me down.

I have known this space many times before, driven by my mother's almost daily bombardment in raising the ante caused by her addiction to alcohol. Unconsciously then, I reached for a mask – it shielded me from the world and, the world from my family secrets.

My system would have imploded, had it not been for my cycling days, where I learnt to push through and overcome the relentless onset of fatigue. It became my reflexive way of survival. I merely persevered, knowing no better. I pushed myself ever onwards and always hopeful.

There were consequences later – the cracks slowly showed. No one intervened – fair weather friends took the line of least resistance and even partners often remained oblivious. A world of denial developed, except I never saw it as such.

"Fight or flight" said Richard Olivier many years later in a one-line response to my rather long intertwined emotional outpouring relating to my marriage. Again, I donned a different mask, a pretence of understanding, even though I was unfamiliar with those terms, the territory, or its relevance.

Perhaps Beth's expression of the collective guilt of the Thornhill family was her view only or a way of hiding behind other family members. My mother's rendition of Selina and Adrian's insensitive attempt to adopt me and the conditional offer to pay for my university education, makes me think that it was only her view – I would like to believe that.

Beth did not need to continue, but did, "We abandoned you!"

This realisation hit me hard, somewhere deep down, and like a punch-drunk boxer struggling to stand upright, I clung on – wondering when this ordeal would be over?

The gist was clear, and my emotional shutters had closed, obfuscating reality. My *inner child* had the upper hand and we both drifted unconsciously in the vast ocean, rudderless.

After all, was I not a man of the world with strong shoulders? My illusory world imploded, the one I created for my *inner child's* survival. Now there was nowhere to hide as Beth had become the arbiter and harbinger of the truth. The adult receded; my hurt and wounded *inner child* still needed much embracing. I feel the pain exploring that previously denied but now evident injured place deep within, and while writing the tears slowly, trickled down my cheeks.

Condescendingly, Beth's words ebbed in disbelief, "Well who would believe it, look at you now, you are all right while we have all the problems."

Of course, the point was missed – we all have relative issues – neither a competition; rather how we chose to weave our fabric of existence. *Who was expiating whom*?

The crux was that I held my *overseas* aunt Beth and her husband in high regard even though I never remember meeting them as a child. He, the *professor,* and *an author*, a sociological book about a distant place, Stanleyville, in the Congo. It conjured up images of wildness and savagery.

His imagined success allowed me to bathe in his achievements, feeling a glimmer of respectability as if I too belonged to and was part of it. It was that link to the greater family group, but it would not be until my mid-forties that I better understood how well indigenous people naturally grasp and absorb the benefits of bonding, without needing to rationalise it.

For the moment, my imagined ivory tower had imploded!

I had tried to reunite and reclaim my relatives, meeting Beth for the first time at her home in Didsbury, Manchester – I was twenty-two, my gap year, while backpacking in Europe.

Julia and I first met when we were both thirteen. She was visiting Cape Town and staying with Adrian and Selina, supposedly on holiday but actually under his watchful professional eye.

They were always trying to coerce her away from being a vegetarian, her choice. Adrian let me into his cruel, deceptive plan to feed her meat. "It's good for her health, and this vegetarian stuff is a lot of nonsense." I was sworn to secrecy, became an uncomfortable accomplice and accepted that what he said must be true; but my gut did not agree.

Under the guise of an African pumpkin fritter, Frikkadels were served. The gods were on Julia's side and curtailed Adrian's ploy. She ate half of one and disdainfully declared, "I don't like them." Promptly, they were pushed aside and not a morsel more eaten – I smiled. Adrian's bulbous eyes remained bulbous, but he was crestfallen.

We met again during my gap year. Julia and her boyfriend were on holiday, staying in a quaint cottage on the beautiful, desolate and wind-swept western side of the Ring of Kerry, in Dingle Bay, Ireland.

We spent a delightful few days together, walking for miles over beautiful green rolling hills to a distant isolated pub. With our fill of Guinness, we merrily weaved our way home in the middle of the night, arm in arm, singing and cavorting. Our laughter echoed down the valley, softened by the gentle rain as if it were an Irish blessing; then, home to the warmth of the peat-fired Aga.

She married, had two children, but realised that the pain of doing the *right thing* was unbearable. *Out* she came, divulging her secret about her true sexuality – I was not surprised.

There were lovely touches and an amelioration to the *evening of spoken truths* as Beth and Julia found their way to the Manchester Stadium on the last night of the championships; a complete surprise. The glow and expression of enjoyment beamed on their enthusiastic faces, cheering me on as if I were their world champion. We were all blessed, emotional frontiers redressed and all was possible again. My bereft *inner child* was happy too, embraced by the adult recognition and I felt complete.

Another day and a new hope – the breeze blows, and the sun continues to shine. Meanwhile, the disguised damage quietly rests in the repressive halls of the subconscious. It becomes the precursor to the emotional havoc caused by the unexpected periodic eruptions.

The *wounded soul* awaits the healing balm of recognition of unresolved matters. While the fearful wounded *inner child*, shouldering them, needs to be seen, embraced and loved by its *own adult*. This continual process is fed with compassion until a sense of well-being is achieved and a healthy *inner child – adult integration* takes place.

This is a journey I have undertaken.

CHAPTER 6

CYCLING

There were colourful, inspiring characters in the cycling world. Pioneering men like Gotty, already mentioned (Tour de Jugend), and Raoul de Villiers, driven by a vision and love for the sport. Voluntarily, they gave of their time to our sport of naked, raw energy, encapsulated in a *can-do attitude*, endeavouring to achieve a similar fanatical following to that which dominates the European psyche.

Raoul, a newspaper man, worked for *Rapport,* a new Afrikaans conservative weekly newspaper launched in 1970 to rival the more liberal English-speaking *Sunday Times.* In '73 the longest amateur stage race in the world was born – the prestigious *Rapport Tour.*

Styled on the Tour de France, different sponsored teams of riders were invited to compete over a distance of some 1,500 kilometres with the start and finish alternating annually between Johannesburg and Cape Town.

Gotty and Raoul were my early role models. Their examples of commitment, enthusiasm and vision helped me enormously in ways they never knew. First, though, they had to overcome the stalwart, Cyril Geoghegan, from Natal, the English enclave of South Africa. He had been the president of the South African Cycling Federation for twelve years, and the young Turks knew now what was necessary. Men like Raoul and Gotty, driven by a passion, took up the cudgels, and our sport flourished.

Then there was Harry Bloomfield, an ex-British professional cyclist, whose stewardship was instrumental in Southern Transvaal's (the province I lived in) team domination of interprovincial and national championships. The reigning champions were nevertheless scattered throughout the four provinces of South Africa: Transvaal, Orange Free State, Natal and the Cape.

Shrewd Harry, our doyen and a great tactician, always wore a black French beret – his distinctive hallmark – which complimented his protruding tummy. Like a baguette or the Eiffel Tower, his spirit encapsulated my imagination and allowed me to dream of the greatest race ever, the Tour de France.

I liked Nic Nolte, a Hollander and a spectator – a bricklayer by day – and at times, my informal track coach being of great psychological help. English-Dutch pidgin was our modus operandi, complimented only by intense stares and physical gesticulations. His friendly and generous spirit nourished and encouraged me to do my best. Other cyclists were dismissive of him.

A comforting hand on my back steadied my nerves as he held my cycle upright against the steeply inclined track. His short, stocky body and strength was our secret weapon. We deployed our perfected technique: feet strapped in for the 400 metre event, pressure on the pedals, while he held me back – pistol fired – an almighty powerful thrust propelled me advantageously forward.

Jack Lester, a Springbok cyclist (the highest accolade for representing the country), six years older than me, was my mentor and friend. We were playfully dubbed *the intellectuals* in this predominantly blue-collar sport. We studied the constitution, understood the election process and on occasions stirred the political pot.

We were spoilt in South Africa, where we could race all year round; track in the warmer months and road during winter. University years were helpful with copious free time to pursue my cycling dreams – racing the South African circuit and annual invitations to the Somorel and Fagor Tours in Mozambique.

This changed in my twenty-first year, articled to a firm of Chartered Accountants – work in the day and lectures in the evenings. Meaningful road racing was hampered – there is no substitute for the *base-miles* needed. But for track racing, I devised a shortcut incorporating competitive events skilfully as part of my training regime – I never let on. The type and duration were changed closer to targeted premier events like the sought-after annual Minnaar 25 mile track trophy held in Paarl or the South African Track Championships over Easter weekends.

My intent to peak was sometimes hindered by misjudgement or illness. There is a fine line in achieving and sustaining peak performance – helped only by a strong psychological makeup. My way was more intuitive, rather than scientifically proven. Not surprising, at times my erratic track performances were responsible for the many random drug tests even when not in contention.

In 1971, my second year at university, a contingent of seven riders was chosen by Harry Bloomfield, our team manager and coach, to become the unofficial South African team competing in the annual Fagor Tour in Mozambique. This mini Tour de France – from the starting point in Lourenco Marques, now Maputo, the capital – took seven days; the real Tour, three weeks.

The General Assembly of the United Nations had just passed a resolution calling on all member states to shun sporting activities with South Africa. We slipped under the international radar, a lesson in subterfuge, by being invited as a club rather than as an official team.

It was my second trip to Mozambique, having ridden in the shorter four-day Somorel Tour the year before, where I finished ninth in the overall classifications. The Fagor Tour was a quantum leap and a taste of what it is to be a professional – racing daily and touching the area of pain and suffering known only too well by all racing cyclists.

This pain and suffering is seldom talked about as if it would detract from the fulfilment of dreams; dreams powerful enough to override the discomfort experienced along the way. It is its own silent lore – it was for me. The focus needed is singular, demanding, continual and feeds from a special place in the psyche that encourages this discipline.

Some of the cast of characters in our team for that Fagor Tour included stylish Jeff Lincoln, always impeccably attired. He rode an imported Masi bespoke cycle – the only one in South Africa. The atmosphere buzzed as we reverently unwrapped this pinnacle of Italian design and beauty. It was as if we were in the pupillage of the great designers like Cinelli and Colnago.

Jeff drew from its mystical powers, performing better than he had ever done previously. Encouraged by his effortless, smooth pedalling action, it was always pleasurable riding in his slipstream. Alas, without him in sight, it was back to my old habits.

Wolfie Landgrebe, the son of a German immigrant, was the most unusual lanky cyclist. The Tour became a playground for his comical collective nouns and mixed metaphors, which always had us in fits of laughter as we struggled to hold on to our handlebars. It happened during the dull moments while the peloton rolled listlessly along. He would *jump* – a colloquial term for sprinting away. And it was as if in cajoling and encouraging our spirits, he would howl in his inimitable voice, *come on let's go like a herd of turtles!*

His indomitable spirit never tired of this energy-sapping practice. Normally, a *jump* has an element of surprise, but his shout always gave it away. His tactics and timing were questionable, yet undeterred he persisted, notwithstanding his challenges quickly petered out. Perhaps, a change of metaphor may have helped, then again it may have been for his amusement; it certainly was for ours.

Joe Knobblespies was the eldest, thirty-two years old. A few years prior, Joe immigrated from Austria with his clipped German accent and his love of our sport. A colourful character, sanguine, and a seasoned road rider with a pugnacious look, robust and reliable but lacked a good sprint finish. Characteristically, he wore a cycling cap perched on top of his head – the two were inseparable, and the slightest puff of wind might have blown it away. He filled the role of a *domestique*; prized in European racing, and relentlessly, he closed the gaps in many breakaway attempts.

Alan van Heerden, Jeff and I were still juniors (I was eighteen). How might we fare was still unknown. *The Van*, his nickname, was a phenomenal natural athlete and became a legend in South African cycling. Four years later, he turned professional and raced in Europe under a pseudonym. His '76 successes stand out: a stage win in the '76 Giro de Italia, a placing in the Paris-Roubais and to compete in the greatest Tour – just before the start, his cover was blown. By comparison, I worked hard on every aspect of myself. At the same time, I raced in Belgium and Holland, under the wile of being a British cyclist.

The overall victory for the Fagor Tour was his; the accolade for the longest day of racing, mine. Often, emotively, certain stage wins are important – such was Alan's plight as I was soon to find out. It was a dual stage of some two hundred and twenty kilometres, ending in João Belo (Xai Xai).

Road sprinters edge forward towards the end of any race. We swept around the final bend towards the looming finishing line, a Portuguese rider hugging Alan's wheel. A journalist had labelled me *mercurial wily Walter* – Alan drifted, an opportunity spotted – I held my line forcing the Portuguese rider to surrender his.

Alan *jumped*. I clung to his wheel for dear life in those nerve-racking moments, as we simply accelerated away from an exhausted peloton, nipping at our heels.

The advantage garnered – my attack – unfolded instinctively; accelerating and hurtling past Alan as if he were standing still. Adrenaline gushed, astonished, my victory had not quite sunk in, while my lungs screamed.

Having not even dismounted, Alan conducted his inquisition. "Where were you? I had all my bases covered, you were not in my slipstream." Suddenly, he burst into tears – years later, I understood the power of those emotions.

The rest of the Fagor Tour was peppered with many vignettes. We all wanted to believe in some magic that would give us a beneficial advantage – Joe's was a swift, deft movement of cracking an egg over his handlebars at the start of each stage and swallowing the contents in one gulp. His showmanship preceded with utterances of *"das ist sehr gut . . . wunderbar . . . ich bin sehr schnell, Champion"*. I barely understood the gist but loved the theatrics.

Now our German Commandant was about to perpetuate another war at the start of the second stage of the longest day's racing that I had won. Perhaps it was the heat of the afternoon, or an apprehension for the distance still to be covered – nerves were tinged and a little frayed – suddenly, insults were flying.

"*Porre*", followed by "*German Schweinehund*" – bikes fell to the ground. Gesticulating fists – tempers only assuaged by restraint to an ebb of soft mutterings. The starter could not wait to fire his gun. A few kilometres was all that was needed to dissipate *our international incident*.

The traditional start of the Tour commenced with a celebratory ride around the Salazar track stadium. No huge crowds were hanging over the rails, cheering us along like in the Tour de France, but merely a handful of aficionados and sponsors. Quite unlike our raucous pavement send-off outside our lodgings beforehand by a crowd of local women as our cycles were loaded onto an open truck. Our sponsored accommodation was in a very shabby hotel, in *Sin Street* as it was colloquially known, directly opposite the professional ladies' parlour.

Cyclists' shoes have cleats underneath and in order not to damage them, we often walked on our toes. The ladies clearly enjoyed the spectacle of a colourful rotation of ballerina-cyclists prancing about; they continued to jeer and laugh.

Joe was clearly well known to them. While travelling by car to Mozambique he would regale us with the delights to be had in Lourenco Marques. Clearly, he had a predilection for professional ladies and was an expert – we were young and naive. In his insistent Germanic way, he encouraged Alan to partake. Alan was hesitant, but the consistent ribbing by the rest of the team, in our playful ignorance, seemed to convince him. They visited the parlour.

We laughed, and were just too scared to join, hoping that the nocturnal activities would be detrimental. Of course, Harry had insisted on a good night's rest for all and knew nothing of this. Alan proved us wrong and won the first stage effortlessly.

Perhaps it was Alan's first time – he escaped unscathed, but not Joe. He tasted *the ladies'* derision: they bent forward over an imaginary racing cycle holding on to the handlebars, and with a mocking of the appropriate pelvic thrusts of their profession, pointed at him falling about in uncontrollable spasms of laughter.

Incited further only by his protests, Joe was on trial. He did his best to pretend to ignore their scorn with appropriate dismissive hand gestures . . . this merely goaded them on, while we hysterically joined in – pandemonium ensued – they fell about the sidewalks, their bellies trembling, our sides aching.

This was child's play compared to the flippant scorn Joe still had to contend with from his team-mates, while on the way to the stadium. Joe wore it well – no wonder he needed a raw egg at the start of each stage.

Our paths crossed again some ten years later. His indomitable *playful spirit* remained. Despite being a leg amputee from a mining accident, he continued to cycle with a prosthesis. We reminisced and playfully jibed each other, drifting deliriously back to the Fagor Tour. In that moment, it was Joe who had won the longest stage and the overall tour; his victory complete – the subsequent mishap a mere incident.

It seems that the João Belo stage was my crowning glory; the rest of the tour was rather difficult for I had developed a saddle sore on my crotch that became an abscess. After that, each day I bravely mounted in excruciating pain. Ten kilometres of riding through that barrier, my brain anesthetised, but not sufficiently to halt the relentless gnawing thought – *to quit*! I was driven, not wanting to let my team-mates down.

It was an exceptionally hot day; the heat, reflected off the tarmac, created images of shimmering lakes of water on the distant horizon that became the mirages of my mind. I persevered somehow – mindlessly trying to count to a hundred – forgetting where I was, starting over or just in the middle of a sequence. Adrift, in and out of my numbed state, hanging on, with time passing slowly in my state of delirium.

Finally, that stage ended, the relief from a hot shower, palpable. We slept in a make-shift, stark and unfriendly dormitory, consisting of orderly rows of beds, under the huge vaulted cement ceiling of an enormous old aircraft hangar, then used as an Agricultural school – I never knew such schools existed.

It served its purpose; but I could not help but feel overwhelmed by a sense of oppression. Was it the cold smell of concrete, a dictator state or a family void of love? Was I drifting back, unconsciously into memories of my convent days, or was it an early premonition of my time to come in the military?

Joe Knobelspies leading the bunch

Jack Lester – 1968

1971 - Somorel Tour (L to R) Rodney Emmenes, Raymond Hogg, me, Martin Thomas, Jeff Lincoln, Wolfgang Landgreber and Harry Bloomfield, with his characteristic beret (photo courtesy of Ron Thompson)

CHAPTER 7
NEW BEGINNINGS

PERSPECTIVES AND PRESENTS

Surprises awaited. George and my mom were now married – we would live together, and I would go to a school that was across the road from our new home. I would even have my own bedroom. Life was different and good. Perhaps God had read my thoughts – no more convent days and the chance to be a family. While acclimatising, an adorable brown mongrel puppy arrived. It could not get much better.

George, in his capacity as chairman of the baseball association, attended the South African *Sportsman of the Year Award*. Perchance, sitting next to the winner Sandra Reynolds, the tennis player, he excitedly shared snippets of the ceremony. We were spellbound. I was proud of him, and naturally we called our puppy, Sandra; a beautiful Ridgeback and Golden Retriever cross and like an ancient Greek goddess, she bestowed her importance into our world.

My mother and I spent a lot of time playing with her where spoken and unspoken thoughts were seemingly understood. My true mother – kind, compassionate and playful – worthy of emulating.

Sandra, my new confidant, became a master at tricks – she sat up, shook paws, waited attentively until instructed to eat her titbits and could even roll over onto her back, on demand. She loved having her tummy tickled – a specific spot caused her back leg to involuntarily scratch – so funny and a source of endless amusement.

She did not always learn the tricks I taught her, and at times was quite disobedient. Quizzically, she raised an eyebrow or both, as if encouraging me to explain myself better.

Our house was small but adequate: a typical lower-middle-class suburban home, utilitarian rather than aesthetically pleasing. A compact backyard with few shrubs, flowers and a solitary fruit tree awkwardly planted in the middle of the lawn: 53 Cambridge Road, Kensington, bordering Bezvalley, the poorer predominantly Afrikaans suburb. It was as though these white suburb names dictated where an English or Afrikaans person might reside.

Allan de Roche and Gavin Beetge from the *Bezvalley gang* lived in Bezvalley, but I would not meet them until in my early teens, and only because of cycling. Sport, the leveller, transcended social boundaries – except racially – played separately in apartheid South Africa. Other than our privileged white skins, we were at the lower part of the rung.

The suburb was named after Frederick Bezuidenhout, a belligerent Boer – he defied the rule of law, resisted arrest and refused to surrender to the British authorities – he was shot dead. His brother vowed to avenge his death and the incited community of sixty burghers took an oath of vengeance and loyalty – the British clumsily handled the ensuing Slagtersnek Rebellion of 1815, which acquired more importance as a struggle of Afrikanerdom against British domination. Perhaps it added fuel to the general discontent that led to the Great Trek twenty-six years later.

The story of Hillary's ascension of the tallest mountain in the world was told by our school principal at Sir Edmund Hillary Primary School, where I completed standard two and three. It left me with a sense of awe and exhilaration as my imagination soared. The seeds of human endeavour were planted – my association of numbers like his ascension in the year of my birth were omens and portents equipping and signposting my life ahead.

Tenzing Norgay, the Nepalese Sherpa, who accompanied Hillary, was never mentioned, although it is often said that technically he was the first person on the summit – if anything, the honours should have been shared.

There were other artificial social boundaries – a mesh fence separated our school playgrounds – yet, raucous laughter and playful taunts from the English and Afrikaans children still penetrated. Unconsciously, an ancient territorial challenge ensued.

> *Afrikaner, Afrikaner, vrot banana*
> *(Afrikaner, Afrikaner, rotten banana)*
>
> *Engelsman, Englesman, rooi nek*
> *(Englishman, Englishman, red neck)*

Soutie, soutie, julle is soutpiele
(Salty, salty, you are salty cocks)

The first sentence of the rhyme is nonsensical; the second a reference to a sunburnt Englishman, ignorant of the strength of the African sun, followed by a feistier insult reflective of the pioneering Englishman's indecisiveness: one foot in England and the other in Africa.

Our *separateness* was exacerbated. True of all kids, we just wanted to play and know each other better – except – the legislated division between blacks and whites was even greater, forestalling integration.

My sheltered life behind the cloistered walls of the convent was overtaken by taunts and our seasonal game of conkers. No longer would the good Lord God overcome the forces of evil, supported by his cadre of devoted Saints.

Acorns bathed in vinegar embodied the conker with strength and invincibility; not too green or overly dry. Some lasted forever, complemented by the mastery of the deft flick of the boy's wrist, delivered with deadly accuracy. A superior *conker boy* emerged, and further informal inter-school battles ensued immediately after the final school bell. Cherished conkers made their debut. On the whole, sportsmanship prevailed, but there were the odd fisticuffs. Soon school break times were changed, making contact increasingly difficult – perhaps, unconsciously, more deep-seated grievances were prevented from being aired.

The Afrikaner's history started with the landing and occupation of the Cape by the Dutch East Indian Company in 1652. Jan van Riebeck and his entourage established a refreshment supply station for the Dutch ships on their way to the East. Restlessly, those early pioneers, wishing to initially free themselves of the Dutch and, subsequently, the British domination, trekked into the hinterland.

The devastating family stories, repeatedly heard over the dinner table about the Anglo-Boer War, inflamed and kept memories alive (that same war my paternal grandfather fought in). Kitchener's Scorched Earth Policy burnt over thirty thousand farmhouses to the ground. The Boers hid and buried family jewellery and precious mementoes, often never to be retrieved, for the places the survivors returned to were no longer recognisable.

The women, children, and servants were forcefully removed and sent to the British concentration camps; segregated even then between blacks and whites. Incomplete records suggest that of the 115,000 interned, over a third died (26,000 white women and children, and 14,000 black and coloured people). It would have been far worse had it not been for the continual lobbying by Emily Hobhouse, the British humanitarian, to the Members of Parliament back in the United Kingdom.

It was a disastrous war for Britain – their troops grew to outnumber the Boers by ten to one with deaths of over twenty-one thousand, to the Boers' six thousand.

After the war, the colonial confidence continued a silent endorsing of an unwritten separatist policy. This changed upon the Afrikaner's ascent to power in 1948. Still smarting from their treatment as second-class citizens and to bolster their insecurity, they went about legislating and enforcing the policy of apartheid.

The political success of those elections was predicated on a strategic re-enactment of the Great Trek, a hundred plus years later as a centenary celebration. Dressed as Voortrekkers they trekked with their replica ox-wagons across the country, passing through every Afrikaner dorp, creating a historical fervour.

It became a remembrance of forefathers – what they stood for, their strength of character, the hardships endured in assembling and disassembling the wagons as the oxen pulled chattels and possessions up and over the foreboding Drakensberg mountains into the interior, away from the rule of law and the control of the Cape.

The visual and visceral effects worked; the National Party won. Jan Smuts, the then prime minister's United Party was unexpectedly defeated. It was demoralising, especially as his party had more individual votes. The rejuvenated Afrikaner became the Phoenix rising from the ashes; first united as a volk with political party ideology second.

Smuts, an Afrikaner and a prominent statesman, military leader, philosopher and botanist, first fought for the Boers when he led the Boer Commando in the 1899-1902 Anglo-Boer War. Subsequently, for the Commonwealth during the First World War, leading the armies of South Africa against the Germans, capturing German South West Africa.

His statesman existence spanned the two World Wars, and as a member of Churchill's War Cabinet, he had a strong hand in the drafting of the League of Nations Charter that later became the United Nations. He was a vocal supporter of the segregation of the races while extolling virtues of humanitarianism and liberalism abroad, incongruous really.

My mother was born in 1926, the year he wrote *Holism and Evolution*. Einstein remarked that there would be two mental constructs that will direct human thinking into the next millennium, his own on relativity and that of Smuts' Holism (Einstein, 24 June 1936).

Smuts and Gandhi were political adversaries, respectful and admiring of each other. Initially, Gandhi extolled the virtues of British Democracy, but his views changed possibly because of the countless re-reading of Leo Tolstoy's *The God Within* during his various prison stints in South Africa. It became his beacon of *professing change without violence* (Satyagrahi), a tactic that ultimately toppled the British Empire in India with independence granted in 1947.

Before returning to India in 1914, Gandhi presented Smuts with a pair of sandals that he had made. Smuts returned them twenty-five years later for Gandhi's seventieth birthday with the following message – *I have worn these sandals for many a summer, even though I may feel that I am not worthy to stand in the shoes of so great a man* (Following the footsteps of a great man, 1939).

During my primary school years, I never knew much about that early history or the machinery of the Broederbond, an Afrikaner elite secret organisation dedicated to the advancement of the Afrikaner. It wielded power, ensuring that only its members were chosen for key positions in government and corporations. The grip on the country was tightened, the organisation's existence denied until exposed by the press in the late-seventies when the names and addresses of the prominent members were published, devastating the Broederbond.

I did not understand – the Afrikaner dilemma – in a nutshell, a belief and a need to forge their own country. The far-reaching fallout, with all its human difficulties, is well known and documented.

Nor did I understand the intricacies of the country's politics. The *Job Reservation Act*, an example of a fulfilment of an election promise to reserve certain jobs for whites only, while the *Group Areas Act* controlled different race groups places of residency.

What I did know was that the harmless English-Afrikaner schoolboy banter and our conker games were important to us. And, only by the age of fourteen, after a 60 kilometre cycle ride from Johannesburg to Pretoria, staying overnight at the Swanepoel family's home did my views of the Afrikaner change considerably for the better.

Smuts was born on his family farm, *Bovenplaats*, near Malmesbury.

". . . and then there was the purchase of Jan Smuts' Lancaster aircraft which lead to the downfall of Tropic Airways," explained my mother. "There was not one, but two breakdowns in rapid succession. A replacement Rolls Royce engine and spare parts were flown from London – the delays longer than expected." She spoke further of my father's wealth and her dismay when the liquidator walked into our home, marking all items of any meaningful value.

"Even the fur coat your father gave me," said indicative of a loss, another loss, far greater than the coat. "I stood watching, helplessly, as they systematically, like vultures, placed labels on the items. The men instilled fear, instructing me not to touch anything as they were no longer our property. It was awful. I held you in my arms – you were just a few months old!"

There were other snippets, different and romantic, ". . . those were the days when it took four days to fly to London . . . I was married for eight months only, to one of your dad's pilots, but then your dad and I fell in love, and he asked me to marry him." The *only*, I interpreted as an insignificant marriage . . . *was there any animosity? . . . did he remain in the employ of the airline?* While that to my father was meaningful – although it was never discussed.

I mused on their period of courtship, my mom an air hostess on his airline – *was she lured away, did they elope, or did my dad arrange for them to fly to exotic, romantic and mysterious sounding places, like Omar and Jordan, echoing images of Lawrence of Arabia, that must surely have added to their adventure? Could planes actually land and take off in the desert?* I wanted to know about such things, while those distant, untouchable places were beyond my suburban knowledge.

My mom clearly was spunky – Reg Park, an early influence and mentor to Arnold Schwarzenegger, had just won the Mr Universe award in 1951. He was on a return flight to South Africa, compliments of my father, and apparently particularly obnoxious. "I had enough and could not stand by any longer, so I feigned an accidental trip, purposely pouring a drink all over his suit. He remained as meek as a lamb after that," said my mom rather indignantly – I loved hearing her stories.

Numerous times, while in my teens, my mother said she was prepared to stand by my father. But my dad, it seems, became more aggressive, drank more and on occasions vented his frustrations, lashing out with more than just his tongue. Putting more of the pieces together, Monty confirmed that my folks stayed together until I was about four – it made sense.

In those early years during the night, I witnessed a violent argument while walking down the stairs. I stood and watched. Upon being noticed, I was instructed to go back to bed, knowing my father would sleep in the upright armchair.

On many levels, I felt disturbed – subliminally, locked into my subconscious – subsequently, in adulthood tapping on the door of my consciousness, inviting proper integration.

~

Strange, how parents can give the wrong types of presents – I always pretended to be most grateful; instilled from early teaching of manners and a boring continual reinforcement by relatives, *say thank you . . . don't be rude; she's your aunt you know*!

Then one day a great present arrived, my sister, Gayle – the proper spelling as George insisted – born on the 28 January 1961. The eight year age difference was significant; our interests dissimilar, and she was, after all, a girl – cute – although

I did wish she could speak rather than utter those silly gurgling noises; even Sandra looked up, quizzically.

My father's present giving was always a few years out of sync like paint-by-numbers when we all knew that cowboys and Indians were *in*. An Indian and an engine sounded similar – my misuse, much to the merriment and laughter of all, left me feeling humiliated.

Maybe, even then, I may have had a hearing impediment which was only discovered in my fifties. That may have accounted for my flirtation with Mrs Malaprop. In my mid-thirties, a small fish in the sophisticated metropolis of London, worse was to follow. Over lunch with a major client during my banking career, another surfaced – *eminent*. The usually shy and retiring treasurer drew his proverbial sword and delivered his *coup de grâce*, as only the English do so well; *imminent*, surely, raising his eyebrows. I felt his disdain. Daunted, I recovered my composure, concealed my embarrassment, and immediately checked the dictionary upon returning to the office.

George and my mother were not much better – a Zorro suit when all the kids knew Superman was *in*, just sucked. Dutifully, I would don my cape and mask, wield my sword and ride on a ridiculous pedal-tractor to Rhodes Park. Thank goodness, it was in the opposite direction to school for it would not be cool for my classmates to spot me.

Zorro's knees seen before Zorro – the tractor, ludicrously too small and for younger kids, required a Herculean task to awkwardly peddle. Neither farmer nor superhero. Even my toy black Scotty dog, seemingly a remnant of England, was equally irrelevant having never seen one before. Sandra, with real heart and soul, did not approve, and Scotty was banished.

The park was enormous, or so I thought, and the 800 metres peddling there in that peculiar fashion was a long way. The looks I received told me it was better to play Zorro at home, except for the odd creepy man encouraging conversation with the allure of an ice cream – I never accepted. My senses scurried me away from that danger, although there were uncomfortable moments.

Finally, I gave up on my tractor and Zorro's suit, walking instead. There were nooks and crannies to be discovered, getting to know the regular fishermen and, enjoying the playground. The roundabout was a favourite, while the swings were the least enjoyable – the point of equilibrium before the return – my stomach churned. Happily fatigued, I returned home, yet so often with a sense of loneliness. Perhaps, because I did not make any friends during the two years we lived there.

However, raiding the neighbour's apricot tree across the road was a real boon and beckoned when the fruit was ripening. There was much to learn about colour variation, its ripeness and taste: too dark, mushy and beyond its best; too light, acidic and unripe. Biting through a worm was squeamish stuff as it wiggled through my imagination, while sitting in the tree gorging myself, I soon realised *too much of a good thing is no good*. Sharp, decisive stomach pains, and the call of nature – home just in time.

The solitary plum tree in our backyard, besides its delicious offerings, made an excellent prop for a photograph standing carefree in its crook. My Zorro outfit now exchanged for a Cub uniform and a dutiful howl of our Cub promise:

> *I promise to do my best;*
> *To do my duty to God and my country,*
> *To keep the Law of the Wolf Cub Pack,*
> *And to do a good turn to somebody every day.*

I was distinctly uncomfortable with the resonance of the second line; *duty* troubled me, while the third was special; a hint of something mysterious; the other lore. The fellowship, a sense of belonging and the acquisition of skills and badges as a proof of advancement, was compelling and enjoyable.

GAMES

We were upwardly mobile. Two years later, we moved within the suburb of Kensington from the Bezuidenhout border to the posher Bedfordview side. The last house on the corner and at the opposite end of a 4 kilometre road that starts at Jeppe High School, which I attended later – 458 Highland Road. This number took on significance for Piet Jacobus du Rand, my next-door neighbour, in our later lives – he was thirteen years old and I was just about to turn ten.

There were four children in their family, Piet's older brother Andre, and his two younger sisters. It was my first meaningful encounter with Afrikaners besides brief interludes in the games of conkers and early kindergarten, while living in Koch Street. The boys became my new playmates as if providence had thrown us together.

It was strange at first for the unspoken word remained: *they were inferior* to the English-speaking whites. Now, in such proximity, it would become the start of my awareness and dissolve of White separateness.

The Afrikaner *Gereformeerde Kerk's* (Reformed Church's) blood pulsated through their family veins under the iron fist of Piet's laconic father, *old man du Rand*. He appeared to embody the puritanical views and the vows taken by the Afrikaner before the Battle of Blood River in 1838, when praying for deliverance from the onslaught of the attacking hordes of Zulus.

The stern disciplinarian with a powerful handshake, attempted to keep their lives *in balance;* yet it was his buxom caring wife, the embracing mother of mixed Afrikaner and Scottish heritage that held their family together.

I never knew *old man du Rand's* first name, but I did know his stories: an alcoholic who discovered the Lord and never touched another drop, worked for the government as an assay official ensuring weight scales measured accurately. Most intriguingly, his morning exercise and ablution routine – pull-ups on the branch of their distinctive mulberry tree and his preferred toilet *gravity squat,* somehow perched above the seat. After Piet's mind-boggling revelation, the *old man* was viewed differently and I smiled inwardly.

It was as if *old man du Rand* did not want me, the English-speaking kid from next door, to contaminate their home or value system – perhaps he was right. Yet we as children shrugged our shoulders, got on with it, and accepted his ways.

Everything about our larger home and the neighbourhood was uplifting: the different smells and a garden that seemed enormous – Sandra even gave a nodding wink and wagged her tail in approval. We were in heaven, and from the corner house, we had an uninterrupted view of our playground, the disused yellow cyanide mine dump and its peripheries.

Over the next nine years, an array of adventures happened there, including the completion of primary and secondary schooling, and my first degree. Albeit, an emotional sapping roller coaster through adolescence, teenage years and into young adulthood.

In trying to make sense of it all, the older kids knew better, seemingly drawing upon their vast life experiences. Religion and school were embraced and rejected.

It was natural to follow Andre through our private cut away entrance into the Kensington golf course, a street below where we lived. And an annoyance when the wire mesh fence was repaired. Then, we had to traverse the top of the tricky barbed wire. Patiently, Andre would re-open the gap, while we kept *chips,* lest we were spotted. There were few pedestrians or cars on those sleepy suburban roads; their distant engines audible as they groaned up or down the hill.

Andre, lanky and taller by far, was carefree, yet had a nervous disposition. He was our golf pro – we had no golf bag, shared our three irons and a putter: a three, a seven and a wedge, and on occasions we carried a wood. Our game started on the thirteenth hole, a par four. Andre, a natural, showed us the way, then Piet and me. Often, my balls veered with some advantage landing in the rough – other lost balls found were true to our maxim – finders-keepers. The brother's natural bush talent ensured they returned home with a bountiful supply.

An effortless execution down the fairway, followed by a good chip and a putt did wonders for our enjoyment and boyhood friendship as we wandered along, carefree as golf vagabonds: never paying green fees and relying on our cunningness. The eighteenth hole was but a dream – a no-go area – in full view of the clubhouse, and we risked being caught. The seventeenth, less risky, so we thought.

We were spotted. Andre ran like the wind, Piet close behind and my apprehension lengthened my short stubby legs, struggling to keep up our escape. Adrenaline pushed us to safety as we hid in the undergrowth behind the broad-beamed oak trees separating the fairways.

Our hearts pounded, our lungs screamed. We listened attentively to the sounds of abating footsteps. Andre and Piet's stealth, deeply rooted in their Voortrekker survival DNA and, by association, became mine. I never let on that my daringness was wanting. Rather, I basked in their irreverent fearlessness, free and beyond the yoke and control of the iron hand and tyranny of their father.

The sanctity of the course encouraged our spirits to flourish under Nature's protective mantle and we ate her manna: a white, sweet, sticky almond flavoured substance from the blue gum trees. We never knew if it was poisonous, neither did we care; only an overindulgence led to nausea.

Our ritual, of chasing a golf ball and living in the moment, cemented our camaraderie. The perceived lurking danger of being caught would have been, ironically, inconsequential. The Golf Club Secretary was married to Aunty Ronnie's dearest and best friend, Molly – but our tension, and fear, was real.

Aunty, a social golfer, played at that club. After Uncle Jack's death, we continued his Saturday morning tradition, but without the *talent scouting*. Instead, we indulged in tea, scones and toasted cheese-and-tomato sandwiches, my favourite. Afterwards, she would visit Molly while I watched the club pro give Terry lessons. He was about Andre's age, their only child and Aunty's godson.

Years later, he married despite an attempt by his relatives to dissuade him – the occult was consulted – the forceful finger controlling the glass on the Ouija board, hardly even subtle, spelled 'no'. Intrigued and in my twenties, I participated; it was a complete charade. Terry smiled, and politely excused himself; astonished, they soaked in their sweat of failure.

His marital challenge was like my cousin Julia's. He too divorced, and with Ivor, his partner, moved to Cape Town. Back then, gay relationships were frowned upon – perhaps the family knew and unable to air it openly, turned to their subterfuge.

My dear Aunty Ronnie, in her latter years, also moved to Cape Town, while I was in London. Our compassionate contact, circumstantially, was limited to letter writing, telephone calls and infrequent visits, while taking care of her financial responsibilities. Even more so, Terry's and Ivor's friendship and support of Aunty was invaluable. Ivor shared, "Terry is reliving his wounded mother-son relationship through Aunty as a surrogate mother, and, sometimes it is hard for me to stand by, witnessing it all as he goes about his resolve of sorts . . . but, I care and love him dearly!"

~

It was January, the middle of summer – a clean slate, new beginnings and a different uniform accompanied my eager anticipation to hear which sporting house I would be in. My new school, Kensington Ridge Primary, was within walking distance from our home. A plethora of discovery and exploration beckoned.

The good climate encouraged afternoon sporting activities. My quandary and disappointment was in not being able to play every school sport – there was something about games, the friendships and the certainty of rules. Uncle Jack's guiding hand, in between our Wanderers Club talent-scouting outings, became my comfort blanket: "Sometimes in life, you simply cannot do everything you please, and that is all right."

School work was acceptable but compared to sport a necessary evil. I was diligent and always did the homework my teachers set, although the concept of studying for exams eluded me until my first year of high school, some three years later. Unexpectedly, for the first time, I failed History; it was quite a shock.

Mrs Orbach, nicknamed *Allbubs*, because of her predominant upper anatomy, asked me to stay behind after school. My schoolmates' laughter and jibing resounded down the corridor, *Allbubs is going to give it to you . . . you're in for it now.*

Sheepishly, I returned awaiting my punishment. She looked at me quizzically, "You are one of my best students, homework always done, what happened?" Dazed, I looked on for I loved History – those exciting stories of the past. However, to recall the numerous dates of events and foreign names like Robespierre, Garibaldi and Byzantine were beyond me and impossible to pronounce. Seeing my stunned look, she enquired, "Did you not study for the exam?" Narrowing my eyes, thinking, she again noticed my confused look, "You know what it means to study, don't you? You must revisit the work continuously." In that split second, sensing her curiosity, the penny dropped – grateful for her guidance, I still had to figure out the *study thing*!

Anyhow, I am ahead of myself, back to primary school where the sandy shaded alley, adjoining the sporting playground, was our mecca. It was a favourite spot to indulge our afternoon passion of marbles where the in-house rules were orally handed down from one boy to the other and, in the event of an unforeseen altercation, made up on the spot. We could have stayed there forever. Either sport intervened, or the teachers ushered us along when we had overstayed our welcome.

Games commenced within seconds with the old familiar cry, *shaya, shaya,* (strike in Zulu). Pyramid castles were won if the stack was collapsed. School shoes had many uses: a quick game of football, to kick loose stones or pine cones while walking home but, most importantly, to haphazardly draw the demarcated line for our game in the loose red sand.

A win was only valid if the *shaya's* feet remained behind the line – easy to monitor . . . well up to a point. In the heat of the moment, the frenzy grew with each throw; excitement mounted, a magnetic effect edged the *shayas* closer to the cherished prize. Admonishments were yelled, like, *toe your ticks*, but mostly fell on deaf ears. We did not know where the colloquial term came from, but we certainly knew its meaning – our feet had to be behind the line. A castle of twenty marbles always attracted a big crowd – the ultimate prize dreamed of – the allure and risk of a solitary marble, most compelling.

The sound of rapid marble fire from a group of boys all throwing at the same time was music to the *keeper*, our term for the owner of a castle. It was only stopped by a successful hit, and any sane *keeper* would protect the marbles from being pilfered by sitting flat on the ground with outstretched splayed legs. A wayward marble, like a missile, could strike a *goolie* – ouch!

A keeper had to have eyes everywhere for deviant tricksters knew no bounds. The *line* creep by excited *shayas* was innocent enough, but not the sly throw of an accomplice, standing close to the target. Cheating was frowned upon and – if spotted – the marbles were not handed over; consequently, it died a natural death. A *keeper's* role was passive, but more lucrative, except if there were successive early hits by the *shayas*.

At times, it was like a cattle market: a cacophony of different excited cries from simultaneous games, *shaya, shaya . . . toe your ticks . . . that's unfair . . . wow, great hit,* and so on. We were hooked and tried distinctive styles like over-or-underhand. Girls were definitely not allowed, although their glaringly attractive long outstretched limbs were spotted while they played netball.

My bulging white cotton flour bag, discoloured by the hues of red sand and full of marbles, was a beacon revealing my prowess – marbles sold became a useful source of pocket money. But the real thrill was a big hit on the first throw, which always received vocal admiration – priceless, like floating on air, and life was great. Not surprisingly, I conveniently forgot to go home straight after school, a mere ten-minute walk.

A reproach, "Marbles again?" – I feigned surprise – the undusted red sand on my navy-blue shorts betrayed me. I wised up, but no matter how hard I tried to dust them off, the sand with a mind of its own remained, albeit a touch lighter.

One afternoon we all painfully witnessed a ruthless rebuke. An Afrikaans lad, at our school, in itself rather unusual, was seemingly instructed to go straight home but, like us all, was attracted to the companionship of the game. We watched in disbelief – his father, in a fit of anger, grabbed his son by the ear, twisting and holding it, as he wrenched him away – we were ignored completely.

Twenty or thirty paces away, he released his stronghold and made his son bend over and touch his toes. With a menacing look of cruelty, he unbuckled his thick postman's belt. It seemed an eternity as he deliberately and slowly pulled it through the loops as if each loop had to acknowledge the master's brutal ensuing act of carnage – I was frightened and stood frozen to the spot, not knowing what to do.

The heightened tension was not relieved by the brutal, deliberate *thud . . . thud . . . thud*, as he whacked the daylights out of his son. The shudder of the thick two-inch wide leather belt went through my body as well. Finally, it stopped, and he looked at us with a warning glare, *we would be next if we were not careful*. Deathly silence followed as a gallery of appalled perplexed eyes just gawked.

The incident affected us; a boy collecting his discarded marbles, uttered, "I will keep these for him and give them to him tomorrow" – there was no tomorrow; rumour had it he moved to an Afrikaans school, but in our game at least, he had a home. This early witnessing of the shadow side of mankind left another indelible imprint on my psyche.

~

My primary school years were always in twos; the Sacred Heart, Sir Edmund Hillary and Kensington Ridge, and were embraced through games, jocularity and ribaldry.

We still had those old-fashioned wooden desks that seated two students side by side, an inkwell on either side, a hinged desktop to store books neatly below and a solid backrest.

The punishment regime for talkativeness was having to share a desk with someone of the opposite sex. Soon, I was in the front row next to Susan, the ugliest girl in the school. My wings were clipped, enduring the scorn amongst the boys, mocking me.

She, however, was in seventh heaven, plying me with sweets and hand drawn love cards covered with hearts each day. I was having none of it and was simply imprisoned.

At the end of the first term, Mrs Barker wrote, *Walter works hard, and his books are reasonably neat. His main fault is that he loves talking even when someone else is talking.* There was some redemption; *Walter has done well and deserved his average. He must, however, control his tongue, which is continually being overworked.* By the third term even my form teacher, Mr Smith picked up on the theme, *Walter is a very promising pupil, who sometimes tries to control the class and unfortunately the teacher. Try to improve your handwriting, please.* That upset me as I liked Mr Smith.

While at Sir Edmund Hillary, two years prior, Mrs Bosman also spotted my affinity to talk, *work is good – must talk less and attend more.* That school's motto was *Vincit Qui Se Vincit* (He Conquers Who Conquers Himself); an apt mountaineering ethos for Hillary's conquest of Everest and a modest nudge to adjust my sights on loquaciousness.

I made it to the next year, and after the first term Mr Smith commented, *Walter is working satisfactorily. His arithmetic is excellent, but more time should be devoted to Afrikaans. It is a joy to teach Walter this year.* Clearly, I was out of jail and no longer sitting next to broken-hearted Susan, who I hope was not put off by my lack of sensitivity.

~

There was many an occasion for Sandra, my friend and confidant, to enjoy our newfound freedom as we explored the small forest area that abutted the mine dump. She had a mind of her own and tugged me along. My mom insisted she was kept on a leash – unsure, I never let her roam freely, fearful she might not return.

Then one day, on a balmy summer afternoon, with my pockets bulging from the spoils of my marble exploits and my seat, the tell-tale evidence, I found Trixie on the way home from school – a small mongrel, and a stray, with some Pekinese in her. She was petrified and shivering, and had probably not eaten for days.

Trixie was delighted to meet Sandra and have a square meal of whatever I could find. We awaited my mother's return – a perfect foil – my dusty shorts ignored, but not the arrival of Trixie.

"We already have Sandra, we can't have another."

"Only for a day or two, while we look for her owners," I pleaded.

The days moved on, and my mom softened. Trixie's name had more to do with my aspirations: a circus dog, her size perfect for the tricks to be taught – she sat up well and pleaded with both front paws for a snack, but she could not emulate Sandra's handshake.

On rare occasions, she would allow me to roll her onto her back and gently tickle her tummy – slowly, she trusted our family, but never quite recovered from her previous ordeal. If approached too quickly, she would immediately cower, retracting her tail between her legs – in that instance, I felt sad and wondered about the extent of her previous abuse.

ADVENTURES

My horizons expanded as I made sense of the new neighbourhood, its lore and matters unbeknown to our parents. Our perennial playgrounds were the relatively quiet hilly streets and the mysterious disused iconic yellow cyanide mine dump and its peripheries, across the road in Bedfordview.

The main cast of local characters were Piet, Malcolm Falgate, his elder brother and Peter Botha. Peter and Malcolm were a year older, and Malcolm's brother the eldest. Our natural gravitation was towards the mine dump, shaped like a hilltop which became the pinnacle of our theme park. At its furthest reaches was a forested area where the scary inbred hillbillies lived and at the opposite end was the clay dam that swelled after the summer rains.

Our *foofie slide*, constructed by previous *homo sapiens*, consisted of a makeshift rigged taut steel cable, secured, way up around the trunk of a blue gum tree down to the lower part of another, seemingly a long way away. A simple twelve-inch loose fitting metal cylindrical sheath was held onto for dear life as we took a leap into the unknown.

Being the youngest, I was always looking up to the older boys and learning from them. There was an exhilaration, tinged by initial fear of climbing the tree to the *foofie slide* platform, which as a ten-year-old was exceptionally high, coupled with the possibility of a broken limb should I have fallen. Cautiously, I clambered and clung to the branches, not quite as adept as the older boys, who effortlessly scaled the tree.

The first time was the most nerve-racking in every respect. Hillary's dictum, deep in my subconscious, helped, but the daunting prospect of the descent remained for the ground seemed a long way off and the time on the platform an eternity. The adrenaline pulsated along with my random neurotic thoughts ... *what if I can't hold on ... or my hands slip ... or I travel too fast hitting the other tree ... or even faint*! The chants of the taunting choir broke my thoughts; come on *whosie* (colloquial for coward).

My safety harness was my guts and ability to hold on to the shiny metal pipe, and with that, I leapt – gravity did the rest. I whizzed down to terra firma – the cable slackened for a millisecond before taking my full body weight. My heart raced as I hurtled through space, gaining momentum and sliding ever faster – the trees rushing past. It took a moment longer to realise that the ride was successfully over – my heart still pounded, and my feet dangled slightly above the ground before I finally let go. Everything around me looked much clearer, stimulated by the adrenaline rush – it became another rite of passage.

We never knew who built the slide or whether we might be caught, which only added to the tension and excitement of the adventure. It may have been the poor hillbillies, whom we would spy on. Stealthily, we crept to their place where they kept undernourished emaciated horses, only to be threatened by pellet guns whenever we overstepped an artificial boundary. Actually, I did not enjoy that game and was quite scared of them.

We were always trying out the latest crazes, like skateboarding; not my forte at all, so I was glad when we moved on to go-karts. The neighbourhood kids were quick and ingenious in acquiring the *know-how* to construct them. Parents' garages were raided for encased roller braced stainless steel ball bearings, attached to a plank of wood that became the front steering axle, operated by our feet. Rear pram wheels, which were much larger, created a downward sloping cart, exaggerating further the sense of steepness as we raced down the hill. The thought of pedalling my tractor in my Zorro outfit was pedestrian now and a lifetime away. There were the inevitable spills caused by sliding off the cart while cornering, or by broken axles and collisions – we limped home with grazes and damaged egos, awaiting parental admonishments, insufficient to stop us.

Malcolm's brother led the way and became our champion. *Old Falgate*, our Hercules, bestowed with mythological qualities, and with some encouragement would perform his party trick – by association, his strength became ours as well. It started with a silly dare – could he lift the back wheel of his dilapidated old car off the ground?

Standing with his back flush against the car, he securely grabbed the rim above the right rear wheel. Knees slightly bent, back upright, he braced himself for the feat, like an Olympic weightlifter. Slow, considered and focused, he psyched himself up; concentrating on directing every muscle to coordinate simultaneously. We watched his neck turn red and his veins enlarge. Imbued with the necessary power, slowly but surely, inch by inch, the wheel lifted – he held the pose for a few seconds before dropping the car to the rousing humongous shouts and applause from us all. Deep down he had a heart of gold, his brute strength a mere compensation for his slowness in academic matters – I must admit, I was afraid of him.

Koos, our Scoutmaster, was in his mid-twenties, and had a quality of independence and aloofness that was appealing. He introduced a boxing club to our scouting activities. I hated boxing, not only because of the physical difficulty in keeping my arms up while punching for a minute or two but also because of the senselessness of adversaries throwing punches at each other. I never mastered the art of outwitting a lanky kid, nor did I persevere to learn the subtleties.

My few weeks of attendance were sufficient to earn an entry ticket to Koos's vivid hair-raising rides in his racing green GTS modified Mini with spanking new wheels and leather bucket racing seats. His racetrack – our neighbourhood. While the engine purred, lessons about double-declutching and centre of gravity were imbibed from the luxury of the passenger seat, and although a lot more frightening and potentially more dangerous, they were infinitely preferable to staid classrooms. Newton would have smiled at my graduation into propelled motion, although it was more than my stomach could handle, not that I ever let on.

In all of this, Koos probably thought our guardian angels were cheering spectators, while I was only too glad for their extra vigilance ensuring that we never came to any harm. Royal Oak Street was the main downhill *straight*; cross roads made a perfect ninety-degree bend that only a lunatic might consider. The engine revved, wheels spun and the smell of burning rubber filled our nostrils. We flew down the hill over the slight blind rise, momentarily airborne. My stomach hit the roof of my mouth before the Mini fell back onto the tarmac with a resounding thud – the suspension had *bottomed out*.

Highland Road approached, the engine roared with furious double-declutching: the resistance of gears momentarily slowing us down before turning and drifting the car sideways, while simultaneously accelerating as it straightened out. Koos was in his element, the robustness of the Mini proven, while I attempted to absorb my new experience.

Screeching to a halt – we were home. I stepped out of his highly-polished jewel with boldness, but inwardly was out of my comfort zone and merely glad to have survived the experience. Are there different adrenaline rushes and can they be measured? If so, I had maxed-out . . . the acute power of recall where a second or two stretches into a lifetime. It was no longer fun – I casually thanked him, in time made my excuses, and moved on.

There must have been something about our neighbourhood or the boys' toys – *old Falgate* made the most elaborate go-kart imaginable: essentially a stripped-down car needing a lot of shove-power to push it up the hill and finally back to his home after the rides were over. The rear drum brake was ineffective for the surprising downhill speeds achieved. Instead, we relied more on the laws of gravity and a levelling of the road to bring us, finally, to a natural stop. Only our giant could control and tame the beast he had created; it outclassed all our endeavours and any attempt to race beside him was futile and foolhardy.

Upon the unveiling, we stared in utter admiration, dutifully awaiting our instruction. Now the gods had truly spoken, confirming both his strength and ingenuity.

Old Falgate, our engineer and soon to be test pilot, commenced his maiden voyage and as his confidence improved, the starting point moved ever higher up the hill. His daringness rivalled that of the Wright brothers; *foofie slides* and Koos' recklessness paled into insignificance, while the ineffective handbrake increased the risks, tenfold.

I astutely followed every detail of the test programmes, always a willing participant with my legs chasing after the go-kart as fast as they could carry me. First-hand snippets were like gold dust and absolutely invaluable as the project took on a life of its own. There were the occasional mishaps, but nothing untoward.

Finally, we had the all clear; it was our turn as four or five of us clambered aboard, huddled and clutched on to anything that could be held, including each other. Tinged with Dutch courage, the open platform carried a group of cheerful brave young warriors, going through another rite of passage – our leap into the unknown.

The go-kart rapidly gained speed as we hurtled down the hill. Perhaps the additional weight gave it more momentum for we were now literally flying. My fear and apprehension increased exponentially, petrified that a car might turn out from a side street with the handbrake being of scant help. The road levelled, we slowed down and came to a halt.

I am not sure who was more relieved. Our captain's sheepish grin and words said it all, "I think it is better if we have fewer on next time – it was difficult to control." Thank goodness for his unnerving strength and our *guardian angel protection*.

School terms interrupted our explorations, and by the following holiday we had mostly moved on to the next thing that grabbed our imagination.

Sliding and racing down the yellow dune of the mine dump on corrugated cardboard was a less hazardous pursuit. Even the spills when turning too quickly were harmless. Yet the fun we had was met with another chiding. It seems sand, whether from the marble pits or the mine dumps, behaved similarly – penetrating deep within the weave of my shorts. Any dusting off remained but a feeble attempt.

I tired of that, as well, not because of my mother's tongue lashing, but rather because the enjoyment of the quick descent was outweighed by the laborious effort in climbing while sinking into the loose dune sands. The thrill of the *foofie slide* and go-karting was more memorable.

At times, we ventured up the hill to the natural clay dam – upturned 44-gallon-drums, sawn in half, our Captain Cook boats, and with makeshift oars we set about our crossing. The murky still bracken greenish water scared me – were there monsters in its depths that may swallow us at any moment?

The unspoken law was that we, and our adversaries, the St George's School boys, would remain on our respective sides. Reconnoitring was dangerous:

their scouts detected our incursion, their shouts and gesticulations clear, *move off our turf*. We rowed backwards as fast as we could – they, always in our sights.

Back on our side, we moulded clay – scooped from the banks – into grenades, packing them around the end of the reeds we had cut. With a swift flick of the wrist, they were launched and the battle commenced – this time our accuracy was greater than theirs, giving us the upper hand. Andre was particularly accurate and his hits were followed by our feisty jaunts. Their loss of face was more than they could bear – the battle took a nasty turn – anarchy reigned. They charged around the dam across the demarcated boundary, hurling vitriolic outbursts – no match for our light-hearted banter.

Andre, our leader, without hesitation, shouted, "Run!" We scampered as fast as we could; his swiftness showed us the path home, slowing only when the disgruntled voices faded into the distance. Beaming, this episode was retold, albeit embellished and became our victory – we moved on from that, as well.

The earth gobbling trucks and enormous bulldozers moved in, swallowing part of the mine dump to make way for a new residential and shopping centre; fascinated, I watched them for hours. At the end of a working day, other playful, daring kids used the top of the excavated site as their jumping pad – tragedy struck. The bank collapsed, burying one of them alive – bad news travels fast and soon we were watching the rescue operation; it left me numb and chilled to the bone – our paradise was not as safe as we had imagined.

THE SILK ROAD

The monks' ingenious deviousness, smuggling cocoons out of China in the hollow of their bamboo walking sticks while crossing the border on foot, gave the West the art of silk production – that story always intrigued me. Naturally, when the opportunity arose, I imagined the exotic mysteries of the Silk Road would unfold through my new hobby, *silkworms*.

Neither my mom nor I knew what we were in for over the next three years, but her words of advice were simple, "Your responsibility, OK?"

"Of course, Mom, it will be easy." The famous last words of any eager youngster ensuring no impediments – my determined sights were set.

My mom was always helpful in that way – her enthusiasm was infectious as she raided her wardrobe producing shoe and larger flatter clothing boxes to house my newfound friends. They were strange looking: the ubiquitous creamy whites and the zebra types with their more distinctive circular bands and appearance of greater stature. Fascinated, I watched them for hours as they munched their way through the mulberry leaves.

Watching was one thing, but cleaning their boxes of all the tiny black droppings was another. The still bigger task of finding an endless supply of mulberry leaves was the most difficult, not initially, but soon the neighbours tired of my constant visits. I tried substitutes, like lettuce leaves, which were reluctantly eaten; rather, they implored me to restore their favourite nibble.

The second year and particularly the third were the real test of everyone's patience. My army, on the march, devoured anything in their path, while conquering the alternately stacked boxes – their tower of Babylon.

I was beside myself – their ravenous appetites remained unabated and I could no longer keep up with the daily poop-clean. By then, I knew every mulberry tree, the icon in the du Rand family's backyard. Most neighbours had endured my harassment; their irritation levels guiding my rounds of collection.

I was like a mendicant monk – "*Ja, wat wil jy hê die keer*" (Yes, what do you want, this time) said *old man du Rand* sarcastically – he knew exactly. The deliberate pause after his harsh intonation of *ja*, was used to establish authority. Intimidated and with my pride hurt – which I would not show – I needed to feed my worms. The old man's tree became imperative and was the green leafed gold mine, but how?

Respectfully, I acknowledged him, "*Kan ek asseblief 'n paar blare neem?*" (May I take a few leaves please?), a gross understatement. Perhaps by necessity, diplomacy, or was it deception? He retorted laconically, inviting no further comment, "*Ja, maar dit is nou die laste keer, verstaan jy my?*" (Yes, but this is now the last time, do you understand me?). Sheepishly, I half nodded, refusing to say *ja meneer* (yes Sir), an expected obligation, as I did not want him to have the satisfaction of thinking he could break my spirit. Throughout life, I have purposefully resisted saying, Sir, unless I felt the respect was deserved, and certainly not because of age or hierarchy.

An alternative strategy had to be found – circumvention. When he was not around, a reason was fabricated for a visit. Casually, when the atmosphere seemed appropriate, I would ask Mrs du Rand whether I could take just *a few leaves* as if *old man du Rand's* conversation had never happened. She smiled, and her kind nod gave her blessing. With that, I would scamper and climb into the tree, the deeper the better so that the leaves I stuffed inside my bulging shirt would not be apparent. Of course, when the fruit was ripening and to avoid those indelible stains, the picking had to be done from below. As quickly as I could, I would leave turning sideways, not wishing to betray my deception, and with a friendly wave, said "*totsiens*" (goodbye). She played along, the helmswoman of that ship and the salt of the earth, ensuring our dignities remained intact.

The Curtain boys, our other neighbours, Irish Catholics, had a trick up their sleeve. They knew the brunt of *old man du Rand* and swore me to secrecy – I could not contain my excitement, nor believe my good luck. Their back-garden wall abutted the *gold mine*. The noise level of five siblings detracted from any suspicion relating to our abnormal activity from their backyard – an excellent vantage point to observe the moment to strike. The younger brother, my age, would keep *chips* while the eldest, a year older, with the clever use of a gardener's shears attached to a long pole, adeptly cut and safely retrieved our bounty. Ingenious, and to boot the Roman Catholics had outwitted the *Afrikaanse Gereformeerde Kerk* – our supplies were intact and God smiled, condoning it all.

For a while peace reigned – we continued raiding the precious leaves, the silkworms were well fed, and *old grumps* and Andre looked after their racing pigeons – their husbandry admirable, as they moved effortlessly with an uncanny ability to catch and hold the birds while inspecting them. I was convinced it was an Afrikaner thing, in their blood and part of their Voortrekker DNA.

The pigeons were ringed, registered and raced. Daily, they were released from their roost, winging their way upwards and around. Whenever they landed on a roof, a succession of handclaps would shoo them off, onwards, to keep training. Unexpected strays were welcome, caught and kept in the coop until they had mated; the primal instinct of brood caring ensured they remained. At sunset, *old man du Rand* would open the automatic flap door and could be seen shaking the feeding tin of dried corn, while imitating cooing calls to attract his flock home – all particularly endearing.

As much as I was keen to learn, the noise, flutter and flapping of the wings within the confined roost put me off. It was quite disturbing – Hitchcock too, may well have had a similar experience.

The utopian days of milk and honey never lasted – the cutting shears separated from the wooden pole, and there the evidence remained, dangling. Fortunately, providence prevailed as they were embedded deep within the heart of the mulberry tree and could only really be detected from the Curtain's side of the property. Any attempt to retrieve the evidence failed. It was just too inaccessible and for the moment our earlier skulduggery remained undetected. So, it was back to the begging bowl routine again.

The marching empire had outgrown themselves and their encampment now extended from my bedroom to our enclosed sun porch, which fast became out of bounds to the rest of the family. Shoe and clothing boxes were brimming to capacity and unlike the odd stray pigeon added to the roost, the challenge of my increased army size was more fundamental. The hatchlings of thousands of eggs from the previous year rapidly grew into large silkworms as they devoured their way through the *sweet nectar* from *old grump's* tree – the extent of this invasion reached epidemic proportions.

Worse was to follow – they soon climbed out of their tanks thinking they were ground troops and started exploring every nook and cranny of their extended habitat – the officer had lost control; anarchy and chaos reigned. The special helicopter brigade airlifted them, one by one, carefully working with their squishy diaphragms and ensuring that their delicate aerials at the rear of their bodies remained undamaged – there were casualties, but fortunately the losses were small.

Command headquarters summoned an urgent meeting – the quartermaster complained that the unexpected run on food supplies was depleting the emergency rations and other food sources had to be sourced. Backup plans emerged and one of the best scouts was sent on a mission, beyond borders ventured so far, to ferret out new fodder. Up, down and along the alleyways, risking life and limb, I scaled unknown neighbour's walls, sometimes at significant risk when spotted. Adversity brought rewards – the newly discovered mulberry trees were earmarked for future personal campaigns, while those treasure troves were used to satisfy the troops' immediate pangs of hunger.

Then the most amazing thing happened, completely unprecedented in conventional warfare – the soldiers vanished. Trance-like, their heads swayed from side to side, a marvellous ploy to fool the enemy. Suddenly, they attached a hardly detectable silk thread to the side of the box and slowly but surely the most beautiful yellowish golden coloured cocoons emerged. One became an anchor for another, creating the most exquisite abstract art. The battle was won, and peace reigned.

Then, the next miracle – the chrysalis effect: they ate their way out of the tips of the cocoons and emerged as beautiful stubby pearl white moths; the mating dance followed and locked tail to tail, the seeds of the next generation were ensured.

They could be tricked into spinning flat shapes like a heart or diamond. I experimented placing different shaped cut-outs onto drinking glasses. The unsuspecting soldiers did their best, the heads bobbing from side to side as if in agony, blindly searching and trapped by circumstances – now, the thread could only be attached to the flat surface.

This battle was lost, and the unpleasant tactic deployed did not sit well with me, the unwitting perpetrator – my apologies to all silkworms.

I am not sure if it was trick or treat time for the Curtain boys, it certainly was not Halloween, not that we celebrated or even knew about it, and if silkworms like leaves, we loved delicious, irresistible mouth-watering mulberries. It follows that with a bountiful supply on our doorstep, the pickings were worthy of the challenge and the thrill of the intoxicating dare to take the forbidden fruit from the very jaws of *old grumps*. In the process, the shears might just be retrieved. The first forays were easy, too easy; complacency set in and the need for a lookout – discarded.

Andre, our gazelle, had now acquired the skills of a leopard: silent, solitary and patient. He watched quietly downwind at the pigeon roost, while the Curtain boys raided. He chose to await their return – they brazenly scaled the wall on another warm, inviting summer's night, and while deep in the tree feasting unsuspectingly, a gruff voice admonished, "*En wat doen julle hier?*" (And what are you doing here?). They panicked thinking it was the old man, fell out of the tree, and scarcely looking back they scarpered the fence, but not before Andre, hiding in the shadows, delivered his two prepared buckets of muddy water – bull's eye.

It was Piet's tale; perhaps the Curtain boys were too embarrassed to talk about it. Andre, meanwhile, never let on. If they ever climbed that fence again, it would have been done with extreme caution.

COURTESY OF SOCIAL MEDIA

Piet and I tried our hand at clay modelling, using the mine dump clay – we knew little about the craft, nor that it had to be baked. I was fourteen, Peter Botha fifteen. He watched, indulging in his forbidden pastime of smoking, while Piet creatively made a mug and I an ashtray; a gift for my mom.

Was this a portend for I had hid Peter's twenty pack of Lexington cigarettes in a battery box on top of my wardrobe. One evening, while doing my homework, George barged in wanting a battery.

"In the box", and, as the words slipped out, I realised Peter's stash was there. He looked quizzically with a slight reproach – it only made my sense of guilt worse.

"They're not mine", I spluttered. And without another word he put the pack down, turned and left – had our sense of trust been broken?

Courtesy of social media, we had rekindled our high school friendship after an absence of nearly thirty-five years. Peter had in the meanwhile become an ordained Methodist minister, emigrated to Australia, married with three children and was coping with a rare medical condition that afflicts his wife. In sharing our life experiences, it was clear that he had remained open and inquisitive about other belief systems and philosophies, and that the devil had not managed to devour either of us, although he had left a scratch or two.

What was interesting was his perception of my supposed idyllic home life, compared to his. It was skewed, particularly his view of my mother. Inevitably, as the invisible cogs clicked back to pertinent reminiscences and revelations of my home truths, he suddenly exclaimed, "But she was always so friendly towards us, kind and quick to crack a joke, unlike my father, who I was so ashamed of . . . although it is true she often had a *glass* in her hand. He was an alcoholic you know, who would beat my mother, and that is why my mother never allowed me to have friends at our home."

Vaguely, I remembered; most immediate was the flooding back of the pleasant memories of our childhood – we cruised the neighbourhood on Peter's 50cc Honda motorbike, and whenever we saw Wally Hayward's warm and friendly wave, we would stop. He was a renowned athlete, then sixty years old – from our perspective, ancient – but his stories regaled us. Five times winner of the Comrades Marathon, the first when he was twenty-one, and the holder of the London to Brighton Marathon record, set in the year I was born; a coincidence that captured my imagination.

It dismayed him when he was declared a professional and banned from further participation in amateur athletics because he had inadvertently accepted money towards his living expenses while abroad. The ban was finally dropped. However, the seed of this story was embedded in my psyche as I dreamed of my own nascent cycling prowess, vowing never to be caught in the same trap.

I never became a professional for only amateurs could participate in the Olympics then, yet ever hopeful to partake but that was not to be. South Africa was banned on the 18th August 1964 by the International Olympic Committee until racial discrimination was renounced. Twenty-eight years would pass before the re-admittance to the Barcelona Games in 1992, prompted by the advanced negotiations to end apartheid – by then I was too old, in my late thirties.

I held Wally, a kind, humble and generous man, in awe – it was as if by association my cycling endeavours would accordingly be strengthened, and after all, we had the same name.

A Friday evening's joyride was a necessary step for our talent scouting and an audacious move, particularly as Peter did not have a licence – we were at that testosterone age and *borrowed* his mother's car. My heart raced in apprehension; an accomplice, unsure of his driving skills.

Every boy knew that *detective novels'* caution – leave no clues. The walls heard every step on the creaking floor as we approached his mother's wardrobe – the spare keys hidden under her lingerie. We reversed the Anglia Super 123E out of the garage with the odd jolt or two, while carefully noting the exact parked position. Windows rapidly rolled down with the exhilaration of the air blowing onto our faces, a taste of a different freedom and masters of our own destiny – interrupted by a momentary hint of anxiety – what if we saw a police car, or even had an accident?

A few unsuccessful turns around the block soon dampened our enthusiasm, and we returned the car to its haven, undetected. That very weekend, his mother called us aside; something in her tone and body language suggested otherwise. She beckoned us to follow her to the scene of the crime, her bedroom, which in itself was most unusual.

My mind raced; had we disturbed her clothes, or put the keys back in the wrong spot? We stood, two adolescents not quite knowing what to do with ourselves.

"I know you have been driving my car, but I need to hear you both admit it" – we frowned, feigning innocence as the slow deliberate seconds ticked by – "I will not punish you but I need you to admit it," she admonished. We were crestfallen and with our mouths agape, not a word passed our lips – her eyes narrowed as we shuffled our feet – surely not Alcatraz or St George's Home.

Not wishing to betray Peter, I waited patiently until his mother's way had worked his conscience to the point of no return. Then in unison we blurted out, admitting our deed, hoping it would assuage our sense of guilt. It seemed like an eternity as we promised never to do it again. The scoreboard flashed – God 1, Devil 0.

When things had calmed down a bit, the Devil confided that he thought all bases were covered bar a delinquent disciple who had forgotten to warn us that the passenger window needed to remain two inches ajar, an old habit of Peter's mom – the devil was indeed in the detail; I had wound the window to the top.

We were not really delinquent. Had we been Guatemalan Mayans, we would unwittingly have followed a rite of passage, where the initial task involves the theft of your mother's large earthenware cooking pot and then putting it back again, without being caught or her knowing that it had been taken. It requires stealth to return to the village undetected under the cover of night for the barking dogs have forgotten the youth living away from their families during this period of initiation. Next is to learn to speak eloquently and elegantly and after that, and most importantly, finding the gods and goddesses in Nature. This ensures that partners are seen as having only some attributes from the pantheon, not all – in stark contrast to Hollywood's portrayal of the pursuit of the perfect other. Perhaps, we were tapping into mankind's collective unconscious, for these rituals are designed to make the individual safer to themselves, and, in so doing, to the greater community at large.

At cinemas, besides the movie or the newsreel, alluring advertisements really caught my attention in my early teens. The infamous cigarette industry: masters at encouraging beliefs and value systems, while projecting dreams and unrealistic lifestyles portrayed in exotic places like Acapulco. The backdrop of glorious sunsets viewed from the deck of a magnificent yacht, adorned with beautiful women sipping champagne with a casual offering of a cigarette – so powerful.

Notwithstanding, I never succumbed, but it had ignited a hankering for a glamorous lifestyle, worthy of pursuit, when contrasted against the continual roller coaster emotional rides at home. Later in life, through more meaningful exposures to other cultures and belief systems this view changed. I must admit though to having developed a penchant for cigars – more to do with introspection and creating a meditative space.

Finally, we managed to put Peter's mom's car back undetected on subsequent joyrides. God and the Devil smiled in cahoots, ensuring our world was in balance and that we were becoming safer to ourselves, except we still had the matric dance to think about and neither of us had girlfriends. To boot we were clumsy in conversation and friendships with the opposite sex, a consequence of attending an all-boys' school.

The daily excited schoolboy banter was mixed with huge dashes of arrogance, sobered only by the persistent teachers' harassment, *study for your impending final university entrance examinations*! We managed, somehow, to persuade Peter's neighbours to accompany us. Not an easy task, particularly as Margaret, my date, had a steady boyfriend.

The black and white compulsory photograph said it all; four stooges, two in suits and ties, wet behind the ears and pretending they were indeed couples. The thought of risking a kiss was stifled by Margaret's body language and fidelity. Instead I took her cold, lifeless hand, attempting to dance, while going through the charade as bravely as possible – awkward at best. Our schoolmates, assisted by the forbidden consumption of alcohol, believed a marvellous evening was had by all – perhaps it was, but we remained sober, having borrowed Peter's mom's car; this time with her permission.

Peter left school to do his navy military conscription. Being still too young, I went to university. His farewell gift was a copy of the New Testament, Good News for Modern Man, inscribed: *this is just to wish you every success in the future and may God help and guide you* – throughout all my countless cathartic clear-outs, the book remained.

CHAPTER 8
IN THE SHADOW OF DESTINY

CONVENTS

George was an affable person, but like us all, he had his peculiarities. They may well have been exacerbated by our family dynamics. He did his best; but was probably insensitive to how certain of his actions affected my inner turmoil.

I felt an alienation of sorts as George's stepchild, always second best. It was preferable not to be seen unless it suited his sense of well-being; certainly, never to be too demanding. I tired of his off-putting responses – it left me bereft and in nowhere land.

Desiree's behaviour, too, had its effect on me. Their individual unconscious styles of manipulation and behaviour, accompanied by veiled or direct threats, increasingly affected me – my responses became perfunctory.

In a way, it helped develop my negotiating skills, particularly when my needs were paramount, like a lift to a cycling event or a necessary school item. But in another way, it was demeaning – eventually, I found other solutions.

George's aggression was disguised in his passiveness, while Desiree's was fired by her catalyst, alcohol – always only a sip, sufficient to alter her state of consciousness as her demons possessed her and we felt the wrath of her attack.

The consequences of all of this, of course, opens a huge philosophical debate in the rounds of determining destiny. The Jesuits say, *give me a child and I will give you the man*. But what if the child's rebellious spirit continually questions and takes a stance, while clawing his way through the maze of life?

Their backgrounds were similar – a formidable part of their early childhood was spent in orphanages. No doubt, it may have become a part of the empathetic attraction between them – the lack of love and caring, and abandonment that they may have experienced.

It must have been psychologically very tough for them. Even my time at the convents, under far easier circumstances, nevertheless left me feeling alone, as if being punished.

George's family had emigrated from the island of Kasos, the westernmost island of the Dodecanese between Crete and Karpathos. Their story was like most waves of immigration. They set sail with the hopes, dreams and aspirations of a new future. Panayiotopoulos, their surname, became the first obstacle to communication and instead they adopted *Lostramus*, Greek for bosun, George's father's occupation. Subsequently, it was changed to Lostrom – perhaps, a more easily pronounced anglicised name that supported their new identity and future.

George was born in South Africa into a typical Greek family that ran a cafe in East London. Alas, his father died – the four boys were of school-going age and unfortunately, his mother spoke little English. She was pregnant with Demi, his younger sister, not a girl's name but given in honour of their father, Demetrius.

Cheated out of their business and his mother unable to raise the family under the circumstances, the Greek community arranged her marriage to a Mozambican Greek, living in Beira. It heralded another twist – a *Sophie's choice* – only the eldest boy, Tony, accompanied his pregnant mother; the other three brothers were placed in an orphanage.

It is difficult to imagine the scale of this trauma. George was convinced that the community had taken the line of least resistance, and subsequently turned their back on his family.

The boys went to Izele Convent in King William's Town, run by the order of The Sacred Heart, for orphans and underprivileged boys and girls. "They thought I was stupid and unable to learn until they realised I needed glasses. My brothers tried to help me do my homework."

Today, only the derelict ruins of Izele remain, and a Facebook page – perhaps driven by a nostalgic search for an emotional bonding, unconsciously declaring, *we are alive and have made it thus far.*

The boys had each other for emotional and moral support, and there may have been kind and caring nuns. But, it could never be a substitute for the familial warmth and a sense of belonging, snatched away by a cruel card of fate. What a difficult start – I only ever knew him looking through his thick-rimmed spectacles.

Upon the boys passing a rudimentary level of education, they found their way in life as best they could. George was a night-watchman at the East London harbour during the midst of the Great Depression. He pulled himself up by his bootstraps: plumber, electrician and finally a general manager of a medium size electrical firm – his last post before retirement.

While there, he completed a part-time Business Administration course and was clearly the only tradesman attending. I loved hearing his anecdotes about the other corporate participants from diverse industries. The course advanced as did the renewed twinkle in his eye – I was proud of him and his achievements.

Desiree's father, Frank Ridewood, died aged fifty-seven when she was only nine. He and Granny Ridewood must have already been divorced for several years, and Desiree was by then already in Nazareth House, another Roman Catholic orphanage. Granny remarried a month before Frank's death, and became Granny Buxley, the only name I ever knew her by. Her mother was a Dutch immigrant to South Africa.

My earliest recollections were that my grandmother was already old and wrinkled. She lived in Troyeville, a very impoverished white suburb of Johannesburg, in a tiny terraced house with the bare essentials. Into my teen years my embarrassment grew as I realised the extent of her poverty, only outweighed by our treat of a baking tin, stacked to the brim, of her crispy homemade apricot jam tarts, baked in her coal stove. As delicious as they were, biting into and discovering a hair of hers, or extracting a protruding one slithering through the jam, simply made my stomach turn. But her recipe was always victorious in overriding my revulsion and squeamishness.

Granny never locked her doors. Pilate, her collie, named after Pontius, was her protector. He lay on her bed and, despite my affinity with animals, would always bare his teeth accompanied by a low guttural growl, a warning to back off. Granny would calm him, but he needed at least two or three of her reassurances before he would reluctantly accept my touch. She encouraged me to curve my fingers inwards in a relaxed fashion, and slowly extend my arm in a non-threatening way so that Pilate could smell the back of my hand. Her teaching, of harmoniously earning his trust and acceptance, was a wonderful gift – I am sure he smelt my fear.

Desiree's sister, Aunty Ronnie, had already left home fending for herself. Little was spoken about their elder brother, William John Ridewood. Perhaps the pain of his premature death in a car accident, at the age of forty-six, was too great. Desiree was twenty-seven and Ronnie forty-five years old. It must have been a momentous shock. I recall my mother telling me that my father broke the unfortunate news to Granny, proffering a stiff scotch as solace. He stayed with her that evening in her inconsolable state.

Gayle and I, in our adult lives, were amazed to learn from Desiree, many years after Ronnie had passed on, about her relationship with Ronnie, whom she viewed as a surrogate mother while in the orphanage. She was disappointed that Ronnie had not done more to remove her from there and, unnecessarily, held a grudge. It manifested in a disguised resentment that showed whenever they were together – Desiree nit-picked at anything Ronnie said within minutes of her arrival. It was uncomfortable to have to witness.

The next revelation was her belief that the sole reason for being in the orphanage was because Granny had too many male partners. Desiree stopped short of saying *she was a prostitute*, but the implication was clear, yet it was also the period shortly after the Great Depression. It might have helped if our mother entertained another possibility, *Granny's friendships were like single parents dating*. She did, after all, marry again, but Desiree's thoughts were her truth, her baggage, and unbeknown to us while we grew up.

Yet Desiree, in her own way after leaving Nazareth House, endeavoured to make the best of her life.

The nuns exacerbated her emotional damage by putting the fear of God into her, *you are here because of the devil's work your mother does*, which must have been a reference to Granny's attendance of the Spiritualist Church of Troyeville and her clairvoyance. I never knew the full extent of her capabilities, but she was always in the know whenever I had had a cycling accident.

Dr Peter Becker and Credo Vusamazulu Mutwa consulted her, probably about esoteric matters. I never met Dr Becker, but often heard my mother say, *he visits Granny and pays her electricity and telephone bills, which helps us with Granny's upkeep*. Becker, the well-known Zulu historian author, was one of two whites only who officially attended King Goodwill Zwelithini's coronation in 1971.

Credo, the High Sanusi of the Zulu Nation and the oral keeper of tribal mythological stories, of which some were recorded in his books, *Indaba, My Children* and *Africa Is My Witness*, resided in a safe house in a white Afrikaner suburb – unusual, during the apartheid days. Our perchance meeting in my mid-thirties, only happened upon mentioning my grandmother's connection to Dr Becker, while on a telephone call – we met the following day.

Credo named my grandmother *Nomthandazo*, daughter of prayer. "She was one of three people that I trusted, her speciality, fertility. My son Innocent was conceived with her help." He shook his head sadly, continuing, "Alas, Innocent was killed . . . *necklaced* . . . in the turbulent change of our country, because I would not take sides." I felt his pain.

Reflecting now – the numerous plights at different points in my mother's life, besides the orphanage and her belief as to why she was placed there – the period immediately after the death of her brother must have been extremely difficult. Not only had she been married for barely a year and a half, but also her protective nurturing instincts were at the fore – she had a three-month-old baby, me. Her marriage was probably under strain. My father's business was placed into liquidation, culminating in his officially declared insolvency in September that year – only seven months after I was born.

There are certain things families want to forget, either because of the severity of the emotional pain experienced, or the simple need to start with a clean slate. Yet the Quechua of Peru, or the Balinese, believe that the past must be acknowledged, ritualised and integrated. This way of being becomes a fundamental cornerstone of existence – otherwise, there is a danger of remaining a prisoner of circumstances, where emotional upheavals like anxiety, panic attacks and depression continue.

OUTINGS

On Saturday mornings, I often accompanied George, an electrician, to his work place. One such day, it was as if he needed to show me his superiority, and I witnessed the inhumanity inflicted upon a black co-worker, another George, who reported to him.

He was summoned as if to be given an instruction, but instead, was told an inappropriate racial joke. Feigned, forced subservient laughter followed; the job worth more than the humiliation suffered. Simultaneously, the sharp psychic blade sliced through my abdomen from the cruelty unleashed. I liked the other George, a strong Zulu man with a powerful spirit and a friendly smile.

The effect of this and other racial inequalities haunted me like floating ghosts that reappeared at different stages of my life. I did not need anyone to tell me it was wrong, even though I was only eight or nine years old; the psychic shock did that. But once that destructive jocular seed was sown, there was no way back. Their relationship would be different, only my stepfather probably never realised it.

Notwithstanding, I loved the outings with George to hot-rod car racing, football matches and professional wrestling, where he was responsible for the working of the floodlights. Wrestling was a fantasy world: the goading of a hysterical audience to the relentless pounding of bodies, accompanied by mock sounds of excruciating pain, the cheers, boos, and the final surrender. In a way colourful, but once I was let into the secret – the results were staged – it became meaningless.

~

Sunday afternoons were special, often spent basking in George's glory, where players and spectators greeted him reverently at different baseball outings. Well-liked, respected and in his element; he knew all the rules and had the power to award *a walk* or *a strikeout*.

The game, renowned for its players' sideline banter and crowd jibing, never left umpires unscathed, and George, not immune, took it in his stride – b*lind as a bat . . . polish those specs of yours . . . give him a walk . . . retire old man* – I knew it was harmless and part of the sporting vernacular.

The Wanderers Club was my favourite: besides a flashback to Saturday morning tea and talent spotting outings with Uncle Jack and his invaluable advice on choice, it became a healthy adjunct to my pocket money – a tickey for every empty cold drink bottle returned.

Strategy and tactics were crucial – too late and it became some other kid's prize. Sometimes, Gayle was my accomplice. While the spectators were engrossed in the game, nonchalantly, like restless vultures with the cunning of a leopard, we would snatch the empty bottles. When we were caught, we had to surrender our gains, feigning our innocence. Of greater concern was, *who are your parents*? Then, the gauntlet of the vendors – *you sure these bottles are all yours*? *Were you not here ten minutes ago*?

The end of the game curtailed this lucrative activity. Teams, partners and staunch supporters retired to the clubhouse. For us it was treats like a kola-tonic-and-lemonade and delicious club French fries with plenty of oozing tomato sauce. They were happy times – in and out of the rumble of adult conversations, cavorting and doing our own thing. Best of all, and nobody knew, was the sneaking of another plate of fries paid with the gains from the afternoon's *bottle-running*.

Soon, I knew the baseball rules backwards and that the game originated in America, somewhere far away. I wanted to play, perhaps motivated by the legendary Babe Ruth story that George told so well, or simply my admiration for George even though he had never played. A few more happy years passed, then it all changed.

Our neighbourhood team practised on Thursday evenings at Rhodes Park, well known to Zorro on his tractor. George assisted with their training sessions, and I would regularly accompany him. My eagerness to try my hand at swinging a bat or pitching a ball, knew no bounds. Persistently, I asked George, "Can I play?"

"No, you don't have an eye for the ball!" The unequivocal answer was always the same.

Confusion reigned. Why was he so adamant? Was it true, or might I tarnish his reputation? Was he embarrassed that I was his stepson? I felt unwanted, unseen and no longer part of the baseball scene. My disappointment –

enormous. The joy previously experienced, ebbed away – the club fries never quite tasted the same again. Finally, I stopped asking and gave up on the Wanderers Club outings.

His blatant favouritism and adoration of Gayle, now four years old, was increasingly evident – I felt I was an unnecessary part of the equation.

~

Yet, social family outings remained an integral part of my sense of belonging. The Greek Club in Bedfordview encapsulated this – intriguing, slow, spirited dancing that accelerated into energetic rapid movements, and in the background the sound of excited Greek babbling.

George only responded in English. What surprised me was that I never knew he understood the language. It transpires, he vowed never to speak it because of his belief that the Greek community had betrayed his family after his father's death. Notwithstanding, it was clear that they liked him and respected his judgement.

There were other joyous occasions – Greek Orthodox baptisms and weddings and the ritual knocking of each other's coloured eggs at Easter time – it reminded me of our game of conkers.

Best of all was escaping into a fantasy world during *movie evenings*, where George was the projectionist at his boss's home. I marvelled at his knowledge and dexterity as he carefully threaded the film through all the spindles. A click and the governor was shut. The film ran along the track until the inevitable slipping and the ratcheting sound, as the screen images jumped, George's cue to fix it. I smiled and was proud of him, and in that moment, glad to be his stepson.

Two of George's brothers lived in Johannesburg. Johnny, younger than George, was single and never had a girlfriend. He was rather creepy, had putrid breath, and delighted in indulging in inane conversation while drinking with Desiree. Gayle, in our adult lives, confirmed her similar aversion, declaring, *I did not like, but tolerated him*!

Visiting Nicky, the youngest who was married to Irene, was always a pleasure. They were childless and Irene's Greek mother, always dressed in black, lived with them. The first thing I noticed when entering their home was the pervading smell of round shortbreads, topped with aniseed, far preferable to the overripe melons of Adrian and Selina's place.

Then, that inevitable Greek grandmother greeting, secretly feared, but enjoyed. She approached slowly, rotund and demonstrative with sprouting moustache hairs, calling, *oggie, oggie*. There was no way to escape her large smile of erupting strong emotions – my cheek grabbed between her thumb and forefinger, a simultaneous passionate squeeze and a tug, while my head was buffeted by the repeated slapping of my cheek with her free hand.

Their house was immaculately clean, adequately furnished and tea times were the highlight. Spoilt for choice: baklava laden with syrup, my favourite, and many varieties of olives, hummus and dolmades, my least favourite.

Nicky, slender and shorter than George, had a groovy set of drums. He played them, while twiddling the drumsticks between his fingers and simultaneously pounding the pedal of the large bass drum with great coordination. The sound boomed in his minute practice room and reverberated through my body – I was fascinated and loved watching him.

He worked for a Greek businessman who had two adjoining stores, a carpet shop and a delicatessen. The latter perfumed by the brine in the large oak barrels of the different types of green and black olives, while a step into the carpet shop through the connecting door was like entering a pristine fantasy world. Rolls and rolls of carpets of a variety of colours and types, neatly stacked on aluminium rollers at various heights, decorated the walls.

One school holiday, needing to supplement my pocket money to replace my stolen bicycle, I worked as a checkout packer, and when there were no customers I would replenish the shelves. Strong brown paper bags were de rigueur, a time before plastic bags. I soon learnt the art of packing, like with like, and my quickness improved to keep up with the groceries pushed my way. Initially, it was quite daunting. Then, it became a fun game to see if I could pack as quickly as Nicky keyed in the items. Busy times were best, otherwise the day dragged, prompting me to question why anyone would do this type of menial work, unless they had no other option.

Lunchtime was the highlight of each day. The tantalising smell of fried chops and eggs reached my nostrils. My Pavlovian response confirmed that I was indeed hungry, and a good hour beforehand, my stomach was already rumbling. Uncle Nicky, the chef, cooked on a single plate gas stove at the back of the shop. Sometimes, we even had baklava for dessert – what a treat. He always completed his meal with a Greek coffee, boiled in a little copper urn.

Enjoyable family outings were habitually disrupted and destroyed in an instant by my mother – a sip was all that was needed. Sometimes, her taunting demons rested, despite a sip or two. Perhaps, in those instances, she felt sufficiently secure, but mostly we could not rely on her uncontrollable side remaining dormant.

At times, it would start with a simple nag, "George, you're always fixing things in other people's homes, but never in ours." He was good at letting the first thrust brush over, but my mother would goad further – a confrontation ensued – soon, the atmosphere could be cut with a knife. The joy and frivolity of the occasion evaporated instantly, and we drove home in silence.

It was not always like that, and I have hinted about the special qualities my mother had – the true mother, the one not possessed. When I was about nine and Gayle nearly two years old, judging by the photo of Gayle standing on the beach next to George clutching seashells, we spent a delightful family summer holiday at Morgans Bay, on the Wild Coast of the Transkei, in the only home upon the hill overlooking the Kei Mouth lagoon. Access was via a single dirt road.

Trevor Miller, a larger than life South African Englishman, dressed in khaki, was reminiscent of hunters and prospectors depicted in *Out of Africa* type colonial films. He relentlessly sought an efficient way to recover titanium dioxide from the local beach sand in his makeshift workshop, using a vibrating table that separated the different particles, airing his dreams of riches. I never understood much more about it, but he muttered, "It's like gold – if I can recover it, I'll make my fortune!" It was so exciting and in sharp contrast to our urban existence. The ruggedness and natural beauty of the setting, his dreams and a seagoing fishing boat, built by him and aptly named the Viking – only fanned my imagination.

His wife was placid, caring and most likeable, but of a nervous disposition. I was not surprised overhearing my Mom . . . *she is recovering from a nervous breakdown*, and Trevor's abrupt attitude and behaviour with her was noticeable when reprimanding her. It startled her and me, and I could see she was upset. I felt sorry for her, seemingly trapped in their relationship, in this scenically beautiful yet desolate place; their children, grown up, had already fled the nest.

Mandela was born into the Thembu royal family from Mvezo, the heartland of the Xhosa, some eighty kilometres from there.

I loved spending time with the earthy Xhosa women – warm and friendly with instant smiles, seemingly without a care in the world. Their rhythm was different, living in the moment. They taught me the familiar Xhosa Click Song, *Qongqothwane*, about a little beetle – Miriam Makeba, the civil rights activist nicknamed Mama Africa, made it famous internationally. I never knew the English translation, although I thoroughly enjoyed singing along while learning the different tongue clicks, an integral part of the Xhosa tonal language.

Whenever I would hear that song, at different stages of my life, I contentedly burst forth, singing along as best as I could. The effect, immediate – a seamless flight back to a glimpse and an experience of those moments of warmth and happiness that coursed through my veins.

A time of belonging before having to face and challenge my mother's demons. Her love was displayed in many ways, and in Morgans Bay it was wrapped in tenacity. Santa Claus would be at the local hotel's Christmas party. It had rained heavily the previous evening; the lagoon had burst its banks, creating a rivulet to the sea – the hotel was on the other side of the lagoon.

"It'll take hours to drive around by road and you'll never cross the river by foot", Trevor said dismissively as he walked away.

"I promised Walter, and I don't wish to break my promise. I'll get across," responded my mother with verve and determination.

The short walk down the hill was accompanied by encouragement and support of the Xhosa ladies.

Determined, my mother looked so radiant and beautiful in her summer dress, which she rolled-up and tucked into her underwear. She took off her shoes and hoisted me onto her shoulders, starting to cross the ever-broadening stream. I looked ahead at the hotel on the other side, noticing a small crowd gathering. They watched our progress. I was a little scared and apprehensive, for I never wanted anything to happen to my mother, particularly as Trevor had remonstrated, "It's far too strong and will wash you away." She tentatively moved forward, finding her footing as the water slowly rose, the further we crossed. We were nearly midstream, the water almost touching her tucked dress. She never hesitated and moved forward into the deeper part of the water now swirling around her waist – then slowly but surely it receded as we made our way to the other side.

By that time, the onlookers had entered the river. They welcomed my mother like a heroine and assisted her by lifting me from her shoulders, carrying me ashore. I was so proud of my mother – we did it, or should I say, she did. That experience has encouraged me, many times when faced with adversity.

I was glad to have a sister, it added to my gravitas as if part of something bigger, except for the peculiarity of hearing that she was my half-sister. This exactness of social convention was misplaced; the colour and flow of conversation being far more important. That said, my son, at a tender age, would never allow me to deviate an iota in the retelling of a story involving the two of us. Minutiae, seemingly important for his sense of security. I tried to convince him otherwise, but he would not budge; meanwhile, I enjoyed referring to Gayle as *my sister*.

A few years after our holiday, I started to notice a difference between how we were treated – I was the stepchild. This feeling was exacerbated subsequently by George's continued attention bestowed on Gayle as if I never existed. I felt increasingly alienated from the intimacy of our family, and my loneliness grew.

George was a keen photographer. He had a Leica, a Hasselblad and an 8mm cine camera in his armoury. The Leica was intuitive – point and photograph, while the Hasselblad was more interesting – look down and photograph. I was fascinated by his explanations on the principles of light refraction, the inversion of the image through the aperture and that the angle of incidence equals the angle of refraction.

My mother, a glass in hand during her argumentative moments, challenged, "No wonder we don't have any money, you waste it all on this stupid photographic stuff of yours", her tone telling me this was no ordinary conversation.

"Don't be silly Desiree", George calmly replied.

But with her unconscious agenda assured, she remained oblivious and continued to raise the ante, provocatively attacking, "That's all you do, sitting here, night after night, reading your stupid newspaper." He mostly continued and ignored her.

We were at a wedding one day, George happily snapped photographs of all and sundry – the unofficial self-appointed photographer. I knew how many spools he had and that each could take thirty-six photographs. Umpteen photographs later of Gayle, in many different poses, my mother, equally aware, interceded light-heartedly, "George, why don't you take a photograph of Walter, as well?" Slightly irritated, he begrudgingly took a single photograph, then continued to snap away at Gayle again.

The impact was hurtful and reinforced a message, *you are the stepchild*! Bravely I feigned a smile, turned and walked away, pretending it was unimportant. But that was not true – I felt alone, unseen and insignificant – there were other such occasions.

When the family gathered to look at the developed photographs, it was painfully obvious how few there were of me – a double whammy of emotional turmoil. Even my mother, in her rational moments, encouragingly commented, "George, you should take more photographs of Walter, there are hardly any here." The same was true of any cine film. His behaviour continued – it remained glaringly obvious and hurtful.

My sense of alienation persisted – whenever we were in a shop and Gayle asked for an item of sorts, George willingly obliged. Thinking he was in a generous mood, I asked for something specifically needed for school.

His immediate, reflexive retort was, "You don't need that", said in a gruff voice, yet he never responded to Gayle in that tone. It was blatant, yet in the presence of my mother he was a little more cautious, particularly when she reinforced my request, "That's right, Walter does need an eraser."

Our family dynamics were awkward and skewed.

I had a thing with shoes – struggling to know whether they fitted properly or not. It stems from when I was about four years old and had to have specially adapted heels, preventing me from walking pronate. The cobbler would remove the existing heels from my new shoes, such a waste, and would replace them with peculiar wedge-shaped ones that made walking difficult.

When I was five, still living across the road from Aunty Ronnie, I adored the outings with my mom to those big departmental stores. The shop assistants had a knack, *this fits well and looks good on you*, which always became the clincher; but at times my indecisive grimace, *not these Mom*, succeeded. My mother smiled and with the patience of Job we would go to another store.

John Orrs was our favourite. Both the quality of merchandise and the better calibre of staff were obvious, and my mother, so eloquent in the way she conducted herself, knew where to locate all the different merchandise. I was impressed and loved her dearly.

We frequently charged purchases to Aunty Ronnie's account.

"Cash, cheque or charge, madam?"

"Charge please, Mrs Prentice."

Perhaps my mom and Aunty had an arrangement. Better still was when we paid in cash and the strange array of pneumatic tubes would gobble up the inserted docket and money with a whoosh! The cylindrical see-through spaceship container would disappear and magically reappear shortly thereafter. How it knew where to go and to return so quickly, with the correct change in it, always amazed me.

Then there were treats like meeting Aunty Ronnie in the cafeteria for waffles and ice cream with lots of syrup – these were happy times. A treasured black and white photograph, snapped by a street photographer, tells the tale: my mom and I walking hand in hand, carefree, while I look adoringly at her, so elegantly dressed with her fashionable high heel stilettos and a handbag draped over her arm.

This was in stark contrast to shopping with George when I was twelve, my first year at high school. He was impatient and kept insisting on a size or two bigger. "You will grow into them. It is a waste of money taking a pair that fit well." Being strong willed, I resisted for a while but finally gave in.

I looked down at my floating clown feet, which did not go unnoticed by the other schoolboys, goading, *here comes big feet*. Feeling humiliated, the taunts were ignored as best I could. But in my adult years, I never quite resolved my dilemma – looks versus comfort – frequently making disastrous choices.

PASSION AND HUMILIATION

During my forties, Piet and I went on a spiritual trip to Giza, in Egypt – he reminded me of many childhood incidents. One, completely forgotten, was masked by my sheer embarrassment.

"We hid behind the lace curtains with the lights turned off so that your mom could not see us. We looked down upon her standing between our houses." It started flooding back, the more he spoke. My mother, in her drunken stupor, would go on a rampage hurling insults at our immediate adjoining neighbours.

No doubt, they were listening to her prior out of control ranting and raging already happening at our home.

Piet's family was first, "You fucking hypocrites pretending to be so religious going to your *Gereformeerde* Church on Sundays; you're no better. Don't pretend you are not listening and that you're asleep." With that she would pick up a stone and throw it onto their corrugated roof as it clunked its way down. "If you are asleep, now you are fucking awake!"

Next, she went to the Curtain's side, yelling, "You're equally as bad, no wonder you have so many children. That stupid religion of yours doesn't allow contraception." And on and on – of course, neither neighbour showed themselves, and finally she ran out of steam.

The next morning, the two equidistant bus stops from our corner home posed a quandary – *which gauntlet to run*? I was most preoccupied that I might bump into the neighbours. My shame was still raw.

On the lighter side, Piet recalled George's driving, an adventure that could be titled, *at your peril*! We were on our way to a road cycle race around the Indian township of Lenasia, some thirty kilometres southwest of Johannesburg.

Travelling there allowed a peek into apartheid reality, not that I comprehended its complexities. We skirted the areas where the Black and Indian populations lived. Lenasia was more affluent, akin to and in instances, better than some middle-class White suburbs, while Soweto's bleak concrete matchbox homes were depressingly visible for as far as the eye could see.

A sad wave enveloped, and I felt a visceral chill inside. It was as if I could sense a hopelessness brought about by the unnecessary displacement in being evicted, sometimes forcefully, in making way for the newly demarcated White areas. What must have been endured – or did it become of necessity an adaptation to survive?

Piet continued, "I was sitting in the back of that black Citroën and thought it was the last day of my life. I wondered what it was that George could see from behind his thickset glasses."

George was his own Stirling Moss, refusing to recognise his limitations or those of the Citroën, his pride and joy. Once he had decided to overtake, there was no stopping him, except he forgot that speed and power were an integral part of the equation, as was his judgement of the depth of field – impaired, as was his ability to admit defeat.

There was a funny side to his antics though – always the same, every time he attempted his strategic manoeuvre. He grabbed the wheel more tightly than necessary and proceeded to rhythmically pull and push his upper torso, forward and backwards. The increasing tempo reflected his determination and will to physically propel the car to go faster – of course, foolhardy.

At times, I am sure the other drivers spotted his theatrics, and for their amusement would accelerate just a bit, frustrating George's efforts further. Like a gladiator, he remained locked in mortal battle. Furtively, he looked out of the corner of his eye while muttering under his breath, "Come on you silly goat, out of the way", as though the utterance would influence the predictable outcome during his gymnastic routine.

We anxiously lived each moment as the oncoming vehicle was not that distant any more. We were still only neck and neck with the car we were trying to overtake, which either forced George to brake hard and drop back or otherwise, with his left indicator flashing, he simply cut across the other driver. All the while cursing, "Now, move over you bloody goat. Look at him, bloody idiot." We were left in no doubt that it must be the other driver's fault and that his words had our concurrence.

Piet finished his rendition, which only encouraged us to mimic George's motion – our fits of laughter magnified until our aching sides could handle it no more. George's absurd *overtaking manoeuvres* have gained epic proportions. When retold, Gayle still spontaneously breaks out into irresistible, uncontrollable laughter, but those journeys could so easily have ended differently.

The resounding laughter that occurs in the retelling of the story compensated for the weakness of our young voices, not able to engage with, or dissuade George from his dangerous driving practices. We were dependent on him for transport. Desiree tried, but was met by his irritated voice in its defensive retort. She never learnt to drive, and handled her fear by sometimes sitting in the back, shielding herself from an eagle's view of unfolding events. Perhaps, her evening indulgences, unconsciously attempted to do the same, albeit for different reasons.

George's passion for his 1948 black Citroën knew no bounds – it was the model with the gear lever protruding from the middle of the dashboard and indicators that flicked out between the front and rear doors. There was only one problem: it often broke down. Understandable, unlike George's hallmark, stubbornness.

The Transvaal Highveld, notorious for its intermittent below zero winter snaps, frequently meant that the water in the radiator was partly or wholly frozen. Common sense dictates idling for a few minutes to allow the frozen water to thaw. George's impatience knew otherwise. Sure enough, it was not the first, but the second time that the cylinder head gasket blew – the car grounding to a halt. Frozen in time, we waited for the tow truck, while the passing traffic continued its carefree journey.

Long-distance vacations were another time of breakdowns, and strangely, never on the way home. It annoyed my mother no end, while I rather enjoyed the adventure, but not when it was early evening, already dark and freezing cold. Soon, I knew about the quick fix solutions: *Bars-leak* and *guffer-tape* for radiators and rubber pipes; best of all was the ingenious use of tightly twisted pantyhose to replace a broken fan belt.

This new-found knowledge encouraged my watchful eye to cast furtive glances at the old-fashioned oil pressure and water temperature gauges, a favourite pastime of mine lest something was awry, while the purr of the engine was always comforting.

Once, we stayed in a truly one-horse town for a day too many awaiting the arrival of a spare part. An exercise in patience, until we were on our way, accompanied by George's usual symphonic array of flatulence, often disguised by knowing the terrain.

"George, was that you?", my mother innocently enquired. He feigned surprise; she continued, "The smell."

Vaguely, he nodded. "Ah yes, the Lion Park over there," pointing distantly as we travelled through the Valley of a Thousand Hills. The ruse worked for a while, and, encouraged by his cloud of deception, a few more silent friends played hide and seek.

Finally, my mother in a genial manner, exclaimed, "This must be one enormous Park!"

Relieved, we rapidly wound our windows down to the welcome breeze.

George's natural ebullience and indulgence in his humour left none of us immune. His boyish prank and infectious laughter cajoled the Citroën merrily along.

Sometimes a stranger in the street asked him a question. When they were out of earshot he would idiosyncratically say to himself, *now that is what I think of them*, emitting an enormous *derriere* roar. He was always chuffed with his ability to let them rip on demand, which amused Gayle no end. She was unable to stop chuckling. Perhaps by then, my familiarity with his caper had run its course and it no longer seemed quite so funny.

The Citroën, on death's doorstep, finally gave up the ghost and lay lifeless in our garage, awaiting resurrection. There was nothing to do but rebuild the engine, a task George set about over weekends, occasionally with help from his friends. The weeks turned into months – I asked the odd question and was baffled by all the parts that lay around. The head off the block with four pistons staring. Spark plugs jutting out, a carburettor valve winking as George showed me how it opened and closed, and the distributor cap with octopus's tentacles protruding, now no longer attached to the spark plugs – could it be put together again?

The evocative smell of the leather seats remained, while the forlorn silver headlights on the Citroën's black body patiently awaited George's restorative loving care to put all the parts together again. Confidentially, the Citroën confided: *his playful coaxing thrusts, to greater speeds, were missed; alas, she had tried, but upon acceleration was not built for George's ambition, although on the open road she came into her own, and enjoyed their reign*!

Finally, to everyone's delight, the Citroën burst back into life as did George's smile. A continual grin from ear to ear, except the few extra nuts and bolts laying about, which perturbed me. Their relationship continued for a few more years – the old larks prevailed. Inevitably, a younger model, floating on hydraulic suspension, won the day. With a bit of luck, the '48 Citroën may well have found her way to a vintage collector – George would have been pleased.

Meanwhile, his initial infatuation peppered all conversations . . . *the latest technology . . . the aerodynamics . . . the best car in the world*. Such novelty and excitement. Upon starting the engine, our spaceship rose – first the rear then the front end, and could be set to varying heights depending on the terrain. Now I no longer minded arriving earlier for school, even finding excuses as to why I could not cycle. The only pity was he never outgrew his *overtaking torso habit*, and I feared for his new bride's curvaceous body and our survival.

My dismantled track bicycle only just fitted into the peculiarly shaped boot. George, understandably, was most preoccupied lest any chain oil touch the interior.

There were many facets to George, endearing and irritating – perhaps, the latter exacerbated by the emotional stimuli swirling around our home. Mostly, I dreaded having to have my homework checked by him – my mother, busy with other chores, fobbed me off; *Go to George he is much cleverer with things like that*. He was, but therein was the nub – his barrage of belittlement and how it affected me. Slowly, the enjoyment or wish to continue exploring creative subjects, like languages or art, dissipated. Instead, I focused on exactitude: arithmetic, mathematics and science; there were no shades of grey, and I did not need George to help me.

On the other hand, he would share charming anecdotes of his school days: *he was the only boy who knew the meaning of certain words, like how to pronounce and spell 'rendezvous'*. In that moment of the telling, I admired George and his learnedness was worthy of emulation.

But . . . in the next breath, I was put down. His gestures, like a disapproving sideways nod, communicated his scorn looking from behind those thick glasses, while I recited or read my English homework.

"You'll never be able to spell." Dismissively, he would pick up his newspaper, hand me back my book and carry on reading.

His misplaced sense of humour embedded with overtures of disdain became humiliating: *you bloody goat . . . you stupid donkey*! Mostly these painfully pierced my spirit. It was not his words but his tone, differently from when he was driving the Citroën – those were often rather funny.

I would like to think it was an unconscious hiding behind a shield of ambiguity. Yet, my impression was that the reviewing or assisting with homework was an annoying interruption of his leisure time. I felt inhibited – it was hurtful, as if my heart had been ripped and my soul squashed.

After that, it was difficult to muster any further enthusiasm to continue reading or recite any verses. My voice lost its strength and any homework bonding dissipated as I completed my tasks on my own.

My earlier diligence changed, partly because of George's behaviour. Cribbing crept in, but was accompanied by a sense of guilt – there was an art to convince my classmates, and I knew only too well my reluctance when it was the other way around, particularly if I did not like the person.

Inevitably, I started to pretend: *did it at school, during breaks . . . no homework today,* and so on. He never asked to see what had supposedly been done, so I relied on this ploy. But there were times I needed additional help and reluctantly, I ate humble pie. Of course, my confusion reigned for there were moments when my *homework experience* was pleasant, possibly because he was in a better space or perhaps because I had not pestered him for a while.

Mostly, it was an emotional tug of war.

KALI AND ANGELS

The sibling age gap of eight years, between Gayle and myself, determined our different views of the turmoil witnessed from our mother's strewn path of nocturnal havoc. In our adult years, comparing notes, we realised that the fallout from the trauma was not dissimilar.

Our *family baggage*, unchecked, running rife and unattended was drenched with Kali's energy. In our formative years, we never knew about Kali, that devouring timeless Hindu Goddess of creation and destruction. Neither did we have the tools to appease her. Psychologically, she has aspects of the Jungian *shadow within* and, venerated with tinctures of deepest recognition, whether by way of a simple or an elaborate ritual, creates rather than destroys. Integrated and recognised by our psyche, the shadow side is less disruptive – otherwise, our dark side, like Kali's wrath, waits like a time bomb and will erupt, explosively.

Christian religions do not recognise the *shadow*, rather it is more absolute: good or evil, heaven or hell. Sin and repent, accept the penance, a few coins in the confession box – and start with a clean slate. Is it not preferable to recognise and honour the *shadow within* as an integral part of our existence, rather than as the work of the devil? Is it not better to have another way of dealing with this energy, rather than denying it, and, repeating it, repeatedly?

A solitary sip ignited my mother's affliction and evening activity; the ante raised until the smothering pervasive cloud of doom, gloom and sheer hopelessness descended upon the family – invariably, I felt quite despondent.

In those heavier moments, George, who seldom drank nor rose to my mother's bait, would sit in his favourite armchair, placidly reading the evening newspaper, while I challenged her, particularly if a principle was at stake.

"Shut up, don't answer your mother back, it will blow over by tomorrow" – George's words of reprimand never deterred me.

There was an occasion when he saved me from my mother's violent actions and I was grateful. She was ranting and raving in her drunken stupor and had decided to beat me with my scout leather belt for a misdemeanour undeserving of punishment. She was completely out of control – perhaps, her vicissitudes were not even directed at me.

He physically came between Desiree and me, instructing in a surprisingly strong decisive voice, rare for him, "Lock yourself in your room and don't open the door until tomorrow morning, when all of this will have blown over."

The key turned, and in my absolute fear I felt safe and protected by him in that instance, listening as his voice trailed down the corridor, "Desiree, leave the boy alone and don't be so ridiculous!" I tried to make sense of it all, listening for a while longer. Then, a certain numbness crept over me, and sleep finally shut me down for that night.

The morning after any episode my mother would always greet us as though nothing untoward had happened. Meanwhile, I was still gripped by the continual confusion of the previous evening's occurrences and at times lucky to be alive.

Sometimes there were recurring nightmares. What was worse? Falling off a cliff and awakening just before hitting the bottom or beating off assailants, only to realise that I was punching my wall.

Sleepwalking was equally scary: finding myself in Gayle's spare bed in the morning. My sleep world frightened me and was beyond my control.

Gayle reminded me of an incident, only heard in my adult years, that shocked me, and forced a lens adjustment of what she had endured – her fear to fall asleep at night in case Desiree killed us. Our age gap allowed me to ignore some of those reckless utterances by our mother, while Gayle literally clung to every word; a dangerous psychological arena that should not be treated lightly.

Sharing further, "I would go to bed praying not to fall asleep so that I could remain alert and stop Des if she tried to kill any one of us. My eyes became heavier and heavier, fighting to stay awake. I listened to the corridor sounds of our mom romping around the house. Inevitably, I fell asleep and awoke the next morning wondering if I was the only one still alive. I soon discovered that everyone was fine. Life carried on, only I was still reeling."

Our sibling bond was strengthened during our adult lives, driven by our incessant need to understand our emotional reactions to these home events, and how it had subsequently affected us. Our trauma was indeed deep.

It was not Gayle's time to die then, or even when she nearly drowned during a family holiday down in Natal. She had been playing in the shallow end and while edging towards the deep end, lost her footing. The more she tried to reach the surface, the more water she took in and slowly started to sink to the bottom. "I was laying there with my eyes open looking upwards at the sky wondering if anyone could see me. Next thing I was hauled out." A quick-witted waiter jumped in and saved her life.

And on the seventh day, the *Lord's Day*, not a solitary *drop* was consumed. I guess it was steeped in her fervent biblical belief and in a way an unconscious hoodwinking, her denial, not that she or any of us recognised it as such. Strangely enough, Sundays always allowed me to see my real mother: the caring one with her beautiful heart and shining soul; but only for that day. So I lived in hope for a reprieve of another day – the Monday – but it was seldom beyond that.

For nine formative years, from eleven onwards, this became our skewed saturated dance. It may seem trivial during a lifespan, but those important years opened a psychological corridor that determined my unconscious future adult behaviour. The real issue was the witnessing of my mother's habitual second nature verbal attacks, her ancient reptilian *fight* mentality, lashing out whenever insecure. It embedded into my psyche, and unknowingly, I too was capable of this destructive behaviour, even without alcohol.

It was as if a voice deep inside suggested, *you have to break the genetic curse and inherited pattern of behaviour, to ensure that more of the same is not passed on to your children, at whatever cost.* Many different terrains were traversed in an endeavour to come to grips with *our family baggage.* The benefits from these journeys were apparent later.

A lot happened in Kensington. Initially, my father and mother lived there, then later, George and my mom. The local hub was St Andrews Anglican Church – my baptism and confirmation, church for my mother and me, and scouting activities, a natural progression from Cubs.

Expeditions with my mom to the Scout shop, stocked with paraphernalia, were magical and a time of joy. Her soul and inner beauty shone forth, my true mother. The different uniform and the shaping of the large brimmed Rocky Mountain felt hat that protected me was a sense of graduation.

However, the bonding and joy were mostly transitory; always that dreaded first sip, followed by the hurtful actual or veiled threats that dangled in the air. In a way, like Gayle, how was I to know that some would never be fulfilled? Instead, the impact of her piercing words was absorbed, and I became downhearted.

The Scouts badge system was interesting, enjoyable and tested an enormous variety of skills across a spectrum from sewing, gardening and cooking to compass, map reading and camping. Had some slipped across from the Girl Guide's manual? Over time, the importance of those vital skills was realised, and badges earned became a stepping stone to recognition as either a Bushman or Springbok Scout, the ultimate accolade. Some were easy pickings, while others were more daunting and challenging.

Camping and surviving a few days on our own was such a task. Our Zebra Patrol created its boisterous fun, cooked over an open fire, and never forgot the chores of cleaning the blackened pots and pans with grit. My Patrol leader's handcrafted six-foot stave, burnt with twelve-inch black ringed intervals, accompanied me like a badge of honour, and doubled as an invaluable measuring tool, as did my thumb.

The other animal patrol names were more powerful. Eagle, Lion, Cheetah, even Kudu, also my high school house name, was preferable; always alert, and ready to dash at the slightest whiff of danger.

My most memorable badge was for gardening as I tended my vegetable patch of potatoes and tomatoes in our forlorn backyard. By contrast, my mother had passionately created a most beautiful front garden, a joy to behold. Hours were spent on Sundays, her day of reprieve from her evening habits.

The true loving mother was again revealed. The care and delight taken in sharing her knowledge: the preparation of the soil, when to plant, how to cultivate, water, and maintain the crops.

The speed of growth fascinated me, and at regular intervals I attended to the necessary covering of the branches and stems of the potatoes with a pyramid mound of soil. The beautiful eruption of the delicate yellow flowers, the subsequent birth of tiny red tomatoes and their swelling as the sun's energy was absorbed, was enchanting. The moment arrived when the distinctive fragrance of the vine filled the air – a signal that the fruit would soon be ready and my efforts judged.

Harvested potatoes and healthy sun-ripened tomatoes, guided by my mother's love and filled with my care and attention, greeted the examiner. The three of us stood there – the first shared bite. Intoxicating and lingering . . . endorsed by his approving nod and echoing words, *absolutely delicious*. I could not contain my immediate smile, which reflected my delight better than any badge.

I only made it to the Bushman Scout level – over time my interest waned as my increased cycling activities took precedence. Marie-Louise von Franz, the renowned Swiss Jungian psychologist, made her patients and students, after interpreting their dreams, ritualise them – a vital step in enforcing the bridging of the unconscious to the conscious. Mine was the plaiting of the Bushman thong and wearing it proudly, an encapsulation of all my Scouting efforts.

A flashback – I'm eight years old, in our Cambridge Road home, a time before the onset of my mother's demons. Treasured moments – tucked in with a simple prayer we recited together; our special quiet time.

> *Matthew Mark Luke and John,*
> *Guard the bed that I lay on,*
> *Four corners to my bed,*
> *Four angels around my head,*
> *Amen.*

My hands rested together, palm to palm, on my chest like a cherub; during *the amen*, we both crossed ourselves – a calmness pervaded, a befitting end to the adventures of the day.

Best of all was when she sang in such a soothing, beautiful voice, *Little boy you're tired, tell you what I'll do, mommy put all your toys away; the soldiers were fighting, one by one, little boy, it's been a busy day*! I did what most children do, using that powerful word, *again*. It did the trick; my eyes gently closed to my favourite lullaby, content in a sense of her love and essence which enveloped the room, seeping into my pores – our true heartfelt bonding.

I was probably sound asleep within seconds, but that period of contentment was subsequently shattered in the Highland Road years. No longer would I fall asleep instantly, rather I would lie awake . . . my radar scanning, listening and anticipating every sound indicative of the developing state of play of my mother's behaviour. And if not doing that, a silly tale about *our eyes rolling back into our heads at the point of falling asleep*, would preoccupy me in trying to pinpoint that exact moment – instead, I often awoke with a jolt.

Those types of anxieties had their roots much earlier. Notwithstanding feeling quite grown-up flying to Cape Town, as an unaccompanied minor, to visit my Dad on an evening flight, I thought the exhaust flames from the prop engines may be the start of a fire. No one else seemed to have noticed. My strategy to attract the stewardess's attention was to request a soft drink, while furtively casting a sideways glance as if warning of an impending disaster – it never worked, and my silent apprehension remained.

A touch of St Vitus, silly phobias and another weird habit – in total darkness I would listen to *The Creaking Door is Opening*, Saturday night's Springbok Radio's 9 o'clock broadcast. The jingle, an eerie sound of the creaking door slowly opening, was accompanied by an equally exaggerated scary voice – "Do come in!"

The mottled moonlight, filtering through the oak branches, gave a slight reprieve to my fear, but not before slowing my breathing to an undetectable level, purposefully, lest any ghosts detected me. If I kept absolutely still, I was convinced that they would not notice and move on. The tension created terrified me as the darkness engulfed.

The programme ended, but I remained frozen, still petrified. Relief slowly ebbed in through the comedy show, *Leave it to Van der Merwe*, a satirical depiction of the Afrikaner – Springbok Radio was an English station.

Sometimes it took me a while longer to thaw, particularly, when there were strong winds swaying the heavy branches of our huge oak tree. The scratching over our corrugated iron roof, exacerbated the storm of my frightened mind – thoughts that swirled to their darkest depths.

Church was always welcome; seemingly safe from the ghosts of my mind. I loved the social activity, the orderly behaviour of the congregation, the ritual aspects of the body of Christ and his blood, the wine, but mostly the mystique conjured from the burning of incense; the smell intoxicating. I dreamt of being an altar boy, dressed angelically in a white robe with a red collar, a pathway to the revelations of more mysterious matters of the Church. It was never pursued – emotional confusion around home conflicts intervened and weakened my interest.

However, not so my keen observation of the stoic men, standing in the aisle on either side of the pew, passing the collection plate . . . row by row . . . projecting an enveloping sense-of-shame to ensure a coin of the right denomination was given. Could I put one in and remove another of a higher denomination – I never had the guts to try it.

I saw angels once, and what better place than in the sanctity of the Lord's home. It happened between the infernal genuflecting. Was it God or the Devil that struck first? I awoke, prostrate on the floor; a circle of friendly, yet concerned faces, looking down upon me below. A whisper, *are you alright?* My mind raced remembering my last thoughts about the collection plate – was I in heaven or hell? I quickly made a mental apology, *I wasn't really going to remove any money, promise*, but before I received an absolution, another distant voice echoed, *he fainted*!

Trying to comprehend, my body was lifted and carried out, like on a funeral pyre. I lay on the hands carrying me, looking up at the ceiling – was this Michelangelo's inspiration? Our Sistine Chapel was bare. Perplexed, I thought I had had a religious experience. Slowly, it dawned on me that I was still in the church. It was the first time I had ever fainted.

Subsequently, I tested that brink – it caught me – weeks later. I fainted again in the church. On that occasion, it caused a little more distress to my caring mother. She hurried me to our family doctor, and onwards to other specialists for various tests. All of which offered no real explanation – I guess it was just one of those things and part of growing up.

George and his Citroën

Boy Scout days - 'planning the recce'

Boy Scout days - 'carefree'

CHAPTER 9
ROLLER COASTER RIDES

HIGH SCHOOL, PINBALL AND KARMA

There was something about the first day at a new school, that was like leapfrogging time. It happened at the Ridge and again at Jeppe High School for Boys – a kind of graduation into the unknown, tinged with anxieties and excitement; as if a quantum leap in maturity was being made from only the day before.

Perhaps the new uniform did it; a blazer of black and white vertical stripes, a badge depicting the gold ore of the Witwatersrand (Gold Rush of 1886) and a junior boy's tie – all set off by long grey flannels. The colour of the blazer was originally from a former headmaster, James Humphrey Allen Payne's, *alma mater*, Trinity Hall at Cambridge University. Donning the kit changed my demeanour, making me feel grown up and ready to tackle this new world, with fortitude. In the new democratic South Africa, the school has adopted the slogan, *let's turn black and white into gold*!

The school's motto, *Forti Nihil Difficilius* (for the brave nothing is too difficult), was commendable, but not yet ingrained for I was still at an early stage of my warrior's journey. The magnificent school stone buildings, built in 1909 on land donated by Sir Julius Jeppe and designed by Ralston, a student of Sir Herbert Baker, was traditional and awe-inspiring as if taking me back into antiquity.

The playgrounds seemed enormous. Vast sporting facilities flanked either side of a koppie, still wild, desolate and untouched. Koppies like this, where battles were fought between the English and the Afrikaners during the

Anglo-Boer War, made history lessons more real. Little did I know I would have my boy fight there, a few years later.

I was always ready to try any school sport. My first ever cricket practice, having never seen practice nets, was during the first week of high school. The boys lined up and took turns to bowl – I noted their action and thought nothing of it. It was beginner's luck: first ball, batsmen bowled with the wicket tumbling.

"We have a bowler here," said a teacher. Try as I would, I could not repeat my fluke.

Maybe, if I had known that practice was necessary, like finding out the hard way about studying for examinations, there might have been an outside chance. But with no further guidance and, naturally being impatient, I quit bowling.

Instead, I defended and played 'point', a position requiring lightning reflexes – pity George never saw any of my school cricket matches, a far cry from his hurtful comment, *you have no eye for the ball*. I never bothered to correct him.

Tennis was attempted in my second last year of school, but the players seemed precious and rather aloof. Feeling threatened and not part of their social standing, I gave it a miss, but mainly because it conflicted with my afternoon cycling training sessions.

Jeppe was a rugby school. Mr Stander, my sports, form and Afrikaans teacher, played me as a flank in the under 13A rugby team. I liked that position; extremely quick and often successful in tackling the opposition scrum-half.

This may have been attributed to my approach to scrumming, not that I ever let on to the teachers or the other team members – I pushed, but not as hard as I should – instead, remaining spring loaded.

One of our locks, affectionately known as Puppy, probably because of his *puppy fat*, was solid. When he had the ball pounding forward, few schoolboys, hanging on while being dragged along, were able to tackle or stop him. Our secret weapon, encouraged by our shouts from behind, *go Puppy go*, and only when we had a sense that he was overwhelmed would we shout, *pass*.

Stander taught us that even the meekest rugby player could tackle Puppy, but it needed decisiveness, courage, good execution and then letting gravity do the rest. A charging buffalo was daunting; yet, the bigger they were, the harder they fell. Surprisingly, we were unhurt, which is more than I can say for some of the tumbles during my cycling days.

Things were not always pleasant in the scrum. One lock never seemed to wash between his buttocks, a dreaded occasion when attaching myself to him – at times I thought I would retch. No one had the wherewithal to say anything. Perhaps, it may have accounted for my quickness out of the scrum.

Important matches were between the triangle: Jeppe, King Edward and Parktown North – compulsory attendance, and a time to hear the mighty Jeppe Zulu war cry. Our first team was strengthened by exceptional rugby players, needing better marks, who were encouraged to repeat their final year.

Players, locked arm in arm, roared – as powerful as any Maori's haka. The strong resonance pulsated through our bodies – it was earthy and ancient – beefed up, the opposition were hopefully intimidated, and not knowing the meaning of the Zulu words, only added to the mystique.

War cry practice days had an initiatory aspect – new boys in the middle, enclosed by a massive outer ring of senior rugby players. Quickly, I learned to duck into the inner core of the huddled boys to avoid the weaving onslaught as they gave us the boot. Bullying types vented their frustrations, while the sportsmen gave a symbolic playful kick. Instinctively, I disapproved of this form of behaviour, and like many had my share of being bullied at school and in the corporate world.

Tea, after matches, was special. It had a distinctive smell and a satisfying taste; made with condense milk. Only a slice of home baked cake was allowed, but we could always come back for another cup poured from the long spouted aluminium bottomless teapots. The robust mothers greeted us with the same warm, friendly smiles, inviting conversation . . . *good game* . . . *did we win*? A perfunctory nod on our part acknowledged this tea drinking ceremony.

Half time orange wedges, served on a tray during a game, were a close second. We could rip the inner out in one go, which allowed another to be guzzled until none were left – it hit the spot perfectly.

Victory or otherwise, the comradeship and chit-chatter, while quenching our thirsts, was the most satisfying end to any match; a time of emotional sustenance, where life was relatively carefree and uncluttered. My only real responsibility was to pass the examinations.

On the other hand, the changing room and communal showers were dank and disagreeable, as if infused by the stale smell of dirty socks and underpants. Might the rotting cells of ghosts that haunted the school also be there? The boarders were full of such stories and I was glad to be a day boy.

While the sociocultural revolution of the '60s was underway, I was locked into my addictive practice of playing pinball. Some of the boys were absolute wizards, and with a solitary sixpence they would win countless free games ensuring an afternoon of sheer delight. How I admired their skill and mastery, and watched their techniques deployed to defy gravity's hold of the rapidly zig-zagging iron ball electronically propelled in a myriad of endless permutations. At times, the machine's rhythm and flow was altered with a gentle nudge, shake or cunning bump. It necessitated remaining calm under pressure as the hidden secrets were discovered the more it was played.

These behemoths would spew out their symphony of sounds, indicative of the state of the game and the tasks achieved. This only encouraged and excited us. Frenzied continual eye and muscular coordination culminated in either a *downward spiral ring* of a tilt, which automatically ceased play for that ball, or the satisfactory *deep cluck* of a free game awarded; better still, a succession of *clucks*.

We all fell prey to the monster when taken to the brink of sheer frustration – an occasional banging of a fist on the wooden surround or a kick to the underside. It never met with the cafe owner's approval; his glancing look of admonishment, sufficient. At times I was a *groupie*, just watching, while at others, a *player*, signifying my intent by putting my sixpence on the front of the table.

The pinball machines ironically were owned by another Greek immigrant family, whose three sons also attended Jeppe, one of them in my class. We were fascinated when the machine mechanic opened the table and we could peer inside the electronic brain. Before leaving, having collected the takings and ensuring that the machine was fully operational, he would touch the tripwire a few times producing that familiar *cluck* sound. Smiling, while locking the machine, he indicated that the free games were ours to play.

What a gift – the power of observation – soon the older boys were prising a tiny opening at the bottom of the coin return slot. Deftly, a stiff wire was inserted through the small aperture, triggering the tripwire, which immediately awarded more games. Now, I was always on the lookout for a new pinball cafe where the return slot had already been doctored. Of course, craftiness was necessary to allay suspicion, for cafe owners had a nose for sniffing out misdemeanours.

However, like all things that are too good to be true, they end for one reason or another. Inserting the wire sometimes met with disappointment for the circuitry had been altered, or we forgot the foresight bit, like asking for more change, but rather greedily notching up five or six games at a time. In our excitement, we had failed to notice the strategically placed horizontal mirror in the gaming area – our giveaway. In a wink, the cafe owner grabbed my ear, twisting it so hard I thought it would tear from my head. Frogmarched from the premises, he shouted in a stern voice, "Don't you ever come back to this shop again, boy!" I never did.

The ear, an icon of reprimand, first the nuns, now the Greek cafe owner – I was let off lightly. It became a deterrent and my energies were focused elsewhere, although when opportunity knocked, I could not resist the odd game or two. This continued into adulthood where Stefan and I enjoyed the early laptop versions, but the subsequent ubiquitous electronic games, challenging man's continued insatiable appetite, were left to him.

I had never heard of karma, being more steeped in Christian ideology, although like many my innate sense of right and wrong was present. Could what happened next be a retribution for my prior misconduct?

My cycle, unlocked for a few minutes at the entrance of a shop, upon return, was gone. Panicking, I ran hither and thither, hopeful that someone may have placed it around the corner. Deep down, I knew. Crowning it all, fully clad in cycling gear, I ludicrously hobbled home in sheer disbelief on my cleated cycling shoes. It was embarrassing – how I wished I could turn the clock back, just a little.

The dread of having to tell George and Desiree lingered, while remembering another occasion when a quick neighbourhood game of garden cricket went awry – an enthusiastic full swipe. I had been warned – *it damages the flowers.* It was not *the flowers*, but *Gayle's bedroom window*.

Desperately, I attempted to reverse the slow-motion passage of time of the unstoppable sound of breaking glass. Examining the large shards, my act of concentration could not put them together again, as much as I tried – the same was true of the rumination around the theft.

That evening, fearing the worst, I presented the facts as skilfully as I could, and was taken aback. No reprimand, merely a slight admonishment and a proviso, *you'll have to save your pocket money if you want another bike.*

Fortuitously, a neighbour wished to sell his immaculately cared for and accessorised pale blue racing cycle, dressed in the finest and most efficient Campagnolo equipment – a dream machine. Startled out of my reverie, I faintly heard, *why don't you take it for a ride?*

Responsive and smooth, and the effortless changing of the gears made my stolen bicycle with its heavy high-pressure tyres seem archaic. And, even though the frame was slightly too large, this time, unlike the shoes George made me have, I certainly did not mind.

The days passed and my fervent excitement waned, while the monotony of a bus trip or George's embarrassing overtaking theatrics had to be endured.

My lifetime savings fell short of the asking price. Providence smiled through my mother, who recognised my enthusiasm, confirming that I would have to pay back the difference – and in that flash my dream came true. Sheer joy surged. My magic carpet would pedal its way to victories – I soon learnt otherwise.

Restraining my enormous smile but not my gleaming eyes, I remained attentive to the rest of her conversation, "George has spoken to Uncle Nicky. You can help out at the delicatessen during your next school holiday."

My earnings from that stint were more than sufficient to repay their kind loan with another surprise afoot – *you only need to repay part of the loan, the balance to be kept towards the upkeep of your bicycle.* Their generosity and their unexpected act of kindness was staggering.

At such times, the more gracious and caring side of my mother's genuine personality shone forth. I held on to those moments, while trying to balance the equation of our otherwise skewed home dynamics.

At break times, we naturally gravitated to our favourite nooks on the adjoining smaller koppie at the back of the school – mostly, frivolity prevailed. The rocks, although uncomfortable, allowed a vantage point to look down upon the quadrangle where my newly acquired dream machine was locked.

Unfortunately, the *drawing pin malicious virus* unexpectedly struck, and my tyre was not immune. A cruel spark had been ignited and the culprit's senseless act saddened me. It belonged to the shadow side of the human psyche and was quickly checked by the principal's announcement, *henceforth the quad would be out of bounds and that any boy caught tampering with cycles would be punished* – music to my ears.

Being a year younger in my class, sport field bonding enabled me to maintain contact with my peers but, for the first year only. By my second, my newfound passion for cycling had taken root. Muscles used in the other sports impeded, rather than enhanced my cycling performance. It was my first taste of the absolute dedication necessary to compete effectively.

The better junior and senior cyclists in my club became my idols – attentively, I listened to their experiences and training tips, while dreaming of becoming as good as them. The imagined road ahead seemed a long way off and at times impossible.

We tried different training techniques. It was sheer trial and error, some of which later proved to be scientifically correct. I kept a rudimentary race diary and smiled upon recently reviewing some of the remarks – *strong winds*, *very strong winds*, or *no one would work*. The latter, needed a Wolfie and his herd of turtles to cajole the peloton along. On awakening, I recorded my resting pulse rate; a useful guide to my training regime.

Besides the necessary physical fitness and stamina needed, there was much to learn about reading a race. It would be a few years still before I watched, hawk-like, every determined thrust and ounce of energy expended by the other cyclists, while noting their strengths and weaknesses balanced against my progression. Theory was easy, practice something else. In those early days, being rather puny, it was somewhat academic. I would find out about the sheer human endeavour necessary to achieve the ultimate podium of success.

Friendships happened by chance, and were aided by an understanding of the tribulations necessary. The depth and diversity of the charismatic characters added much colour to our camaraderie.

Johannesburg is much hillier than people realise. If I was unable to get a lift to Hector Norris Park to compete in the Sunday afternoon track meetings, I would cycle the 13 kilometres there on my fixed wheel track bike – no brakes nor gears – the safest way to race, but not so on the road. Stopping was achieved by a peculiar backpedalling action assisted by a temporary fitted ineffective front brake (the shape of the rim was the issue). Also, the awkward strain on my leg muscles was detrimental before a competition.

There was a particularly flat stretch of road, where the rhythm and cadence of the ride was conducive to the catchy phrases of the sixties' pop revolution that flooded my mind. Singing lyrics like Bob Dylan's *how many roads must a man walk down, before you can call him a man . . .* became a temporary respite from my home turmoil and a landscape of other possibilities, but never the panacea.

A simple request to George for a lift often created emotional confusion. His indecisiveness left me in no man's land, complemented by a laconic response, *we'll see.* I tried tactics like asking in the earlier part of the week, or even on the weekend – it made no difference. Even a nudge on a Sunday, *it's already eleven thirty,* was greeted with an impatient glare as if to say there is still plenty of time to await his decision. I was left dangling, and always had to judge and anticipate his, or Desiree's prevailing mood. I tired of this continual charade and used him only as a desperate last resort.

Reluctantly, I resorted to calling Cliffie Steward, also a Jeppe boy, to see if I could scrounge a lift from his family. They lived two streets away. Debbie, his attractive girlfriend, was like Lady Godiva: long blonde hair trailing way past her waist and her different coloured eyes, rather than detract, added to her enigmatic mystique. Cliffie became a good sprinter, probably inspired by his need to get back to her sooner, and was dubbed by the press as the *Kensington Cannonball.* He did well in his cycling career, won many titles and represented South Africa.

Inveigling a lift was barely tolerated by his father. Post mortems were intolerable, only ever about Cliffie and with scant regard for my efforts, even when I did well – I felt unseen and superfluous. They epitomised a perfect respectable suburban family.

After a while, his father's polite excuses followed, *I don't think we'll be able to squeeze you in today, the car is full.* It was so evident when subsequently seen at the track; they could have. I gave up on them as well, and reluctantly had to either cycle there or rely on George.

Sometimes, half way through fitting the front brake, his friendly bark ensued as if my earlier requests for a lift had already been agreed.

"Come on, get your bike in the car, and let's go, you silly goat."

Other times my mother heard my plea and would eagerly jump into the fray.

"George, why don't you give Walter a lift, you don't have anything to do, and in any case, I've lots more gardening." Sunday, her day of rest and her nocturnal demons off duty.

I was mostly grateful, but the emotional rollercoaster sapped my mental energy. Ironically, once we were on our way, George's mood changed for the better, and inevitably he enjoyed the outing. What a peculiar dichotomy, and why did it always have to be so complicated?

INFLUENCES

The '60s lyrics were seemingly pertinent to my emotional deficits. I held on to the songs' aphorisms, marvelling at the foresight to write them and the ability to compose such catchy jingles.

The advertising industry understood this. Many stuck, one particular – *the Boeing's great, the goings great, when you fly with South African Airways, up and high, in the sky, must be SA Airways; from Rome, Lisbon, Paris* . . . and as the cadence soothingly descended, I dreamt that one day it may just be.

Perhaps, the industry had a hand in shaping my ideas and precepts. Indeed, when my emotional shutters came sliding down in moments of disquiet, a line from a song would pop into my head. A temporary succour from the emotional dysfunction at home. The subliminal or actual effect would be challenged in my adult life.

We used to have a daily morning school assembly, and on the more important occasions, the resident teachers' wives would attend as well. My form teacher and science teacher that year, Mr Loots, was a short, stocky man, who displayed admirable attributes.

Once the stampeding herd of boys were seated, he would patiently and caringly help his physically challenged wife to walk the short distance to the back row. Discreetly, out the corner of my eye, I watched him walking backwards while she held onto his outstretched arms, slowly hobbling forward. I reflected upon the depth of their love, and tried to make sense of their world. Meanwhile, witnessing his compassion, my admiration grew, engendering respect, and as such I strove to do my very best in his class.

Assemblies kept us informed about school and other topical issues. Our delightful ex-deputy head, Mr Gass, close to retirement age, was more in tune with the times than we realised, perhaps hinting at Steiner or Montessori ideology whereby the kernel of the child is encouraged to grow and flourish.

Incongruity followed his pep talks – a stern look and an admonishing finger, while attempting to sing Ned Miller's soppy lyrics, *do what you do do well boy* – did not quite hit the spot. Psychologists and advertising executives know only too well – *the catchier the tune and lyrics, the greater the likelihood of influence*!

I was never quite the *Saint*: there were other sides to my personality, which showed themselves with ramifications then and later in my adult life. I rode through the consequences, not having a frame of reference to correct my behaviour. At times, it was as though I faced my day of judgement or indeed was judging others in seeking an exactitude of *truth*.

Chess was my game. I played for the school team from my first year. By standard eight, the third last year of school, having turned fourteen and the time of an *undeclared warfare* with my mother, a classmate was made chess captain. I was peeved – on ability it should have been me.

My sensitivity triggered my ill-founded stubbornness. So whenever I was asked to play for the team, if I disagreed with my ranked position, I would obstinately hide behind my cycling commitments. Our dance continued until I gave up on chess, or the chess captain on me.

With hindsight, his appointment was correct. Then, I did not realise other qualities were needed to lead and motivate the team, neither did I learn from the lesson while younger. *The learning is never done until done*, a shamanic friend once reminded me. What I did know was that when trespassing into any of these territories my energy flow felt recognisably different.

The question begged at so many of these junctures – *what is truth and what is right or wrong*? I grappled with these precepts while trying to find my way through the maze, and was influenced by those I admired or held in high regard. At school, teachers played a pivotal role, appearing to be fonts of all knowledge. They appeared worldly and infinitely smarter than parents – is that not why they were the teachers?

There was a larger koppie outside the school grounds, ideal for schoolboy fights. On the whole, I kept my nose clean. That year John provocatively smeared oil on my white shirt during our metal work lesson. I took the bait, and a few sabre-rattling sentences later, encouraged by my fellow student's quick repartee, it soon escalated to a point of no return. Whispers spread, *fight on the koppie after school: Thornhill versus Ohlsen.*

My classroom concentration went out the window. The impending fight preoccupied my thoughts and feigned bravado; only made worse by acknowledging the other boys' encouragement to beat him up. The added twist was that the boys in my class were all a year older and physically stronger.

I had watched other koppie fights, but it was not my sort of thing. Neither did I enjoy the brutality, nor the spectator's stupidity as the frenzied crowd took on a life of its own. Sometimes another spontaneous fight erupted. The unspoken edict was *not to withdraw*, and I did not want to be perceived as a coward.

The school rules were strict about fighting at school and could lead to expulsion. The outside koppie was a safer bet. It was also a shortcut to the school's dormitories, which the masters regularly used as did the spectators now walking with an excited gait. Bundled along to the beckoning arena, I noticed an eerie transformation taking place like vultures to the kill. A makeshift circle appeared as the boys parted. Our blazers and ties were thrown casually to the ground, sleeves rolled up to the collective chorus, *fight, fight, hit him now* as we circled each other. A quick punch, one to the other, then another. A stinging sensation – how would this end, I thought, as I tried to remain alert?

A sharp piercing cry split the air – *chips, chips, a Master is coming, quick, quick, break it up*! And as quickly as it started, it was over. The boys casually meandered off as though returning from some sporting activity, the fight already forgotten. We were left to dust off our egos, nodding to each other and although not admitting it, I was glad it was over.

Some forty years on, brought together by the class of '69 reunion, we caught up telephonically. John was a leading criminologist. Somewhere amid our conversation, I casually asked whether he remembered the incident. He thought about it for a moment or two, then casually said, "I remember something of the sort, but it is very vague."

He may well have been Japanese face-saving polite. Why were our recalls so different? Was it the significance I had placed upon it in my dislike for the senseless brutality?

Warren Boden, my history teacher from standard nine onwards, treated us like young adults, was never belittling, had a friendly manner and encouraged our independent thinking to ensure we had a balanced view of South African history – Van Jaarsveld was the prescribed syllabus book, written by a biased Afrikaner, and Boyce by an Englishman, Boden's suggested read. Their contradictory perspectives were clearly shown in the Battle of Blood River. Examinations were set by the government, and Mr Boden's advice was to answer the questions treating *Van Jaarsveld* as gospel – an important and cunning lesson in duplicitousness, to survive within a system while having another view.

He enthused us with a zest for life and was passionate about hockey. My admiration for him influenced my unquestioning acceptance of one of his axiomatic statements: *the enjoyment of watching a film is no more than a substitute for the emotional deprivations not experienced in life*. This profound sounding concept became my misinformed beacon that only a hands-on experience of life was meaningful, and sadly was never clarified. It became my dichotomy, for actually I enjoyed the sheer escapism of movies, but my admiration for him, left me feeling a tad guilty, not realising I could do both.

Soon, I would star in my own mid-year drama testing honesty and self-judgement.

"Walter, I don't seem to have your preparatory examination paper here. Did you not perhaps take it home with you by mistake after the examination?"

"No Sir," my immediate defensive response.

"Check again, and don't forget to look inside your blazer pocket. Let me know tomorrow morning if you find it. Otherwise, you must write another", all said unthreateningly.

Sure enough, upon returning home, it was where he had suggested. I was astounded by his foresight and my inadvertent action – seventeen out of twenty, not bad. If I returned the multiple-choice paper, would he believe that I had not purposefully amended the answers?

The next day, not admitting my faux pas as I had lost my confidence, I bravely blurted, "Looked all over Sir, couldn't find it."

"OK, stay behind and you will do another paper now during break time."

I felt acutely embarrassed – my deliberate lie; the other boys gave me a quizzical look upon leaving the emptying classroom. My sleeves rolled up; amazingly, the test was the same. Purposefully, I kept my three previous incorrect answers, but unfortunately made another.

Marked straight away – "There you go, sixteen out of twenty, that's good."

I walked away with a heavy heart knowing my actual mark was higher and was concerned lest he thought that the mark obtained was only because of seeing the previous day's answers.

A good rapport and empathy with my teachers always brought the best out. The opposite was equally true as my shutters came down, making the learning of other subjects tedious – only the necessity to pass my examinations kept me partly attentive.

My friend, Winston Churchill, the second eldest of his five siblings from the colourful Churchill family, was unassuming and considerate. They lived in Malvern, the poorer suburb where my bicycle was stolen. Visits were always enjoyable, their home hospitable.

Chris was the eldest and the protagonist of the unusual Churchill lift club – unique – like dropping through Alice's rabbit-hole – cocooned and bizarre. The Humber Saloon, a noisy place with abundant banter where anarchy reigned, was free of parental control and Chris, only fifteen, was the king.

It had been a while since my last lift as mostly I cycled to school. The route's two ninety-degree hairpin bends skirted the Ash's residence on the edge of the

Kensington Golf Club, where the odd drunk who failed to turn in time went crashing into their property. Chris's cautionary speed was completely ignored. Instead, the car broadsided through the first bend, accelerated and rectified the slide with a repeat on the next. There were screams of delight by all except me, taken by complete surprise. When had this racing madness crept into their daily routine?

Rumour had it that his parents were cautioned not to let Chris drive the kids to school. He was a few years under the legal driving age, and the Churchill family fended for themselves as needs must.

While Stefan was a teenager, some harsh sounding advise was shared – *you may visit and test the edge a few times, but never remain there indefinitely; it has its consequences, and, in the extreme, leads to death*! I am not sure whether this was an original thought or heard at a men's workshop.

Rites of passage are used to ensure an individual's safety to themselves. In the Guatemalan Mayan society, a role of a village elder is to ensure that the youth, between the ages of thirteen to twenty-seven, stay alive. They are taught through ritual to contain and use this powerful *fire energy* that makes us feel invincible. Rites of passages nurture and make the initiate safer to themselves, to their families, the village and society at large. I too felt relatively invincible. Do you remember your sense of invincibility? Everything was possible, dreams were alive and life was forever. My universe was my immediate age group – those in their thirties were old and those in their sixties, ancient.

My first dramatic exposure to death, other than Uncle Jack's, was one evening strolling along Green Point Esplanade in the Cape, while visiting my father. I was thirteen and came across a crowd of onlookers, an ambulance and a sombre atmosphere. A group of inebriated youngsters were walking along the parapet of the seawall, when one of them slipped and fell, hitting his head on the rocks fourteen feet below and dying shortly thereafter. I watched as the stretcher was lowered and raised, realising he was my age with no second chance. My stomach turned, and the walk back to my dad's flat was quite disconcerting as I struggled to comprehend it all.

Chris, just seventeen, met a similar fate – he kept pushing the boundaries, and the car came to rest wrapped around a tree in Kitchener Avenue, close to our first home in Kensington – he was on his own.

Whenever I cycled past that spot, time bizarrely froze – a reminder – life, taken for granted, is so fragile. Their family wrench must have been enormous; I never knew as I had by then lost touch.

Our cycling club had Springbok riders Jimmy Swift and Mike Payne and an up and coming rider Stephen Lipa, who went on to represent South Africa at the 1969 Maccabi Games. He had a friendly disposition, was a good track sprinter, and it was a pleasure being in his company.

Basil Cohen, the commentator previously mentioned, was also the owner of a bicycle shop and the chairman of our club. He regaled us with the story of Stephen's mother's ethical and moral behaviour at the Games when she was asked to step in as one of three judges due to a shortage of cycling officials.

What a predicament: a tightly contested sprint final with millimetres separating the winner. She had the casting vote and chose to err even though she believed her son had won. These types of stories became embedded in my psyche.

The opposite side of human behaviour showed itself in the tandem final of the '76 South African Cycling Championships held in Bloemfontein, where an official's biased decision in favour of the local tandem riders was absolutely blatant. It related to an infringement by the winners during the last two hundred metres. Jack Lester suggested that on principle we should not mount the podium nor accept our second-place medals. We never did, but that story for another day.

LIFE'S SPICES

I enjoyed the camaraderie of my cycling buddies, cemented by the rigorous training regimes. There were two groups: the *Bezvalley gang* for Wednesday morning winter rides, *bunking* school, and our main *Kensington gang* of Rory Budler, Albert Styger, Willy Dawson, and on occasions, Piet, for our regular after school sessions.

Our usual route was from Kensington to the airport along a dual roadway and back again. We rode as a peloton, necessary for our training – quite dangerous because of the traffic. Once, on the way back we witnessed the death of an African man who had misjudged the distance and speed of the approaching car, while attempting to cross the road. The thud off the bumper and the bounce off the windscreen left only a crumpled body, like a bag of potatoes. Shocked and sickened to the core, we stopped and could not believe what we had just witnessed. We rode home in silence, contemplative of the continual road dangers we faced every day.

Being the eldest, I took on the role of mentor, contrasted to school where I was often the youngest. Delighted and in my element, I taught them all I knew. Albert, nearly a year younger than me, worked harder and was better suited to longer distance track events, pursuits and road racing. He became an outstanding cyclist, was calm and considered. His pinnacle moments were representing our province and winning numerous Championship medals. Unfortunately, due to a severe back injury during his Air Force military service, he was unable to compete at his former level.

Rory was an only child with delightful skinny parents – his father sporting a Spitfire pilot-type moustache. Rory had tremendous potential, was cunning, incredibly daring and developed a superb sprint finish. There was never an immediate threat to my edge, but things changed as his turn of speed developed.

We bid farewell to Albert upon our return ride for he lived in Germiston. Sometimes Rory, and on occasions Piet or Willie, would stay on to enjoy a concocted recovery drink made from an Italian family's recipe, handed down the generations. It was a gift from Biaggio, one of my two *colourful* Italian classmates, the other Franco.

Under the fear of rebuke by his parents, Franco did what it took to pass his examinations – the giveaway under such strain was his rippling eyebrows, an intense frown and an unusual ear twitch. His reflexive action made my earlier St Vitus dance look like child's play. How he managed to contort all those muscles simultaneously, remains a mystery.

He studied medicine, specialised as a gynaecologist and became a professor. Academia had to be the best choice – imagine his patients seeing those twitches while conducting an examination – they would surely run for their lives.

Biaggio was one of the brightest pupils, but more importantly were his mother's delicious elongated sandwiches filled with white cheese and salamis that I had never seen nor tasted before – an extra one on offer had my taste buds zinging, and I became every bit an Italian. Her culinary secrets included the formula of our recovery drink, handwritten as if confirming its authenticity, and that only added to its magical powers. My mother, showing the loving side of her nature, helped decipher the recipe and assist in the brewing of the ingredients: milk, sugar, cinnamon, eggs, masala and brandy – gently heated and simmered – cooled, and refrigerated.

Naturally, after our long training rides, exhausted and dehydrated, our medicinal elixir would have another effect. *In vino veritas,* and Rory challenged, "You don't help us as much as you used to" and, it was true. My feigned innocence was an endeavour to hold on to my advantage for as long as possible, fearing that he or Albert might soon eclipse me. Rory never let me off the hook that easily – at the very next opportunity with Albert present, the inquisition continued – I felt uncomfortable and guilty as charged.

There's a love story in all of this – Gayle's. Unbeknown to me, she had a crush on Rory and for that matter, on Albert as well. This I only knew years later when she reminded me of an incident one afternoon when she took Rory's cycling gloves and hid them under her pillow, promptly falling asleep. When it was time for Rory to go, we looked all over the house, thinking we should not have had that second homeopathic medicinal portion – were we going crazy?

In desperation, I awoke Gayle telling her of our plight.

Her sleepy eyes opened and with her Mona Lisa smile she reached under her pillow; magically, they reappeared. What dreams she must have had, shattered only by my angry rebuke, "What do you think you're doing? We have been searching all over for them!"

Many, many years later Gayle recounted the day's event, remembering my chagrin and said, "You were horrible when you told me to beetle off, and leave the two of you alone. So I hatched my plan, thinking I would spitefully get my revenge while also winning Rory's attention. I was fed up parading in front of you two on some pretence or other. You ignored me and told me to go and play elsewhere. In desperation, I thought I'll take his gloves, imagining that, when you start searching, I would pretend to find them, and that is how he would notice me. Alas, it backfired but it was all worthwhile!"

Rory rode well as a juvenile and even better in his last year as a junior. As Norman Crews, a sports journalist of that time put it, *Budler was involved in another fine finish in the match sprint with Walter Thornhill. These two, raced neck and neck for the line and only after some consultation did the judges award the race to Budler. He made himself a strong candidate for the Southern Transvaal team to meet Western Province.* Incidentally, his time of 11.4 seconds was world class; no wonder I stopped showing him the tricks of the trade.

The slightness of his body was deceptive – a possible precursor to a new breed of sprinter. He had superb acceleration, was exceptionally quick and created non-existent gaps as he mercurially moved through the field during track races – some say he was reckless. Sadly, his senior cycling days were numbered; conscripted military service during the time of increased skirmishes on South Africa's borders and his subsequent psychological fallout took its toll.

It made sense that he was chosen to join an elite clandestine unit, operating off the main military radar screen. "We did not need to wear uniforms, nor salute officers, nor did they know our rank or our mission . . . we were based in the Caprivi Strip on the Angolan border. In preparation for incursions, we would not shave, wash, use creams or eat any foods that could betray our presence merely from our body smells . . . in the clean bush air, it is possible to pick up scents of animals and men from a great distance. We smelt the enemy, and they, us!"

His unit was highly trained in bushcraft and survival, and penetrated deep into Angola causing havoc between the villages and different tribes in covert counter-propaganda campaigns. Some of the stories do not need repeating – they belong to the darkest canyon of mankind, safe to say they were atrocious.

It is no wonder that he could not quite recover and rehabilitate into normal civilian life after his ordeal. He became increasingly reckless, had a bad motorcycle accident, broke a leg and lost an eye. He recovered from that but was in poor shape. His great human potential had been misused, and for what gain? We lost touch – recently Albert confirmed that he had died, and that subsequent to the military he had had acute psychological challenges including dipping in and out of alcoholism.

Willie's physique was the exact opposite of Rory's: short, stocky and better suited to sprinting. His presence was always uplifting – he had a huge heart, was courageous and tried everything the sport had to offer, as did we all. His crowning glory was winning titles and representing our province as a junior. Although not a regular to our afternoon rides, only because he lived further away, his warm and friendly smile was a beacon that reminded us that every bit of life is precious and needed to be lived to the full.

Moving forward to my university years, he took me for a spin in his *tuned pair of wheels*, a hot-rod type car with a green elongated front body. It was his new passion, as his cycling days had waned.

Late one evening, close to the witching hour, he prompted, "Why don't we see how quickly we can do our old training ride?"

Why not, I thought.

"Are you ready?" he commanded.

I bravely nodded, unsure what to expect other than to anticipate this new adventure. He looked at his watch, revved the engine a few times, dropped the clutch, the tyres screeched and we lurched forward as though the very devil himself was on our tail.

Straight down the hill picking up more and more speed, we absorbed the undulating fall of the hill and passed the first green traffic light. A negotiated fast approaching left and right-hand sweep followed, then the next traffic lights – all red – and without Willie flinching or missing a heartbeat, nor slowing down, we went straight through. Meanwhile, my heart pounded – an adrenaline rush from this sheer recklessness – what if another car traversed our path? Two more sweeps near the Kensington golf course where Willie was forced to double declutch and slow down, and then on to the finishing straight, the highway, where fortunately there were no more traffic lights.

At that time of night, few cars were about. Notwithstanding, my eyes remained peeled as I watched for any hint of danger. A sneak sideways glance – the speedometer was nudging 200 kilometres per hour. Finally, the airport turn off, a throttle back and a beaming Willie in his comfort zone, exclaiming, "Not bad, just over 12 minutes!"

The engine creaked and the smell of burning oil filled our nostrils. We had a more sedate and chatty ride on the way home, although it was filled for my part with a false sense of daring and a gratitude that we were alive.

Relentless afternoon training sessions continued. I was fifteen, my third year of cycling and our Kensington gang were in for a delightful surprise. Basil Cohen, who was always in the know, let us in on a secret that the legendary sprinter, Tommy Shardelow, Springbok cyclist and Olympian, at the age of thirty-seven was about to make a track cycling comeback – I was awestruck.

Tommy, his wife Margaret, and kids lived relatively close by in a modest home with an expansive view from the top of a koppie; the rewards of his efforts as a manager of a nuts-and-bolts sales team. "Not only is he a great sprinter, but he has the gift of the gab as well," said Basil.

Soon, we were training with him. On one occasion, only Tommy and I were riding side by side along a desolate monotonous road, *doing miles*, when he nostalgically reminisced about his early cycling experiences – he was twenty-one, a member of the 1952 Olympic squad – I was not even born.

Spellbound, I listened, "We spent six weeks before the Helsinki Games living and training together as a team. We ate, drank and slept cycling, like true professionals. The benefits were overwhelming and surprised us. Just before leaving we competed in an open meeting and were amazed at how dramatically our performance had improved. Other cyclists simply struggled to keep our pace. We were in a class of our own!"

In the Olympics, the team achieved spectacular results. They qualified with the fastest time in the 4000 metre team pursuit and came second in the final, narrowly beaten by the Italians. Victory seemed assured, Tommy explained, "The final should have been ours. We had already beaten them in the prior week during a friendly invitation. After our defeat the Italian team manager confirmed, 'You guys over-trained and should have stopped after the invitation event. You were the better team.' And that was our mistake!"

Another silver medal followed, this time for the Tandem Sprint, again Tommy in the saddle with Ray Robinson. After that a bronze for Ray, in the 1000 metre time trial. It was remarkable, and as a British news writer put it, *we are witnessing the birth of a new cycling nation.*

Tommie's silver medals, for me, were like gold. Both by association and because they set an Olympic and subsequent world record during the earlier tandem heats. They were the fastest tandem cyclists in the world. The previous year, Tommy had set a new ¼ mile world record in Italy, beating Mario Ghella, the world sprint champion.

Tommy's sportsmanship had to be admired, giving the accolades to the Olympic tandem winners, specifically Russell Mockridge.

"That Australian, was the greatest in the world, he didn't need Lionel Cox for his partner. He could have ridden it on his own. A big strong guy that drove me crazy when we were touring in Italy the year before. Whenever we were late, he never fussed and took forever to chew his food, while sitting with his countless bibles around him. He was studying to be a minister."

I was enthralled, not only by the reminiscing but to be an Olympian was a worthy goal to strive for. Tommy's stories took on mythical proportions; naturally, I held on to every word uttered as if the cycling gods were talking directly to me through him. Tommy, my cycling hero . . . riding together and chewing the cud was as good as it gets.

Later, much later, when Tommy was eighty-three and while reminiscing I playfully ribbed, "So what happened in that tandem final, Tommy?"

He, like a true gentleman, said, "Well you know Walter, you've been there, you know how it goes," and that is the ethos of a great sportsman – the ability to gracefully accept defeat.

We benefitted greatly from Tommy's training tips – one entailed riding hands-free, sitting in an upright position and using only the thrust pull-push action of the legs to pump away as fast and as hard as humanly possible for a quick explosive burst of ten to fifteen seconds up a slight short incline. It forced the leg muscles to work even harder on their own, while strengthening our core tummy muscles.

Jimmy Swift, the other Olympian, also made a comeback that same year as Tommy, and although we both belonged to the same club, I never had the opportunity to train with him or glean any of his experiences as he lived further away. Men like them I admired. They became the ultimate inspiration of encouragement in a sport starved of any further international competition while boycotted.

A lot happened during standard eight, including a delightful visit to the Swanepoel family in Pretoria during one school holiday. Nico, my cycling buddy, whom I had met while track racing there, invited me to come and stay for a few days. Excited – the prospect of cycling the planned route of some sixty kilometres to Pretoria on my own. His father was a medical doctor and the superintendent of the H. F. Verwoerd Hospital where they lived with the privileges that his position allowed: a big house with many staff to assist in its running. His mother was hospitable, and his elder brother and younger sister had similar attributes – they made me feel welcome – a reaffirmation of how I imagined a family could be.

Thus, besides our neighbours, the Swanepoels were my next meaningful exposure to an Afrikaans family – a pivot point – the estrangement experienced at Sir Edmund Hillary School was over – the Afrikaners were a very friendly folk.

They introduced me to magic, interspersed with Afrikaner culinary delights: mashed vegetables like pumpkin and squash enhanced with spices of cinnamon, nutmeg and sugar. The sweetness made it seem unrefined, yet I imagined that with a few sticks of biltong, it could have been the Voortrekker's survival food in the early 19th century. My muscles were most grateful for the rapid energy fix needed after my long ride there.

The magic had to do with the summoning of the staff during the family dinner and Nico's father anticipated my curiosity.

"Watch my fingers carefully."

Intrigued, I did – his hand held at about eye level, the forefinger slowly joined his thumb. At the very point of contact, the bell rang, repeated a few times for my pleasure and their amusement. I could not work it out. Enchanted, my eyes sparkled at the incredulity of it all.

Nico's elder brother attended *Tuks*, the affectionate nickname for the Afrikaans-speaking University of Pretoria. Over the ensuing months, his entourage, as part of their student life, became our first fan club, cheering us on at the Friday evening track meetings at the Pilditch Stadium. It offered light relief, their collective roars chasing us around the track, "Come on *Doringheuwel, laat waai, papagaai.*" These shouts of encouragement took me a while to fathom; a literal translation of my surname into Afrikaans: *Doring*, thorn and *heuwel*, hill. Meanwhile, lost in translation is the playful thrust of the rhyming slang *laat waai, papagaai*, let rip, parrot. Nevertheless, it became my talisman, pushing me ever onwards, through the pain of my burning lungs and aching legs.

I was not necessarily victorious in those early days, but rather fed and boosted by the strength of their voices and the applause of the crowd. My need to be seen and accepted as part of a community was satisfied, and unwittingly I started playing to the gallery – in subsequent years I would learn about crowd fickleness.

Oh, I nearly forgot – the magic bell, a mere ingenious electronic foot controlled buzzer, rigged under the carpet – next time I will be a better Inspector Clouseau.

The Thomas brothers, who had emigrated from Rhodesia (Zimbabwe), moved into our road and fortuitously took an interest in my cycling and became my lift club to those Pretoria meetings. They seemed knowledgeable, worldly and entrepreneurial and were in their mid to late twenties. Their business was the spray painting of homes and buildings with an innovative external paint application.

In my mid-thirties, I discovered that this product had been introduced to South Africa by a friend of mine's father. His parents divorced – his mother,

Ruth First, an anti-apartheid activist, married Joe Slovo. She was assassinated in 1982 by a parcel bomb, while they were in exile in Mozambique.

Joe, the same age as my mother, was born in Lithuania to a Jewish family that immigrated to South Africa. Subsequently, he became a prominent leader of the South African Communist Party, a leading member of the ANC and a commander of the military wing, *Umkhonto we Sizwe*. In the new democratic government of 1994, he was rewarded with the post of Minister for Housing, dying a year later of cancer.

I often travelled with the eldest Thomas brother. He had an attractive wife that complimented his refreshing disposition. The three of us sat up front, high above the ground in their monstrous Chevrolet pickup truck, with a V8 engine. She always sat between us on the bench-like-seat, but he insisted that she sit right next to him with barely an inch to spare – I was the distant gooseberry. His sense of caring as he endearingly patted her on the knee or put his arm around her while driving, sometimes with a quick hug or a kiss, did not go unnoticed. Their relationship seemed ideal – naturally, I wanted such a relationship but remained clueless.

The throaty roar of the exhausts announced our arrival at the Pilditch Stadium. We were like conquistadors, ready to do battle. There was something exciting about night racing. It was as if the floodlights focused my concentration and gave me a special sense of purpose; the cooler air was a better temperature for my racing body, coupled with his words of encouragement, *give it your best*! There was much elation driving home afterwards and plenty of time for a healthy post mortem. These were exciting times – I felt alive and part of something meaningful outside of my family.

The Thomas brothers eventually moved. Somehow, I managed, on occasions, to convince George to fill that gap. In his way, he was proud of me and was tickled by the solidarity of my Afrikaans friends shouting, *come on Doringheuwel*. It was our private time, equally enjoyable, albeit quite different. Here George could be himself, free from Desiree's continual nagging and theatrical antics.

Come to think of it, I cannot remember my mother ever actually coming to a track meeting, but she must have – at least once? This surprising realisation is upsetting; not that it was something I had ever thought about or focused on before.

English lessons with Taffy, our nickname for Mr Jones, the Sable boarding housemaster, were interesting, mainly because of his nervous habit and the boys' capers. While sitting at his rectangular table, in full view of the class, he could not hide the rapid outward and inward movement of his knees, as if fanning his private parts, or so we fabricated.

The dreaded moment to recite a learnt passage was fast approaching – a near loss of confidence surfacing. Perhaps the pranksters smelt my pervading fear, catalysed by some of George's demeaning homework comments. Taffy, in his inimitable way, encouraged their mischievous frolicking only because he remained oblivious to what was happening – forearms splayed, Sphinx-like, propped up his upper body, while he habitually looked down as if this increased his concentration and acute listening.

Meanwhile, a sea of young, eagerly beaming faces awaited the incisive moment to prank. Standing in front, my body posture lacked the necessary strength to spew forth Portia's famous speech addressing Shylock in Shakespeare's Merchant of Venice. Nervously, I anticipated the voracious mischief-makers' appetite and began as best I could.

The quality of mercy is not strained; it droppeth as the gentle rain from heaven upon the place beneath. It is twice blest: it blesseth him that gives and him that takes. I faltered, struggling with the pronunciation, *blesseth*. My tongue had not quite found the right spot even though my lisping gap between my two front teeth had since been closed.

Taffy's head turned slowly and methodically, glancing at me, and with a calm demeanour, gently encouraged, "Do continue."

Finding my second wind, I tried to imbibe the spirit of Portia, *Tis mightiest in the mightiest; it becomes the throned monarch better than his crown; His sceptre shows the force of temporal power, the attribute to awe and majesty, wherein doth sit the dread and fear of kings.*

Hardly having started, a few pupils in the back row partly stood up. Some gesticulated like monkeys; others pulled faces pretending to laugh, while pointing directly at Taffy's flapping legs. This turbulence hit me and crushed my renewed enthusiasm, grinding me to a halt. Whereupon they immediately stopped, lest they be discovered – those uninvolved scanned backwards and forwards, enjoying the spectacle.

The pantomime had taken its toll . . . struggling to recall my lines, I fumbled onwards as best I could, *But mercy is above this sceptred sway; it is enthroned in the hearts of kings, it is an attribute to God himself; and earthly power doth then show likest God's, when mercy seasons justice. Therefore, Jew, though justice be thy plea, consider this, that, in the course of justice, none of us should see salvation; we do pray for mercy.*

I certainly did. They were in full swing pretending to guffaw as if they were about to fall on the floor, repeatedly pointing with their staccato fingers at Taffy's bellows. Suddenly, something deep within triggered and I saw the funny side. My tense face muscles loosened at the incongruity of it all.

They won, I was floored but not knocked out as I lay metaphorically gasping for breath, although with a grin. The increased decibels had attracted Taffy's attention. His head slowly rose scanning the horizon. The predators' innate sense, coupled with imperceptible timing, had them back in their seats like attentive angelic beings.

"Continue!"

I did . . . with lacklustre enthusiasm, limping down the home straight.

Taffy nodded: my cue to return to my desk. I was grateful that the ordeal was over having endured my classmate's lack of *mercy and justice*! Their spunk, bravery and daringness were admirable, although close to the fine line of bullying. Taffy was my Portia; his early teachings embedded in my spirit, while the mockery of the other boys was just playful.

In one way I was very lucky with my school punishments, particularly as I wrote my feeble absentee letters and forged my mother's signature during standard nine, whenever I bunked to join the *Bezvalley gang* on our long Wednesday morning cycle rides to Bapsfontein.

It took courage, *please excuse Walter as he wasn't well yesterday*. Always unimaginatively the same, yet surprisingly it did the trick. Surely it must have been obvious to Mr Stander, my form teacher, who never questioned its validity. Even the signature on the school reports was not the same, and my mother's handwriting was neater and more fluid.

Truth be known, I was petrified that I might be caught; abounding rumours about the powers of harsh truant officers only ignited my fears – a school warning, then expulsion. Was it true? I never knew, nor had the stomach to find out, but imagined the perceived shame and disrepute it would bring upon the family and me. However, my eagerness and belief in the benefits of those rides far outweighed the possible consequences, and it was a risk worthy of taking. Perhaps the teacher tolerated my misdemeanour as my attendance was otherwise impeccable and, despite everything, I was a reasonably diligent student. But that same year I was unfairly punished. The end of break bell had rung – I was still in the ablution area – unfortunately, Mr Schoeman, our deputy head, walked past.

"Bunking, are you boy?" He raised his eyebrows and narrowed his eyes.

"No Sir, just washing my hands."

"Follow me!"

His pace seemed deliberately slow, as his black flowing gown, like the cloth of the Grim Reaper, enveloped my spirit. Walking silently in tow, a thousand thoughts flashed through my mind, like the black and blue welts on caned bottoms, displayed like badges of honour. At times, the line of the cane traversed across the back part of the legs.

Schoeman was well known for his cruelty and our inculcated fear was such that when he was spotted in the distant corridors, the *chips* warning would sound. Immediately our rowdy tones would drop an octave or two, even when entirely innocent.

There was an uncomfortable silence following him into his office; my sentence had already started.

I blurted, pleading, "But Sir, I . . . was only washing my hands" – my last-ditch attempt was silenced by his pointing finger.

"Over there, bend, touch your toes and lift your blazer." Phew, I did not need to put the back of my neck under the lip of his desk, as told by some of the other boys, to hold it firmly in place for that involuntary knee jerk reaction upon being canned. Slowly he walked, and out the corner of my eye, in that bent position, I noticed his array of canes. He pondered, biding his time as if cruelly enjoying the moment before deciding upon the appropriate one. My fear and apprehension mounted, now pulsating through my body – it was my first caning.

Whack – the simultaneous sound, sensation and involuntary muscle reactions ripped through me as my buttocks, jaw and eye muscles clinched before relaxing momentarily until the next resounding whack, whack.

It was incredible how my senses played tricks, seemingly an eternity remaining in that position not knowing the number of cuts I was to receive. Then his bark, "Stand up boy, next time you will ensure that you are not late for class – you can go now!" I left, my tail burning.

The Afrikaners were well known for their use of a sjambok in disciplining, a symbol of power and authority. I was cross with myself for calling him *Sir*, he never deserved the respect, for it was only said out of fear. There and then, I decided never to use that word again unless the circumstances were appropriate.

Mr Hofmeyr, an exceptionally enlightened Afrikaner, became our new principal. The corridors breathed more easily as Mr Schoeman's perverse fun and the days of corporal punishment were numbered – he resigned shortly thereafter.

TUG OF WAR

That December vacation with my Dad, I tried to discuss my mother's nocturnal behaviour – I was fourteen years old.

"Dad, I think Mom's an alcoholic. She drinks every evening except on a Sunday and her mood swings are dramatic – very argumentative, sometimes violent and a little crazy! It's very scary, what can we do?" I implored and gave example as best I could, like the night she tried to burn the house down.

That evening, she set light to the heavy lined curtains – I liked them, even though they seemed a little misplaced in South Africa, depicting an English country fox hunting scene. They seemed regal and complemented our oak dining room suite – a wedding gift from Aunty Ronnie to Desiree and George.

My mother's feeble, half-hearted attempt or maybe George's intervention saved that day – I am not sure which, but the bottom right hand corner, slightly charred, remained – a daily reminder lest we forget.

Not so my father's look of disbelief – "I don't know your mother like that, it can't be true."

I was crestfallen – did my dad think I was lying? Was it too close to home, though their behaviours were quite different when under the influence?

I would like to believe he was shocked and merely stunned, except his body language told me otherwise – again, I felt utterly unseen. If my father did not believe me, what chance would there be that someone else might?

I knew I would be wasting my breath telling him of other episodes, far worse. I never became impervious to them, nor aware of the impact of the trauma, but I certainly felt the acute embarrassment when other people were around.

It was the 4th July – American Independence Day as Desiree always reminded us, and her birthday. The typical cast of characters of family and close friends were all there. The party proceeded as most do – a sense of occasion, frivolity and excited voices, but alas Desiree's demons surfaced and joined in as well. George's care, love and attention of Gayle was used as the pretext to air her grievances about how he never showered her with similar sentiments.

It was her unconscious opportunity – a captive audience for the outrageous behaviour that followed. Desiree performed well, driving the ante higher and higher, the same way it happened most other evenings, except this time it reached a crescendo and a point of no return.

There were other times, when in her habitual state she would spar for a verbal fight. George would be lambasted with comments like, "Everyone knows that your brothers and other men slept with your ex-wife, right under your very nose. She was a whore and a slut. In any case, you are so fucking useless in bed. No wonder she had to resort to other men."

George tried to halt the attack, muttering, "Desiree you don't know what you are talking about, keep quiet."

In those moments, I could not help but feel extremely sorry for him, having to tolerate her belittlement. Gayle and I never knew whether this was true, neither did we actually care or need to know. The enjoyment and love that we imagined or hoped for to just be part of a normal or happy family were more important than anything that may have happened before.

Sometimes in a serious moment, Desiree took me into her confidence about George's inadequacies, as if by telling me it would ease her pain or guide me in the future. *George can't control himself and just comes too quickly . . . you know your father was better . . . you need to make sure you satisfy a woman properly.*

Anyhow, at that infamous party, captive audience in tow, she was on a roll and notwithstanding George's vain attempts to placate and appease her, she finally delivered her death knell.

"You do so much with that daughter of yours that if you could fuck her you would, but you can't even fuck me properly, so there's no danger in that!"

The atmosphere – stunned – complete silence. She was bitter, extremely angry and again out of control. My heart crumbled as the excruciating pain reverberated through my body, while everyone struggled to gather their wits. Then the first polite, *we must be going now, gosh, just look at the time*!

More excuses followed – only Aunty Ronnie remained with our broken family, sitting amongst the charred ruins. Her large, strong presence somehow contained the shattered shards that floated around in that empty space, allowing a faint glimmer of normality to creep back in. My sense of embarrassment and shame felt for both my mother and our family was paramount – slowly, I tried to step back from an abyss of emptiness and a sense of feeling utterly alone.

Our private family secret, if you could even call it that, had escaped – no, actually blasted into space. The remnant dust particles covered us as though the world knew, and George's fate and ours were sealed in a time capsule.

Aunty stayed that night. It was comforting to know she would be there the following morning.

Gayle's recall years later was not of the incident, but rather of the suddenness with which the party was over. Perhaps it was fortunate that she pranced about in her party dress in her world of fantasy, and was spared the damaging knife that pierced my heart.

~

How much further do I venture, or dare to tell of some of the other happenings? What were the repercussions, and what may you think of me? For that matter, what did I think of myself, or did I merely put it out of my mind as I continued with my survival as best I could? Perhaps the pulling down of the shutters was necessary.

~

Another evening she locked herself in the kitchen, rambling away in her threatening way at the top of her voice. It took a while before I realised what was happening . . . a threat to take her life!

The mutterings about the concoction she was preparing – hot water and ammonia, and how we would have to watch her die. There is a fine line between pretending, a cry for help or the reality of the threat. George must have been concerned – he bashed the door down and restrained her – the kettle had boiled and the potion, already mixed, stood alongside.

The unhinged frame and broken door greeted us for days as if emphasizing the heaviness of the pervading atmosphere. We tried to continue our lives normally, whatever that means. It was never spoken about again; not to my friends, nor even Aunty Ronnie – it was as if the door knew all of this, while waiting to be repaired.

~

Many a morning, I still carried the trauma of the previous evening, but it was not so for Desiree.

"What's the matter with you, can't you see what a beautiful day it is?" Indeed, I could, the sun was shining as it so often does in South Africa but, I was still wallowing in the aftermath – Desiree, seemingly had scant recall.

Sometimes I quipped, "Don't you remember last night?"

She raised her eyebrows quizzically; never answered. Perhaps she remembered, or perhaps the pain of her nocturnal patterns was so deep that her shutters of denial remained tightly locked, forever.

The open kitchen door, relieved it had been repaired, now framed Gayle – the silent witness to the dramatic dark event that night – I was oblivious to her presence and stunned by the happening. The caption could well have read *Young boy stabs and kills his mother* or the other way around. Gayle and I discussed this recently. Without any doubt or hesitation, she recalls – *Desiree held the carving knife high above her head as she was trying to stab you, shouting,* "I will kill you, I will kill you." *You held both her wrists restraining her.*

During this writing, I went into a trance-like state, *my heart was very sad and my body very heavy.* I let out one long, primal scream for an uninterrupted period . . . with more breath than I ever knew I had.

Does trauma play its own strange memory tricks? Which way was it?

I was the one holding the knife and was going to stab and kill my mother.

Perhaps, both versions are correct as events overtook themselves in the unfolding drama of our camouflaged Hitchcock scene. Or possibly, I was so traumatised that my imagination told me I was wielding the knife – I do not know.

What I do, is that I cannot bear to see a large knife laying on a kitchen counter when not in use.

Desiree's favourite phrase, *let sleeping dogs lie*, used when not wishing to face her denial or inability to cope, may just be apt. But I could not – I was young, idealistic and desired a righteous world. I challenged her, and George for that matter, whenever I noticed glaring inconsistencies during the innumerable incidents, or afterwards, when sanity had once again returned. It proved to be ineffective.

~

After yet another incident, I tried a different tack one calm Sunday morning. Diplomatically, I confronted my mother, standing on the pathway in front of the black steps leading up to the veranda, where I used to play an invented game on my own for hours. The ball would be thrown at each step's upright from the top to the bottom, and caught with or without a bounce.

"Mom, this stuff that goes on every night, except Sundays, don't you think you should go and see the doctor and get some help?" said in my best concerned, caring voice at that time.

She exploded, "I'm not fucking mad you know, I'm not a loony and they are not going to send me to Tara (a mental therapy centre)."

"I didn't mean it like that Mom," I quickly retorted, hastily trying to find another way to express myself. Her shutters had already descended; ranting and raving awhile longer – I withdrew defeated.

PROJECTION

And my mother's same shutters had another mechanism, *projection*. She sang from the same hymn sheet whenever an opportunity presented itself. "Walter is so intelligent, religious and good at sport," pretentiously rattled off.

The repetitiveness of the mantra became so annoying and embarrassing, when all I wanted was a subtle, more sincere approach. I tried to discuss it when we were alone – that did not work. Even protestations, when family or friends were around, were unsuccessful – her words never changed, not even in the slightest. I squirmed, thinking, *there she goes again – aren't I such a good mother, otherwise how else could he achieve my claims.*

Could I have overlooked it? Sure, but I was mostly smarting from the emotional hurt and confusion from the previous evening's rollercoaster ride, where my mother's mood and behaviour altered almost immediately after her first sip.

Another scripted comment when sober was, "All I ever want from you one day are three things, a bottle of gin, a carton of cigarettes and a hairdo." It seemed so shallow. Intoxicated, the more reckless ones remained locked in a loop.

My confusion reigned, and my sense of not being seen, nor heard, intensified.

There were occasional diligent bursts of academic glory and, as for being religious, well, I had altar boy aspirations once but that soon dissipated. My spirituality probably started in the Athol days, at Aunty's plot and at the Convent, where Nature's magnificence spoke to me. And in sport, I participated and thoroughly enjoyed it, but I had not excelled yet.

Our parish priest visited one afternoon. My mom prepared tea, put on her best face, while he gently prodded about this and that. Grandiosity prevailed, and her mantra was sung but again – "Walter is so intelligent, religious and good at sport." The priest nodded. Did he have an inkling as to the real lie of our land?

The continuous rigidity of her claims upset me. How would I silence her infuriating bragging, and to what end, I was not sure?

My real mother was needed, not the one that put on a show for an audience. The harmonious way witnessed in the Afrikaner Swanepoel family was longed for. My sense of despair deepened, and I commenced my *silent battle*.

What better place to start than attacking the arena of *intelligence*? It was my cry for help and my plan was to fail in my next examination. I purposefully never studied. However, when the time came, something ignited deep within and I did my best. I did fail history, but surprisingly, an overall pass was narrowly scraped for that third term.

The compulsory signing of my examination report by a parent seemed the logical moment for a showdown. Nonchalantly, I even pointed out just how poor my marks were – my mother seemed unconcerned.

My *cry*, in its disguised form, was of no avail. I guess, if I were sufficiently serious I would have spoiled my papers, but I was not that robust. True to form when the next guest arrived, undeterred and as if on cue, she proceeded as before – the same mantra – I could not believe it.

My form teacher, Mr Stander, even enquired, "What happened, this is very unlike you?"

"I don't know, Sir" – I was too ashamed to tell him.

I studied during the last term, passed into standard ten and signed my own report in defiance under *parent's signature*. The mind boggles, all I can say is *thank goodness for cycling*.

~

There were times when I let my guard down and spoke to my classmates about some of the difficulties at home. *Why don't you run away from home* – amazed at their comment, it was unworthy of further consideration for I had no idea where to go. However, one evening matters were out of hand, and the seed planted rose to fruition – I slipped away into the darkness of the night, needing to escape the toxicity at home.

Out alone on the streets, I felt intimidated by my lack of forethought. Aimlessly, I roamed about for a while, then helplessly decided that the forbidding disused milk and coal cart alleyways, at the rear of the properties, would be the place to hide that night. I nestled and lay down against a hedge, and inevitably fell asleep, only to awake in the early hours of the morning to the sound of Desiree and George talking as they ambled down the lane towards me.

I hope he hasn't gone far and will be back before tomorrow. Having come within spitting distance from me, I was convinced that they would spot me. I never flinched a muscle, laying camouflaged in the shadows.

When they had safely departed, I stood up feeling my aching, stiff, cold muscles, and pensively considered the consequences of my escapade, while slowly walking back home. The front door was fortunately left unlocked. I entered, tiptoed down the hallway and slipped into my bed; not a word was ever mentioned, as if it had never happened. Deep down, I knew I had nowhere to run, and would need to solve this dilemma another way.

SEARCHING FOR THE HOLY GRAIL

No boy's school would be complete without the continual fascination for the opposite sex, starting with the passive showmanship of a condom in our wallets. It was a badge of honour and had nothing to do with precautions, rather an outward sign that we were already there, so to speak. The constant nonchalant removal, a kind of show and tell, served only to wear the packaging thin until it became frayed and it too could take the strain no longer. Finally, it burst forth – the seepage, a damp squib thought the wallet.

That same badge and the stories that accompanied the sheriffs were equally ludicrous. My naivety made me an intense listener: *you can tell a girl has had sex the night before by the way she walks.* It was always greeted by excited boys' hollows – *wow really*? Naturally, when our sister school came to visit, curiously, I would be on the lookout for the obvious tell-tale sign. Clearly, there was a knack to it that too had eluded me; like catching fish.

This naivety was superseded by a riskier adventure. I was not a willing participant but coerced into my role, during my favourite subject, arithmetic. I felt incredibly awkward having to ask a stupid question, especially since I had scored full marks previously.

In standard eight, Jeppe struggled to attract permanent teaching staff. We had more free periods and relief teachers than actual classes. In keeping with the times, this younger teacher, who could have been an older sister, was wearing a saucy miniskirt.

Classes consisted of thirty to thirty-five boys. It was not surprising that the voracious testosterone appetite of the boys would encourage this caper. I was a year younger, not that that excuses it. They had noticed that every time she went to a boy's desk to attend to some matter, the mere act of bending over seemed to reveal a little more of her beautiful curvaceous long legs, but now the tantalising teasing thoughts of what lay beyond, surfaced.

The boys behind me urged, *now Walter, now*! I was very uncomfortable.

My task was to delay her for as long as possible. A dress rehearsal may have steadied my nerves. *Do it, do it*, spluttered the excited voices of encouragement from behind. They were crazy and I was sucked into their folly.

Taking a nervous gulp of air, I slowly raised my hand indicating that I had a question to ask. She came over to my desk.

"Miss, I don't understand why if you add this to that it makes that," pointing to the sum I was doing. True to form, standing beside my desk, she bent over as expected, getting closer to look at my supposed problem.

"What do you mean?" she said.

"Here Miss, this bit in the brackets," and as I said it, surely she could hear the nervous quiver in my voice, the giveaway for asking such a feeble question that could blow my cover. I imagined the frogmarch into the headmaster's office with dire consequences, while the other carefree boys would chant in a mocking playful way, *ha, ha – you are in for it this time*!

At that moment, I felt downright stupid, feigning more ignorance, and loathing my part in this lark as every second flashed before my eyes. She attempted to explain and in exasperation finally said, "I'm sure you will work it out!"

During this whole charade, the audacious boy diagonally behind me had a sliver of a broken mirror, cupped in the palm of his hand, and using his outstretched arm across the aisle, like a radar, deftly scanned, searching for the Holy Grail.

We could not wait for the lesson to end, bumbling out of the classroom – our excited cries, hardly containable, echoed down the school's timeless corridors, *did you see it, did you*? Smiling, he held his grin like a Cheshire cat and never said another word.

Thankfully, having paid my dues, I remained a spectator, while the boys' sheer brazenness induced further endeavours; perhaps, seeking and drinking from the chalice had an inebriating effect; its magic potion was to hold us in its ethereal power, forever.

The next bit of fun was a classic or should I say a Mini, an iconoclastic symbol in keeping with the revolution of the time, and like sleuth-hounds, the boys picked up the scent of another attractive relief teacher. Ingeniously, they bounced her car between retainer walls in such a way that she would be unable to drive away – brilliant, and with such nerve.

Not knowing about the art of bouncing cars, I did wonder whether it could have caused any damage – needless to say, my consideration was unnecessary. I am sure the other teachers and possibly even the principal smiled but had to be seen to take a sterner view. Maybe she secretly admired the attention showered on her.

Senior boys were summoned, and dutifully bounced her car out of its impasse, while the offenders were ordered to scrub the quadrangle that afternoon.

Naturally, the old guard whispered, *this would never have happened under Schoeman . . . the punishment is far too lenient.* Mr Hofmeyr, our more enlightened and relaxed principal, may have erred in determining the thin line of appropriateness in a testosterone filled boys' school, but this change in attitude certainly encouraged our individuality to blossom. If I had to wager a bet, even under Schoeman's fear-based regime, the boys' strength of character would have prevailed.

The school's ethos, to encourage everyone to play a sport, went a long way in dissipating some of that boisterous energy. Notwithstanding, most of the younger female relief teachers seemed beautiful, and the boys' ingenious foolhardiness and sheer playfulness ensured that the search for the Grail continued, albeit in a different vein.

We followed our timetable moving from classroom to classroom – the arrival of yet another attractive teacher became a great opportunity for the next ploy, straight after the first break. Tom-tom drums summoned and the hordes of boys from different classes converged, clamouring for their desks. Sheer pandemonium followed. Timetables were pulled out – the teacher flummoxed. It was priceless, her panic, uttering . . . *wait, I'll sort this out,* as she skirted off to the principal's office.

That was our cue – boys dissipated rapidly, while a few remained to show their collective strength under the pretext of a misunderstanding. Mr Hofmeyr dutifully arrived with his master timetable and kindly resolved this supposed predicament to the delight of the angelic flock of boys who could now continue with their studies.

These occurrences could be correlated; the more attractive the female teacher, the greater the likelihood of some concocted plan reflecting the risk undertaken. Fortunately, the gods smiled on us and apparently enjoyed our playfulness. But like all things there came a point it lost its novelty, and perhaps our new headmaster in his wisdom knew this, allowing the natural course of events to play themselves out.

Mr Stander, in my second last year, was again my form teacher. He had a lisp and an unfortunate habit of spitting when he pronounced certain words – the boys mocked him – I refrained. He liked me, I think, and called my name while announcing new junior and senior prefects, but there was a slight glitch – I was not there.

Later in the day, he demanded, "Where were you? I was going to make you a junior prefect, but as you were not about, I chose someone else." My heart sank, as his recognition and accolade were snatched away in the same breath, and I knew by the tone in his voice that the decision was final. He looked annoyed, while waiting for an explanation.

"I never heard the bell, Sir. I was at the memorial dome." Hitherto, out of bounds to junior schoolboys – now, in my first year as a senior it seemed appropriate to explore and understand the mystique of this newfound privilege; my demise. He looked at me quizzically, and I could not tell whether he believed me or not.

The dome was dedicated to the loss of one hundred and seventy lives of former schoolboys and staff who died during the two World Wars and the subsequent border conflicts in South Africa. In 1986, the year of Johannesburg's Centenary, the main school building and the First World War Memorial dome were declared national monuments. Incidentally, Field Marshall Jan Smuts opened them, the year my mother was born. In a peculiar way, I drew comfort from these coincidences as if they were setting out a roadmap of my existence.

My knowledge of the Second World War was rudimentary. Our family never spoke about it, a type of no-go zone, notwithstanding my many questions. Sitting quietly by myself, I mused about the senselessness of warfare and the emotional turmoil for families. My mind drifted to the hearsay stories of schoolboys, who caught the goldfish in the memorial pond, requiring little skill and supposedly throwing them back. This action seemed equally meaningless.

In my reverie, something tugged at my consciousness, *it was just too quiet.* The typical playground din had abated. That was when I bumped into Mr Stander, faced my disappointment and felt his confidence in me had been inadvertently betrayed.

The following year, I hoped that perhaps I might still be made a prefect – it never happened. There was a slight recompense in the last six months, only because I was applying for a scholarship and a reference letter was needed from Mr Hofmeyr. Again, in keeping with his character, Mr Hofmeyr displayed his thoughtfulness and while looking at my application, said, "It would read better if you were a prefect."

In assembly one morning, he announced, "Walter Thornhill will become a sub-prefect with immediate effect." Although some of my mates were congratulatory, knowing the basis of the award, I was disappointed. On the odd occasion that I entered the prefect's room, a privileged sanctuary, they were indifferent to my presence. Perhaps, I was better off as a pupil with the freedom it allowed and the fun we revelled in. The badge was worn with emptiness; I had not earned or deserved it, and neither was I successful in my scholarship application.

ANCHORS

There was another form of separateness created by the day boys and boarders being in different houses. Competition took place in academia and in sport, where most points were awarded at the compulsory inter-house sports days. It was festive with much excitement amongst the animated boys.

Some boys were naturals. I tried all the events: hurdles, running, high jump, javelin and shot-put, but never excelled in any. Nevertheless, the sense of participation was enjoyed, while keeping a keen eye on the scoreboard and noting how Kudu our house, all dressed in green, was performing. The other houses were also antelopes, and for some peculiar reason, the boarding houses dominated – only once, during my time there, did we come second.

The school introduced a compulsory cross-country run – excitement mounted – bussed to a venue which appeared miles away. I had not the foggiest idea of what lay ahead, but that never detracted from my fertile imagination embroiled in pre-race fever.

It was one of those hot summer afternoons. The megaphone hissed and crackled its amplified messages to the excited athletes. *Attention, attention, quiet now . . . the course will be suitably marked . . . there will be teachers at various key points indicating the right direction . . . watch out for the markers. It will be pretty obvious, and there's a watering point halfway!*

The gun was fired. I was swept along by the wave of marauding ants, while preoccupied lest I trip on a loose rock, and trusting that those in front knew where they were going. Besides the sweat of the swarming bodies filling my nostrils, so did the evocative dry grass smell, typical of the Highveld at that time of year.

In the heart of nature my spirit soared, and I did not bother with the half way stop, noticing fewer and fewer boys – the markers now clearly visible.

My legs were aching, and I had a slight taste of blood in my mouth. The dry Transvaal air rushed in and out of the cavities of my heaving chest, making it feel as though it might explode at any moment. The mental terrain was familiar from cycling, although this time, my leg muscles were working awkwardly.

I suddenly felt alone, not lonely, but as if lost. Then, fortunately, another sign, and another . . . and a teacher's encouragement, *keep going boy, you're almost there.*

Across the finish line, it was clear that only a few boys were ahead of me. My legs felt as though they were going to collapse. I tried to regain my equilibrium, fighting away the pulsating pain throughout my body, while steadying my breathing. A teacher approached, *well-done boy, you finished fifth*!

Taken aback, I could scarcely believe it. Slowly the reality sank in, each time I recovered my breath. If I pushed a smidgen harder, not that I had much left, or tried for a better starting position, could I have improved a position or two? Notwithstanding, I was more than satisfied with the unexpected result and secretly, over the moon.

All my cycling endeavours had built up my endurance stamina, which allowed me to successfully compete. It could never become my preferred sport for cycling complexities were far more challenging.

The following day I did not walk with a broad grin. Instead, I hobbled with painful difficulty from classroom to classroom – the delayed onset and stiffening of an entirely different group of muscles set-in. The first day, testing; the second, excruciating. I started to believe the pain would never subside. It became my darkest hour before dawn, and then I was back on my bike again.

~

Hemingway, in *A Moveable Feast*, wrote about his experiences as a young writer in Paris in the early '20s. *There are so many kinds of racing, the straight sprints, raced in heats or in matched races where the two riders will balance for long seconds on their machines for the advantage of making the other rider take the lead – and then the slow circling – and the final plunge into the driving purity of speed.*

Speed – the fastest in the world has always captured man's imagination. So it was for Tommy and Ray, in the tandem Olympics of 1952. Besides their necessary strength, skill and fitness needed for this anaerobic function, sprinting becomes a battle of wits over the 1000 metres, during the best of three rides. The lead out is often no faster than walking pace and can confuse spectators, particularly when balancing dead still as Hemingway mentioned. Adrenaline pulsates; the slow lap is tactical and used to suss out and unnerve the opponent, while anticipating every move. Race tactics unfold, requiring instantaneous visceral responses to the many possible permutations. Then, that explosive burst of raw energy and sheer blinding acceleration in doing battle, elbow to elbow, across the finishing line with the recorded time over the last 200 metres, secondary.

Mistakes are visible, punishable and mostly irretrievable. Sprinters, like Wimbledon tennis players, are seeded; the strongest against the weakest. Upsets happen, and in the *repêchage* the losers have one last chance with the winner re-entering the event.

In the bigger picture, the road to advantage is a continual trade-off involving compromises between psychology, physiology and the best that science and technology has to offer. Differences are imperceptible to an untrained eye, yet they make all the difference to an experienced cyclist in search of victory.

During those earlier years, the older and more experienced club cyclists were my demigods. Subsequently, they were riders from other clubs and provinces. Experience was garnered by listening to their tales and emulating their styles with the finest learning taking place in competitions. My progress seemed slow; even a local club victory within my class, distant.

It was about sheer endeavour, a commitment to the daily training regime and a refinement thereof. The steps were incremental, emotions followed suit: disbelief to elation, a club placing to a win – these changes further kindled my spirit.

Never resting on my laurels, I developed an acute mental map of my competitors' strengths and weaknesses – while reading the race, thoughts about when to attack or to remain sheltered in the pack were recalibrated.

~

I was fifteen years old, in the winter of '68 and my second last year of high school, when four of us were selected to represent our province in the Schoolboy section of the 10 mile South African Road Championships that took place in Natal. Like royalty, a lift with Kevin Alborough – a fellow club member – and his dad in their chauffeur driven car.

Gripped by a mixture of excitement and nerves, I could hardly sleep a wink the night before the big day. The dawn alarm shattered my dream world. I was convinced the turmoil would affect my performance.

Anxiously, we lined up for the massed start – it was freezing cold, neither did we know the capabilities of the other provincial riders. Five laps of the Roy Hesketh motor racing circuit, including a testing hill – then we were at the end, sprinting for the finishing line. I gave it all, clinging to Kevin's wheel – a second and third place. We could not believe our good results and better still, it was a clean sweep for our province in the Junior and Senior sections. This victory helped change my high school's reluctant view of my extramural sporting activity, just a tad.

Kevin would have been world class – his performance kept improving but for the tragedy of an accident while out training later that year – his right arm, severed. The incident affected us and reinforced our awareness of the dangers training on the open roads. He came a few more times to track meetings, a spectator, then was never seen again. Perhaps it was all too painful for him – I was equally saddened by that turn of events.

Looking back at my early performance, I realised that the first clue of something different in my armour was developing. It had made its debut – a good road sprint finish, the envy of every racing cyclist.

~

Road season completed, the onset of spring heralded a new track season. That year I acquired a second-hand track cycle, infinitely better than the previously borrowed, far too big, club bike.

During December, the halfway mark and wind down for Christmas holidays, I overheard Jack Lester, Chris Harvey and Mike Payne talking about the annual pilgrimage to Cape Town. There was a bristle in the air and a declaration – *one of them had to win the coveted Boxing Day, Paarl Minnaar 25 mile trophy*. This race, the oldest cycling event in the world has been contested since its inception in 1897. Its cachet was even greater than winning a South African championship and drew cyclists countrywide to the allure of this prized trophy.

The other prestigious meetings were under atmospheric floodlights at Bellville and the Green Point Stadium in Cape Town. Secretly, I was chuffed by the prospect of a loose affiliation with these older and accomplished riders. My excitement mounted for it would be the first time my dad saw me race; previously, he had only ever heard of my endeavours. It became a gift and I managed a few places in the juvenile events.

My evolving mental map of the cycling arena was fed – different tactics of the Capetonian cyclists were observed while still dreaming of becoming as good and stylish as some of the better riders. Indeed, twenty-seven-year-old Mike, an icon in our sport, obliged. In spectacular fashion, he won this most sought-after crown jewel before a crowd of six thousand. It had been ten years since an upcountry win and it would be another seven before another Transvaal win – that year, local riders did not place in the first three. An impressive 58 minutes and 19.5 seconds was the third fastest time for the then seventy-year-old race. Conditions were testing, exacerbated by the excessive heat reflecting off the iconic Paarl Rock, a granite outcrop, where temperatures can soar upwards to 40°C, even in the shade. Purposefully, the race is ridden in the cooler late afternoon.

It was also the start of a meaningful friendship with Jack. He had an uncanny ability to read a race, a tactician par excellence and an incredible turn of speed when accelerating out of the bunch. But he did not have Mike's sleek style and smooth pedalling action – I tried to mimic the best of both riders.

Returning to the second half of the track season in early January, Mike was my immediate hero. It was my final year at school, turning sixteen that February in '69, and my first year competing in the Junior category. Mike's victory took on epic proportions and just being there made me feel part of the celebration. Fellow cyclists revelled in the story retold, *they dropped off like flies, the heat was unbearable, Mike's formidable strength was just too much for the breakaway splinter group – he simply pedalled away to lap them.*

Besides the regular Sunday league meetings, the impending Southern Transvaal and South African Championships, the overriding excitement that season was the forthcoming trials to select a Springbok team to compete against the visiting Australians. Young and inexperienced, I could only look on from the sideline, in sheer admiration of the prowess of the riders in contention – their ability still a quantum leap away.

I was astonished that only Guy Ferriman, from our province, was selected. Had Mike not just won the most desirable trophy in the land, and what about Jack's lightning ability to accelerate out of the bunch; always an absolute crowd pleaser.

Having only ever heard of the other riders, I would now see them in action. Willie Marx from Port Elizabeth, world class and seven times South African sprint champion, finished in the final eight at the World Championships in Amsterdam in '67. He was a cut above Jack and Joe Billet, *the bullet* from Kimberley as the press dubbed him – his strategic thinking, sheer explosive force and compact sprinter's body made the difference. Yet, on their day, any of them could be sprint champions.

Then there was Theuniss Theart, nicknamed Tin. He was thin and angular and had sleek lengthy calf and thigh muscles, the hallmark of a long-distance athlete. His speciality, like Mike, was the longer events on both track and road.

Hailing from the Cape, quiet yet colourful, he is best remembered for his legendary pact with a bee during a road race. It happened in a lone breakaway, made far too early and into strong buffeting winds. The peloton, confident in their ability to haul him in, let him drift away.

Meanwhile, he began to doubt his tactic, which normally on balance fails, but fate is fate. Unsure whether he was becoming delusionary from fatigue, Tin started to talk to a tired bee that had landed and hitched a ride on his mitt. The more they talked, the more focused and steadfast he remained, vowing to the bee *if you stay with me I will keep going* – they won against all odds.

The Australians had an exceptionally talented all-rounder, Danny Clark, merely two years older than me – it allowed an indulgence – perhaps, with a continued application to training and racing, I too might improve to his standard. For the moment, that was very distant.

Danny was as quick as any of the top riders, but impetuous. Suddenly, he jumped up, grabbed his bike and whacked an opponent, riding slowly by, to the ground. This unsportsmanlike behaviour made me fearful that one day, I might have to compete against someone of his ilk. Cautioned, he raced well in the remainder of the series. In the ensuing years, he won numerous World Championship titles and placed second in the '72 Olympics in Munich, West Germany (1000 metre time trial).

But our series was narrowly lost, and Doug Armstrong, a member of the

Australian side, stayed on to compete in the South African Championships in Bloemfontein later that year – he won the 4000 metre open individual pursuit. At the same time Alan van Heerden was attracting more attention for his outstanding abilities, particularly in that event.

A year later, Alan, only fifteen, unprecedentedly won that event. Fortunately, for the winter road racing season, being nine months older and competing in the Junior category, I did not have to confront this formidable foe just yet. There were many battles to come, the Fagor Tour already mentioned was just one.

There were changes afoot. I switched from my first club, Northern Wheelers, to the newly formed Johannesburg Cycle Racing Club, JCRC as it was known, founded by Owen Diesel, a visionary – he inspired our imagination and introduced an under ten track category. The club's ethos was different and it was closer to home.

The *Kensington gang* followed. In the club's embryonic stage, it had only one notable senior, Springbok Dries Oberholzer, an electrician, nicknamed *Sparky* – twenty-eight, and seemingly ancient.

In my first year as a junior, my last year at school, I merely participated in the '69 Easter weekend South African track championship. There was some redemption in the prior provincial championship – a gold and two bronze medals; the gold, a JCRC team effort in the pursuit.

The awarding of sporting colours at school always left me feeling sad and unseen for non-school extramural activities were not recognised. My efforts were not deterred for my love of the sport, as a way of life, kept me going.

The winter road season followed the track – the highlight, the Bert King Annual Junior Tour, an inter-club, two-day stage race. It was the first time we rode on the well-known Formula One motor racing circuit, Kyalami, 'my home' in Zulu.

That chilly afternoon proved to be the killer – the exceptional, short steep climb Leeukop, 'Lion head' in Afrikaans, had our chests heaving to the point of bursting as we gasped for breath, while our legs screamed from the aching pain. To boot, the adverse weather of searing rain and blustery winds, only exacerbated the wintry cold. Visibility was negligible. The water splashed from the wheels in front into our eyes. We battled our way in a haze of sheer grit and determination through those difficult conditions, completing the forty miles.

After the race, I put on dry clothes, but I could not stop shaking. I felt weird and soon the first aid team covered me in blankets. Barely conscious, I overheard, *he's suffering from hypothermia*. What was that? I had no idea. Rather, in my state, just grateful for their care and attention. A copious supply of warm infusions helped restore my equilibrium and a good night's rest did wonders.

The next day, back into the fray of our old stomping ground, Lenasia, the JCRC team dominated. Overall however, victory belonged to a hitherto unknown cyclist from Rhodesia, the tall Hugo Landsberg, who became known as the *gentle giant*. He leveraged his lanky frame to great advantage, and his calm demeanour and cycling ability became part of the recipe for our subsequent friendship.

~

Six years later, in 1975, most weekday mornings at 5:30 am in the freezing darkness of mid-winter, Hugo, Raymond Hogg and a few other cyclists religiously trained together. It was a challenging year for me: working in the day, while preparing for my Chartered Accountancy Board examination. Tagging along, my aim was to be fit for selection for the prestigious Rapport Tour, its third year since the '73 inauguration. Both Hugo and Raymond had competed previously, and secretly I hoped to be in Hugo's team – he had finished fourth in '74.

There was only one Raymond, an Australian immigrant. The press nicknamed him *the piglet* – at times, apt. His anecdotes relating to his one-man handyman business, Knight Errand caused many a smile: some incredulous, yet perhaps a few true – *a painting that needed a figurative adjustment here and there*!

A large, eye-catching knight chess piece adorned the top of his old beaten up handyman van, while his brother-in-law, copying his idea, had a giant chess bishop. By contrast to Raymond's infectious personality, he was pallid and dull, but no doubt had the keys to many a door.

One morning, only half the training squad arrived – dutifully we left but after a few kilometres, not knowing why and feeling out of sorts, I decided to turn back. Even Raymond's irrepressible sense of *joie de vivre* and rafter of jokes that normally kept our spirits alive on those early morning rides would not have worked.

Driving to work, I spotted a newspaper billboard – *Top SA Cyclist Killed*. I pulled over, bought a newspaper from the street vendor and immediately burst into tears. Hugo, our *gentle giant*, had been struck down by a vehicle the previous evening while out training – I was devastated, he was only twenty-five, and I was twenty-two.

That year, I was a reserve. My disappointment remained, only because I had my heart set on participating, and not one rider dropped out before the start. The race passed through the sleepy town of Oudtshoorn, known for its ostrich farming. But, it was awoken from its slumber by the press' story of Richard Burton and Elizabeth Taylor's surprise remarrying and planned honeymoon stopover there, where they were photographed with the British cycling team.

Tommy managed the team and explained, "The team did not want to be photographed as they were all riding under pseudonyms because of the sporting ban still in place. Instead, a group of local riders were substituted, but their pronounced South African accents gave them away." A little further journalistic scratching lead to a full-page revelation two days later by the Daily Mail, "The Secret Team Who Masquerade as Britain."

The Irish cyclists, Sean Kelly and the McQuaid brothers, who used the race as preparation for the '76 Olympics, were banned initially for six months and subsequently, Sean was barred from ever competing in the Olympics. He then turned professional and became one of the most successful international road cyclists of the '80s, while Pat McQuaid, the President of the UCI from 2005 to 2013.

~

Back to October '69, the next track season started with the emergence of the Emmenes brothers, from a cycling family, Rodney slightly older than me, and Neil, younger. Freddie, their father, as Tommy put it . . . *was a clever bike rider and very tough*. The brothers, built like sprinters, became very good at it, aided by the single-minded ambition of their father, who trained them to the exclusion of others. Any approach received his feigned smile as if, *you are unwelcome and might pose a threat to my sons' supremacy*. They sat separately, an entity, seldom mingling, and ultimately had their successes.

Sixteen-year-old Rodney shocked the Southern Transvaal selectors by winning the open Victor Dos Santos sprint thereby securing his place in the Southern Transvaal team for a forthcoming interprovincial. Despite a glowing press coverage, I never made the team – *to add to the selectors' problems was the performance of another sixteen-year-old, Walter Thornhill, in the 25 mile. The young rider beat Mike Payne and Jimmy Swift in a time of 56 minutes and 7.6 seconds* – the time was a good two minutes quicker than Mike's Paarl victory, barely nine months earlier.

Something was happening amongst our upcoming cadre of young riders: the Emmenes brothers, Cliffie Steward, Alan van Heerden and on our tails, Albert and Rory. Our raw fresh blood was rattling the old guard as we displayed remarkable form and ability for our age. Neither did I applaud myself for my newfound victories, yet clearly, I was exceptionally glad to have achieved them. It is said *the fish swimming in the water is unaware of the greater ocean*. In that vein, I merely kept training and competing while remaining acutely aware that any of us on their day could be equally victorious.

The Johannesburg Grand Prix marked the end of the first half of the track season. It was developing a similar cachet to the prestigious December Cape events and incumbent Joe, *the bullet,* did his legendary trademark trick:

retching before the start of the sprint, such was his state of nervousness. That year, Willie Marx stamped his mark beating Joe. In one of the heats, Willie's time of 11.4 seconds was the fastest then recorded at Hector Norris Park, the stamp of a master. Rory also did this incredible time, as mentioned in our exciting neck and neck sprint finish, albeit a few years later.

The other crowd pleaser that afternoon was the fifty lap Madison – a demanding race, needing good track craft and strategy with two riders per team, one always racing. Changing takes place by slinging your partner into the contest, a technically challenging manoeuvre executed with riders seemingly passing chaotically on either side of the main bunch. Teams were in club pairs, and *Sparky* and I represented the newly formed JCRC against the winners from my former club, Springboks Mike Payne and thirty-eight-year-old veteran Jimmy Swift – Mike's fitness and Jimmy's strategy ensured their win for the second consecutive year.

The press put it this way . . . *they had to battle to recapture their title in a race that was packed with drama. Dries Oberholzer punctured early in the race and had to leave the track. His partner, Walter Thornhill, kept on going alone until Oberholzer was back in the race . . . and sixteen-year-old Alan van Heerden who gave Payne and Swift a torrid time in the last few laps finishing close behind in second place.*

Jimmy, a gentleman, whether on his bike racing or as President of the South African Cycling Federation, was recognised with the Shield of Jove Award in 1956, South Africa's highest sporting award for Olympic athletes. Recently, while discussing facets of *Eye of the Child* with Tommy, he reminded me, "Jimmy also started life in an orphanage."

No season was complete without *the dreaded accidents*, the bane of every cyclist's life. Tarmac road surfaces and concrete tracks are notoriously unforgiving – inflicting, at the very least, grazes to the skin and at times more: broken bones, torn ligaments and concussion – even death. The press dined on crashes – feeding the readers with gory pictures, commenting on the injuries sustained and speculating on the cause. These sensational aspects were attractive to some, not me – I had my fair share of spills.

PERIPHERAL POLITICAL AWARENESS

At the time of completing high school in '69, I only had a peripheral awareness of the politics of the country. Notwithstanding, I certainly knew what was innately wrong.

The country had been under the strong grip of the ruling Nationalist Party since their victory in 1948. Verwoerd, initially Minister of Native Affairs, in the year of my birth, 1953, laid down the groundwork for lesser education of Black citizens.

> Opening a debate in Parliament, he said, *"Racial relations cannot improve if the wrong type of education is given to Natives. They cannot improve if the results of the Native Education is the creation of frustrated people who as a result of the education they receive have expectations in life which circumstances in South Africa do not allow to be fulfilled immediately, when it creates people who are trained for professions not open to them, when there are people who have received a form of cultural training which strengthens their desire for the white-collar occupations to such an extent that there are more such people than openings available. Therefore, good racial relations are spoiled when the correct education is not given."*

> He had more to say, *"What is the use of teaching the Bantu child mathematics when they cannot use it in practice? What is the use of subjecting a Native child to a curriculum which in the first instance is traditionally European? I just want to remind Honourable Members that if the Native inside South Africa today in any kind of school in existence is being taught to expect that he will live his adult life under a policy of equal rights, he is making a big mistake."* (extracts from Hansard, South Africa)

Verwoerd, seen as the *architect of apartheid*, continued to implement and shape policies. Five years later, he became Prime Minister. The government steamrolled a University Educational Bill through Parliament restructuring *open* White universities despite protests from educational institutions throughout the world. Hitherto, students of all races were admitted.

Ethnic tribal colleges were proposed: three for Blacks, one for Indians and one for the Coloureds. The curricula and the appointment of staff were government controlled, making a mockery of tertiary education where a fundamental tenet is the freedom of education and thought.

Verwoerd and his successor John Vorster, as prime ministers, had a long uninterrupted tenure of twenty years between them. Verwoerd had eight, until his eventual assassination in 1966, having survived an earlier attempt in 1960. Together, they enforced their dreams of apartheid throughout my formative years at school, university and beyond.

Vorster further endorsed the concept of Bantustan. The idea was to reduce the number of Black South Africans, then circa five to one, by becoming citizens of their homelands and selling their labour as migratory workers. The infamous passbook, with work permits stamped for specific areas, was obligatory to carry. It was demeaning and became an instrument of apartheid intimidation and harassment by the notorious police inspections.

Robert Sobukwe, Pan-African Congress leader, incited the burning of the passes as an act of defiance in 1960. The Sharpeville crisis followed – sixty-nine people were killed and one hundred and eighty injured. I was seven and unaware that this atrocity had taken place; nor that the Blacks, Coloureds and Indians did not have a vote.

Citizens were treated like children, continually bombarded with propaganda and disinformation like Russians were Communists and all things bad – it never made sense. Silent whispers of the undisclosed agreements between Russia and South Africa to control the world supply of diamonds and Adrian's bold statement during my teenage years: "True Communism is a good thing but too idealistic, and that's why it doesn't work." This only added to my confusion as my thoughts were caught in a struggle with much resolve needed in the ensuing years.

Meanwhile, George and I stood on the sidewalk in Eloff Street, Johannesburg, with the rest of an excited crowd, looking on through a departmental store window on the 20 July 1969 – the authorised Government replay of the moon landing (South Africa still did not have television) – *that's one small step for man, one giant leap for mankind.* The press attacked, *the moon film has proved to be the last straw . . . the situation is becoming a source of embarrassment for the country.*

Verwoerd even spoke about the Government's responsibility for the spiritual and physical well-being of their people, while Dr Albert Hertzog, Minister for Posts and Telegraphs (media) said that it would be over his dead body that the devil's own box (television) would be used for disseminating communism and immorality. Afrikaner patronisation at its best; media censored and controlled. Ultimately, television was introduced in 1976, seven years later.

Fortunately, the one-seat Progressive Party, represented by Helen Suzman, championed the rights of all races. Her voice of resistance prevailed during the darkest hours of the apartheid regime.

Gayle and me
(Jeppe High School uniform)

George, Desiree, Gayle and
Bambi, another mongrel

Jeppe High School U13A Rugby team - Mr Loots on the left
and Mr Stander on the right (I'm below him)

CHAPTER 10
UNIVERSITY DAYS

FRESHMAN

I bumbled into university, a sixteen-year-old, too young to be conscripted. My peer group went off to do their military service. Forgoing Adrian's bribe to study medicine, I followed my illusions of the wealth and success as portrayed by my mother's boss, the accountant, and chose to read a Bachelor of Commerce Degree.

Clueless . . . three compulsory subjects and two optional . . . and overhearing the excited natter during the registration process – *Industrial Psychology is easy, everybody gets a first*. It seemed nefarious to obtain a mark that way, particularly as I did not even know what psychology was. Instead, following a simple line of familiarity, I chose Economic History, mostly because of my fondness of Warren Boden's history lessons, and was pleasantly surprised to learn later about *sex on the factory floor*!

University of the Witwatersrand's campus consisted mostly of day students. The money my mother had given me previously covered my initial annual fees, while incidentals, like haircuts and bus fares, were inadequately supplemented. I never raised this, rather cycled the distance of 25 kilometres, there and back, making light of it by building it into my training regime out of necessity. The fear of *not having*, found roots. Fortunately, there was lots of sunshine, and the summer rains that erupted in the late afternoons, driven by electrical storms, were mostly dodged.

Fearful that the wheel holders in the bicycle racks could have buckled or scratched my thin rims, I found a novel spot to lock my conspicuous bike to a drainpipe, set against the cold grey cement wall of a faculty building. Malicious damage or theft always concerned me. Patiently, my cycle greeted me each day awaiting our embrace of the open roads.

The leaps between primary, secondary and tertiary education were strongly demarcated. Jeppe's school uniform made me feel grown up, but now the unparalleled freedom was a quantum leap. The only accountability was the writing of examinations and assignments to be completed by due dates.

This freedom was counterbalanced by my emotional immaturity and lack of understanding of the workings of the political and economic systems of the country. I was in awe of these great mysteries, feeling quite insignificant amongst the thousands of students, as I climbed the steps of the imposing buildings, but glad to be attending the liberal university Wits, as it was colloquially known.

Mrs Robinson's red Spider, the iconic image in The Graduate, and other Alfa Romeo saloons ostentatiously highlighted the social-financial divide. It was like a territorial stamp that made me feel impoverished, inadequate and intimidated. It was silly to have attached any importance to it, but I did.

By comparison, my faithful *Don Quixote* steed, even in my delusionary state, made me realise it would hardly be suitable for courting the female species, even those daring enough to sit on the crossbar. But the steps of the Great Hall, one hot summer's day, allowed conversation to flow well; only interrupted by nature's intervention – a pigeon-message landing on my knee. Embarrassed, I recalled my mother's words, *a gentleman always carries a handkerchief.* Jane's curious look penetrated Tarzan's fumbling – in desperation, I finally flicked it off. With a decisive pirouette, she casually glanced over her shoulder, "Late for lectures." My heart sank, realising my clumsiness, and to this day I still carry a handkerchief.

Fortunately, I was rescued by a group of engineering students cajoling me to join their team, hopeful that they had acquired a stealth weapon, a proper cyclist, for the annual inter-faculty pedal car competition. They toiled relentlessly, constructing streamlined space-age works of art. I marvelled at their ingenuity as these space rockets emerged, only to be propelled by pedal power.

The students, a few years older than me, who had never cycled before, soon discovered the intricacies of the mechanical functions of a bicycle with surprising alacrity. I was in awe for it had taken me many years in stripping every part to acquire that knowledge, which they had mastered effortlessly.

We had our practice runs – a tweak here and there to the mechanical and aerodynamic designs, a finessing of the change over from rider to rider as we rapidly accelerated away, while mostly learning about our limitations as fatigue set in.

This form of racing was absolutely energy sapping and would test our human endeavour. For me it was particularly difficult as I was not used to using different parts of the leg and calf muscles while pedalling in a half laying down position. My performance lacked the winning formula they desired.

Notwithstanding, we managed the distance, and although not in a podium position, there was a sense of achievement. The banter and camaraderie that followed were aided by the appearance of an enormous keg of beer, which helped replenish our spirits.

~

Aunty Ronnie regularly visited the family, gracing us with her pleasant bonhomie disposition. Inevitably, often without even a sip of alcohol, it was not long before my mother began to nit-pick at anything Aunty said. What triggered her behaviour? Was the cause buried deep within? The atmosphere rapidly became charged, tense and disagreeable. Aunty would naturally direct her attention to the rest of us, as best she could, in trying to maintain the equilibrium and deflect my mother's behaviour.

The incessant petty bickering, the evening antics, and the daily cycle rides to University, each in their way took their toll. One day, I casually asked on the pretext of Aunty's proximity to Wits, "Do you mind if I come and stay with you for a while as it would be so easy to get to University?"

"With pleasure, provided it's OK with Desiree and George."

I took up residency in her one-bedroom flat for the next three months, sleeping in the lounge, while my road bike rested in the entrance hall which also doubled as our dining room. The kitchen was minute. At night Aunty had a need for social company, while my priority was to study. We played musical chairs between the hallway and the lounge, as I tried to keep those interactions to a minimum. The flat that seemed so enormous when I was younger, now proved otherwise. I was encroaching on Aunty's space. She was sixty-two and more set in her ways than my mother.

Somewhere, hidden deep within my consciousness, like a knowing-ache, was the realisation that I was missing the familiarity and sense of security of my previous existence: the afternoon training rides with the Kensington gang; the dogs, neighbours, and family, even with all their peculiarities.

The stay with Aunty was becoming increasingly functional, despite her kindness and generosity. It was better to go back to the devil I knew and find a coping mechanism, for the benefits outweighed the adversity.

The student year rolled by with the canteen a great place to hang out, catching up on the latest gossip or ideas to counter government propaganda and atrocities. Student elections and candidates championing causes – Craig Williamson, a law student, was rising within the Student Union ranks.

Aunty Ronnie always encouraged me to introduce myself to him, the son of her dear friend, Ruth. He was an aloof and large fellow, four years my senior. When I finally did, I felt inferior and intimidated. He was already involved with the student council, had a font of knowledge about politics, while I was still quite ignorant. Some eight years later we met again, also instigated by Aunty.

Craig's mother, the grapevine, let it be known that he was most successful and always in Europe, mostly Switzerland, on business. The idea was to explore mutually beneficial opportunities, and as affable and charming as he was then, something did not feel right. Nothing more transpired, and Aunty kept me apprised of his successes.

A few years later in 1980, Craig, then thirty-one, was exposed – a *super spy*! What a bombshell, he had infiltrated the ANC. Aunty and I were dumbfounded, but thinking about it, it made sense. A home in the affluent northern suburbs and, after our meeting, I left with only a vague understanding of his business ventures within the security industry – hardly surprising.

Four years after the beginnings of the new South Africa, on 20 September 1998, the Sunday Times ran an article – *The spy who never came in from the cold.* It included Craig's statement: *I respect a person who's willing to die for his country, but I admire a person who is prepared to kill for his country.* Three years prior, he had applied for amnesty from the South African Truth and Reconciliation Commission for his various atrocities. He was exposed as a killer and acquitted. Amongst other acts, he had ordered the letter bomb that assassinated Ruth First.

I thought back to my cycling days in Mozambique, when I was seventeen and eighteen, and how Mozambique had played a role as a base for the ANC. I imagined the alienation that Ruth and Joe, as well as other members must have felt. Away from their country, always living with the possibility of a threat against their lives, yet sustained by their fervour and ideals. It did not surprise me that I never had any empathy with Craig, the master of a double life.

Were these linkages and wheels within wheels mere coincidences or a pre-destiny? Notwithstanding my lack of understanding, it impacted me emotionally even though there was no direct link.

~

I always looked forward to Mathematics and Statistics, and the theatrics of my favourite lecturer, Mr Mittermeier. A finger in the air, he proclaimed in his thick German accent as though imparting vital information, "To do this subject, you must draw a perfect circle!" A contented smile and thickset eyebrows, like a nutty professor, he lifted a piece of chalk – we waited with bated breath – "Like this" – a freehand circle emerged.

He stood back in admiration, pausing for a second or two, looking at his handiwork as if to ensure that there were no imperfections. At that moment, it was clearly the most important thing in the world; the lecture paled into insignificance, much to our delight. His eccentricity encapsulated his essence, and it kept me engrossed observing attentively lest he might fail, just once. Sometimes there was a slight overlap, which never fazed him. He merely took his time, carefully erasing the offending bit, before continuing to complete his perfect circle.

Pivoting around to face us, with a warm smile, he nodded "*Ja,* statistics and probability" and the class would begin. It became a perfect place of learning as exciting snippets, imparted conspiratorially, captivated us, like how the theory of probability started.

> *A repeated flick of a coin by a World War prisoner, faithfully recording the results. Alas, a smaller sample gave inconsistent results, but the longer the duration, an interesting phenomenon occurred – a probability of a near equal distribution. After the war, baffled by this slight distortion, he investigated further – the 'head' side being fractionally heavier than the 'tail'.*

My imagination was enthralled by the prisoner's perseverance and ingenuity in what must have been a debilitating and harrowing time. His pertinent discovery echoed Nietzsche's saying, *a dancing star is born out of chaos within.*

Meanwhile, enticed by our Polish lecturer for Economic History declaring, *Next week's lecture is about sex on the factory floor,* pandemonium ensued. Intrigue lured as word spread like wildfire with hardly a seat available in the packed auditorium.

We listened, riveted, but had been hoodwinked – the Industrial Revolution's dramatic productivity increase when women were introduced into the workplace; nothing more.

I was slower in that field, except for my early sexual curiosities at the Convent. Chatting with my friend Benji in our mature adult lives, it appears I missed out on his childhood game, *train in the tunnel,* which made *doctor-doctor* quite ordinary. Anyhow, back to my childhood, one sunny weekend on Aunty Ronnie's Athol plot, a friend introduced me to a strange self-satisfying activity.

We had wandered around the gardens and had played typical boys' games. While sitting in the shade on a low-slung branch of a willow tree, protected from outside prying eyes, he casually enquired . . . and sensed my confusion. How did he know of this self-delight, a hidden sensuous secret? Such was my mysterious initiation, a far cry from the Church's frowning view.

I soon forgot about it; years passed before my teen testosterone stirred again, often during spells of loneliness. Piet, from next door, shared his pearls of wisdom with the neighbourhood – *ejaculation was the equivalent loss of energy to a twenty kilometre cycle ride, but there was a way to prevent it without detracting from the enjoyment.* We eagerly awaited his revelation – thinking back he could have been a monk in a previous life, working with the rise and containment of Kundalini energy.

It became part of the answer not to hamper my training and racing efforts. But God and the Devil were apparently watching, for a preacher had reminded us during preparation for confirmation of this evil. My confusion was exacerbated, and the tussle between palpable guilt, particularly as all those lives and energy were lost, knew no bounds – there were times I allowed my pleasure to overcome Piet's taught monastic practice.

Neither did we have proper sex education at school, nor were my mother's disjointed attempts helpful, however well meaning.

"We don't mind if Walter has sex before marriage, he should be careful. If he gets a girl into trouble, he only needs to tell us."

It may have been sincere, but it was inappropriate. I had neither a girlfriend, nor was I sexually active. The supposed open manner of communication, mostly with an outside audience present, was humiliating. There were variations on the theme over the years – it was her unconscious way of setting our family apart, to display that our family's liberal morals and principles were ahead of the times. These comments were designed to shock – they did, but it was really about my mother's self-portrayal.

A private, sincere conversation about any facet of sexual exploration, whether the emotional aspects or the consequences, would have been far more welcome. My further disappointment, confusion and continual buffeting in this regard will be evident later, particularly around my first sexual encounter.

Albert's twin sister, Cathy, had caught my eye – she was tall and slender, had a slightly natural olive complexion, almost ethereal, and a serene disposition; except, exceptionally shy. I was seventeen and found continual excuses to visit the Styger family, after lectures.

I had never heard of cappuccino, but Cathy had a way of making instant coffee appear just that. Fascinated; coffee, sugar and a dash of milk, mixed into a thick paste; then with an energetic stirring action the ingredients ground together – more boiling water, and hey presto. It was as if her special care was our private communication, especially since we had to endure the frivolity of conversation until her parents retired, and finally, even Albert gave up, leaving us alone.

The conversation was never easy or free flowing, more because of her shyness, interspersed with, *more coffee*? Goodbyes took forever with little said . . . *must go now . . . OK* . . . an embarrassing silence . . . *see you soon*, and another *OK* – how I so wished she would say more. This dance went on for far too long. What lengths to pursue my perception of her beauty, nor knowing how to take that next step. Finally, we managed to hold hands during these interminably painful goodbyes, where the only thing missing was the first kiss.

Yes, my first kiss. Plucking up courage, I leant forward and put my arms around her – our lips met. Confused and frozen in a moment of disbelief, an eternity, well at least 20 minutes. What was wrong; breaking the embrace I tried again. Finally, *see you soon . . . OK*!

Cycling home, rather than feeling exhilarated, only disappointment prevailed – the lonely yellow dimmed streetlights knew, and the quiet roads that accompanied me, confirmed – she did not know how to kiss.

Things move quickly when you are a student – the following week I met an Afrikaans girl, who had recently moved into our neighbourhood. The air carried my need to overcome my disappointment, mixed with her willingness to oblige; after yet another cup of coffee we embraced – finally Nirvana. An immediate emotional warmth pulsated through my body as our hands innocently moved over each other. This time, I bounded home, joyously.

The next evening could not come soon enough; a taste of this newfound pleasure. When it was time to go, she said, "Why did you kiss me like I was your sister last night?" I froze, and in a flash, realised that there was indeed another way. The previous evening's warmth and the electric response as our lips touched, forgave my innocence.

Synaptic pulses fired, "Out of respect, it was our first date", and as if to prove the point I rapidly embraced her, no longer with my lips sealed. Surprising myself, this exciting new world was entered, probably without breathing. Hungrily, we explored each other; this time, I could have flown home.

There was a strange twist – perhaps my voracious appetite and attack, like an oxygen starved submarine desperate to surface, or perhaps her need to go further, inhibited by my sheer inexperience, led her to seek other pastures. Yet, I was grateful and felt grown up.

Life moved on quickly – clearly, Cathy was ahead of me – her lips expectantly ready and inviting, while mine, together, flashed my ignorance like a red beacon. Endearing, yet in another way hilarious – neither knew how to help the other, stumbling along as best we could.

Upon finding these new delights, my spirit believed from that moment onwards that it had always known – perhaps it is like that for all of us?

Jack Lester and I never belonged to the same cycling club; our friendship evolved as he mentored me on many matters, particularly relating to sports psychology. He had such self-belief that he quit his university studies, trained for the Amsterdam World Championship in 1967. Incidentally, the last time Springbok colours were awarded for cycling before the country was banned from international sport. Subsequently he started his own carpet laying business. He was an unknown twenty-year-old and in the ensuing months, he systematically started to annihilate the favourites, thus securing his place in the team.

Such supreme belief, encapsulated in his statement *nothing is beyond an individual's ability*, was spewed like a preacher on the deaf ears of the cycling fraternity except for his one disciple, me. A battered purple-cloth-covered book on mysticism, hypnosis and such similar subjects lay casually in his kitbag. It was his Holy Grail entitling him to be our guru.

Perhaps our friendship was strengthened by the playful prevalent banter of the other cyclists dubbing us, *the intellectuals*. We knew the rules better than most officials, having studied our cycling Mao Tse-tung red book from cover to cover. Our manifesto, used for enforcing our rights, whenever we felt there was an injustice – we lodged appeals in writing, encouraged other cyclists to protest, and delayed the start of meetings by simply sitting on the track, refusing to move, until our collective grievances were addressed.

Jack the legend was known for his inimitable explosive speed. Basil's indomitable excited voice boomed over the loud speakers, with a knack of rousing the crowds to a fervent pitch. Tripping over itself, shrill with excitement and rising to a crescendo, it still rings in my ears: *Jack, the bombshell, powering out of the bunch, just look at him go, such explosive speed, there's no stopping him now*!

Jack once said of Basil, "He could make a pram race the most exciting event in the world!" Sunday afternoons and mid-week evening racing became our adventure playground. Jack was like an elder brother and statesman, an early role model and part of my survival mechanism; a mirror that challenged or confirmed my beliefs.

Intrigued by his own mixed religious background, a Jewish father and a Christian mother, he took comfort in quoting verses from the Torah and the Bible. An amusing habit, while pontificating, was to twist the same lock of jet black hair, his *payot*, except it was far too short.

One evening, after a track training session, while chewing the cud, Jack characteristically frowned and pronounced that we should form our own religion as the easiest way to make money. The thought, without moral foundation, was designed to challenge and set us apart, and perhaps, to garner a slight psychological advantage. Knowingly, eyebrows were raised, looking on with utter disbelief, as if to say, *here he goes again*! Jack remained oblivious to this; sport does accommodate all, even the eccentric.

My seventeenth birthday, in February 1970, coincided with the fervour gripping the cycling fraternity's imagination as it became de rigueur to attempt to better South African records at specially designed invitation events. At the same time, we worked hard at improving our team pursuit abilities, hitherto a weak point in interprovincial competitions; the junior squad against the might of the seniors, which ironically benefitted us more. We never dwelled on the age disparity; our times improved. Meanwhile, media speculated on the possibility of the ace seniors being beating with the added chance of a new record. The journalist's script could not quite be followed, but in an invitation meeting against a Northern Transvaal junior team, we succeeded in establishing a new 4000 metre Junior Pursuit South African record of 4 minutes and 47.8 seconds, eclipsing 3.6 seconds.

A few weeks later, the Junior Pursuit at the South African Championships in Cape Town was ours as well, but best of all was the opportunity to be with my dad, albeit just for a few days. Those trips were always a godsend.

The first drug test for all medal winners was introduced – scary, we gave two urine samples. Four riders tested positive – I was unaware and shocked (methamphetamine, a powerful stimulant, and ephedrine hydrochloride, a lung opener used by asthmatics). The riders were immediately suspended. Ian Coutts, a fellow cyclist, friend and lawyer, defended a Western Province rider, while closer to home an advocate was briefed for a member of our junior pursuit team.

Ultimately, they were all acquitted for one reason or another. Rumours abounded, *it was the cough mixture taken for a cold . . . my asthmatic inhaler*. Tommy recently shared with me that after the results were known, the doctor administering the tests commented, *I've never known so many sick cyclists at a championship*! The doubt created left a bitter taste, making me question the veracity of my team mate's performance, but as time moved on it was forgotten as we busied ourselves with other competitions.

We trained hard, were committed and already good cyclists – drugs do not make phenomenal athletes – they did, however, unfairly alter the playing field.

~

I regularly visited Nic Nolte for a leg massage, particularly after a long training session. It was always a treat, more so for the colourful stories, some implausible but highly entertaining about his time in Holland when the Dutch cycling legend Joop Zoetemelk, who rode the Tour de France sixteen times, would rush over seeking his advice. Repeatedly during the telling, he would suddenly stop massaging. With a curious gesture of touching his forehead with his fingertips while flexing his biceps in rapid succession, as if showing his physical prowess which did impress me, he would utter his well-known phrase – "*Wat heb ik jou gezeg*" (what did I tell you). It was as though his filaments of thought and muscle were all connected, validating his credibility.

Furtively, I smiled, while his gestures continued. Puckering eyebrows holding my absolute attention, and with a stillness of his stare he would let me into another monumental fact: *the number of bricks he had laid that day.* My simple nod of acknowledgment relieved the intensity of the moment with the muscles of his hardened windswept face relaxing as his genuine smile joyously reappeared.

By this stage, my legs were cooling down, while he, in his reverie, mounted the unseen podium lost in some distant recollection of time. How long to wait out of respect and gratitude and when to gently nudge him back to the task at hand was a fine line. His unselfish act of giving, particularly after an exhausting day of physical work, were more than sufficient for me.

Often at the track after a win, he would give me that conspiratorial knowing wink and say, "Ninety-two" as an affirmation of the previous advice given relating to the gear ratio to use. My chain ring number hidden behind the crank, a practise cyclist use, was helpful when it came to Nic. Neither did I have the physical ability for such a gear, the domain of dominant sprinters, nor the heart to tell him.

Perhaps, I was a hint of his Zoetemelk, and he my emotional solace, much like the comfort of a coach. His advice was often wrong, but the victories became ours.

~

The winter months were all about the road season and a variety of races with stage racing the pinnacle. We endeavoured to peak for chosen events, but that year we received a surprise invitation from the Mozambique Cycling Federation inviting a Southern Transvaal team to compete in their Somorel four-day stage race, in Mozambique. There were no trials, just Harry Bloomfield our manager, who selected his team from the best of the riders available and able to participate at such short notice. The allure of competing in a foreign country for a duration longer than I had ever experienced was so exciting and a venture into unknown territory.

We drove there by car. It was late evening when Harry said, "We ought to find a place to sleep and continue tomorrow." The only accommodation at the next dorp was a hotel under renovation – the hard floor with sawdust and the smell of wooden chips laying all around, our bed. We made ourselves as comfortable as we could by using our track suits and the odd discovered moth-eaten blanket to keep ourselves warm, and a rolled-up article of clothing as a pillow. Our enthusiastic spirits and blind faith in Harry could not be dampened.

Up at dawn, after a few hours' sleep and embraced by the heavy early morning dew, we loaded the bikes and gear. Soon, we were on the road again. The previous night's memories of deprivation rapidly evaporated as did the mist, as the early morning sun rose; the promise of a new day. The first pit stop satisfied our ravenous tummies, and our youthful enthusiasm prevailed.

Crossing the border at Komatipoort was my first experience of leaving South Africa. The sound of Portuguese, passports stamped by quizzical officials, and upon arriving in Lourenco Marques (Maputo) we were treated like dignitaries by the cycling community. My eyes scanned the colonial architecture, while my nostrils filled with the tantalising smell of cooked prawns in Portuguese olive oil. Enjoyably overwhelming.

The organisation of the stage racing was superb, the scale of what it took, incomprehensible. Our inexperienced young team did its best, while the Portuguese dominated. The 100 kilometre first stage was back to the border Ressano Garcia. It was an incredibly hot day. The Portuguese instigated the attacking, and on their home turf, smelt blood and wanted victory. Eating and replenishing liquid is vital in this high calorie-burn sport, long before the first pangs of thirst; tough to achieve, while racing hard, as the simple act of swallowing becomes challenging.

Immediately upon crossing the finish line, we were surrounded by an excited local crowd offering a celebratory *cerveja* (beer), while *agua por favor* (water please), seemingly unavailable. My inattentiveness to my liquid intake during the harsh racing conditions, left me parched and quite dehydrated. An ice-cold bottle of beer was shoved into my hand. Looking around, the Portuguese riders' example had to be followed; the first, second and third sip, the most satisfying. My extreme thirst quenched like none other. In no time at all, the first bottle was immediately replaced by another and another. How many I am uncertain. By lunchtime – lightheaded, smiling and musing – the world floated by.

Unfortunately, there was still the forty-kilometre time trial back to Moamba in the late afternoon, an individual race of truth against the clock with each cyclist starting a minute behind the other – the slowest first with the fastest last. The first half went well, probably as I was still tanked up with alcohol. But then, absolute disaster struck – the dreaded *bonk* – the curse of every cyclist, a state of hypoglycaemia. It is like hitting a brick wall, legs turning mechanically. Now no longer with any thrust, no matter how hard I willed them on. First a rider, then another and another passed. Pushing on valiantly as best I could, before Harry drove alongside, perturbed, and enquired, "What's up?"

I gave him a sideways glance, "Not sure, my legs have lost their power." He immediately knew and remained encouraging, "Keep pushing as best you can, it's not far to go now." But it felt like an eternity.

By the fifth and last stage, I was enjoying the racing, and more in my stride, winning the interim sprint at the 20 kilometre mark and placing in the final sprint. A Portuguese rider won the Tour, and two of my team-mates finished ahead of me – overall, I was ninth. Not a bad effort all considered, a seventeen-year-old junior, competing in an open event; the time trial, my nemesis.

There is an old saying amongst cyclists, *put the miles in, it matters.* Besides my training regimen, the inclusion of the Somorel Tour probably made the difference. It allowed me to win the Southern Transvaal 100 kilometre junior road Championship and place third in the South African Road Championship held in Cape Town that year. Again, it meant I saw my father, a windfall, giving us a chance to catch up and exchange stories.

Spring was always welcome as there was a new track season to look forward to, putting an end to the road season and the hard training conditions of the winter months, in the dry, harsh Transvaal air. The two forms of racing are like chalk and cheese with track requiring a different skill set, specifically, an agile and nimble mind. Track cycling was growing in popularity, and the increased number of entrants in the juniors and seniors were accommodated by introducing an open A, B and C-class, irrespective of age.

Southern Transvaal cyclists were spoilt for choice for within a thirty- to fifty-kilometre radius from Johannesburg the season offered Sunday afternoon league meetings, Friday night racing in Pretoria and specialised record attempts in Krugersdorp. The tracks were subtly different: the steepness of the banks, the smoothness of the cement surfaces and the length of the home straight. All of which added another dimension and required a tweaking of tactics. Pretoria, the steepest with a challenging short home straight, Krugersdorp excellent for record attempts and Johannesburg, a good all-rounder.

Perhaps journalist Peter Thomson's rendition, on the 19th October 1970, in the opening weeks of the track season, gave a flavour of my continued improving performance. *Thornhill gives sprinters shock,* writing further, *Walter Thornhill, a seventeen-year-old first year Wits University student, who has always been considered essentially a road and pursuit rider, yesterday stunned a crowd of over three thousand spectators at Hector Norris Park by coming through to win the feature one lap sprint event. Thornhill, who is the club captain of the Johannesburg Cycle Racing Club, produced what was the biggest surprise on a day marked by the eclipse of several established stars. He first signalled his bold sprint threat by downing Guy Ferriman in his heat. Then he won a place in the final after Rodney Emmenes had been disqualified for riding inside the sprinter's line over the final 200 metres. Carey, riding with a newfound confidence, fought his way into the final with a thrilling win over Jackie Lester in his semi-final. However, leading out in the final he allowed young Thornhill to come right around him and storm to the line a clear winner.*

Peet van Staden, writing for the Afrikaans press, had a different headline, *Junior cyclists shine again,* and his slant, *Surprises, drama and excitement were the three hallmarks of the league meeting. The juniors rode as if there were no other competitors and the day belonged to them. Juniors! A person feels nervous to use the word, but there is no other way. A relatively unknown junior defeated two Springboks and one other well-known sprinter in the Sprint event and such a junior's name must be mentioned. He is Walter Thornhill.*

Our club was responsible for the track meeting that day. Perhaps, emotionally motivated and rising to the mantle of club captain, helped.

The interprovincial team, the following weekend under Jack's captaincy, annihilated the Orange Free State who failed to score a point. The press commented on the opposition's lacklustre performance, especially since the huge surprise was that they had dominated the team pursuit on the previous seven occasions and were the incumbent reigning national champions. Southern Transvaal was on a roll, notwithstanding the still scathing attack for our team's lack of coordination in the team pursuit, concluding that despite the win the problems in this event had not been overcome.

This challenging race is about four riders, where three must finish, and of utmost importance, the timely contribution of each. Every two hundred and twenty metres or so, the front rider peels up the track, while the others move through – smoothly – maintaining the rhythm and pace. It is equally crucial to swoop down and reconnect seamlessly onto the rear of the team's slipstream.

There is a momentary reprieve for a few laps before the same rider takes the full brunt of the atmosphere, upfront again. Gaps created become an unnecessary expenditure of energy and destabilise the even flow of the team's performance. It is a race of sheer concentration, involving precise manoeuvres, where riders are within inches of each other's wheels – raced at the maximum speed the team can manifest.

A lot happened in a short period. In an open event, a week later the press sang my praises with giddy headlines, *Thornhill's day* and *Walter steals cycling honours* as I romped home in both the 800 and 1500 metre race, placing my stake to be selected for the next interprovincial. Jack was again at the helm with Northern Transvaal whitewashed as well.

I was still a junior and had joined the hallowed ranks of our senior provincial side. The press by then were delirious, *Southerns still unbeaten,* and wrote further, *after three interprovincials, Southern Transvaal, holders of the Carlton coveted trophy, chalked up one hundred and twenty-one points with only two against. Both the Free State and Northern Transvaal were slammed.* Our province was riding the crest of a wave.

Previously it was the prevail of Western Province, where my father lived, and only a year and a half prior, half of the team members of the six-man Springbok team for the 1969 test match against Australia came from there. Meanwhile, I was tasting a first purple patch with newspaper headlines abounding, *Thornhill in electric finish, junior rider topples aces*, and *Cyclist nearly achieved new record* referring to my win in the 20 kilometres in an impressive time of 26 minutes and 11.5 seconds, a few seconds outside the South African record.

We were not quite halfway through the '70/71 track season and our young cadre of juniors gave Peet all the fodder he needed for his fertile imagination, igniting his Afrikaans readership further, *Cyclists surprises abound*. His theme: our prowess. Now we surprisingly dominated the *A class* league table, and in the latest reshuffle Alan, who was leading, was overtaken by Albert and me with top seniors like Jack and Guy left trailing behind. Of course, journalism is journalism, and the league was ongoing. Rory, still in the juvenile division, was improving in leaps and bounds with prominent placings. Overall, our *Kensington gang's* performance was extraordinary – it may have been a combination of the influence of our hero Tommy, of Olympic fame, and our self-belief as we created our universe.

Finally, the December Johannesburg Grand Prix marked the halfway point. The top sprinters were all there with Guy victorious. Basil, our formidable commentator, was quoted in the press, *if we ever get back into international competition, we have a world champion in Ferriman.*

Meanwhile, having been involved in a nasty accident earlier, I looked on in awe from the sideline, pondering – *might I ever improve sufficiently to become a classy sprinter, even though I lacked a typical sprinter's physique?*

Peet continued to stir the pot of intrigue: *four riders change to other clubs.* The tastier snippet was a conspiracy theory about Chris Harvey's defection to join Northern Wheelers, my former club. Chris's official line was, *the lack of team spirit where each rider had to look after themselves*, while Peet speculated that it was Jack's unsporting withdrawal from the Southern Transvaal team upon Chris's appointment as captain, that did it.

Sometimes, these events take on greater significance. It was like that for me that December as I had to report for military training in early January. The consequences seemed dire. I would not see my father for our annual vacation, nor the following February during an upcoming interprovincial against Western Province. Neither would I be able to defend my league position or my previous year's win in the BSA 40 kilometre (British South Africa – Tommy had in his youth set a world record in that race), nor participate in record breaking invitation meetings.

And what to expect of the Military? It seemed catastrophic, yet in the overall scheme of life, a trifle.

SECOND YEAR

Dutifully, I started my military training at the Danie Theron *Krygskool* (Combat School) in Kimberley in January 1971. Military's initial primary object, we soon realised, was to break our spirit, eliminate all thought and ensure the automatic obeying of orders, unquestioningly and unflinchingly.

Being a fulltime student, I was assigned to the Commandos, not quite as fancy as the name sounds but rather an internal security home guard unit. Conscription was normally for nine months of which three were for basic training – our programme consisted of a concentrated four weeks, followed by a three-week officers' training course later in that year. The purported privileged programme had its sting: a commitment to an annual four-week camp for the next fourteen years.

Meanwhile, we had to endure the bombardment of morale-sapping humiliating insults lavished enthusiastically by those burly permanent force corporals and sergeants. Random surprise inspections in the middle of the night disrupted our sleep as they barked their invectives, delivered like rapid machine gun fire, *Julle fokken betogers, julle moffies, ons gaan julle op vok* (You fucking protestors, you homosexuals, we will fuck you up) – designed to crush our spirit.

Perhaps they felt vindicated; a punishment for our regular liberal university student protests against various political injustices. The predominantly Afrikaans Nationalist Party, who had dominated politics in the absolute for over twenty-three years, were the perpetrators. Liberal whites were tolerated, but the greater perceived threat was *die swart gevaar,* the black danger.

The predominant country politics could not be clearer than two universities standing on opposite sides of Jan Smuts Avenue, the main road that dissected these universities. Our placards denounced contentious political matters. Wits was mostly English and the voice of the opposition, while Rand Afrikaans University (now the University of Johannesburg) was mainly Afrikaans and the voice of the regime.

The Military's need to be obeyed was in such sharp conflict with our university ethos and its fundamental prerequisite *to challenge and question everything*. I struggled with the continual abusive harassment, the Military's necessary evil. Fortunately, my weapon, a simple letter from the Southern Transvaal Provincial Cycling Union requesting permission to allow me to train for the upcoming Interprovincial Championships, and coupled with the Afrikaner's passion for sport, did the trick. A daily military pass permitted my absence from the camp from 5 p.m. until 7 p.m., except for the first week – it was my saviour and ensured my spirit survived.

Exhausted by the end of a military day, training was the furthest thing from my mind – but, it became my safety valve to mental freedom, pedalling the fifteen kilometres to a cyclist's home. There, the Military's proverbial three S's were indulged: shit, shave and shampoo, and under the circumstances, an unbridled luxury.

Completing basic training and toughening up was a big step in becoming a man, and indeed I felt different.

~

A week later, I returned to commence my second year at university. Now, it was back to the abundance of choice – float-building, social and sporting club outings or lazing about the student canteen, all within the wrappings of intellectual freedom.

I excelled in company law and thoroughly enjoyed the continuation of legal lectures. It was as if an understanding of the law and its ramifications gave me an edifice of confidence in knowing my rights. Accountancy, by comparison, was dull and methodical; the maxim, *whatever you do to the one side you do to the other,* was applied. At first, I never understood why anyone would go through such a rigmarole to record a snapshot of profits and losses, or the accretion of wealth. The mystery of *an interested party's reliance on the signed audited financial statements* would become apparent upon studying further for my Chartered Accountancy.

The theory of Business Administration and Economics seemed simple enough. Economic cycles, business failures, recessions, product obsolescence – but again, I never fully comprehended it until experienced first-hand some eight years later. In a similar vein, the economic maxim seemed inconceivable – *demand and supply will always find its equilibrium in the best interest of an economy, except for political manipulation to win votes.* I still had a lot to learn about politicians and human nature.

Meanwhile, fellow students suggested the use of a secluded soundproof language room, void of any natural light, as an excellent way to facilitate study; the learning process and the retention of information supposedly substantially enhanced. An hour was extremely exhausting. My body objected to the artificial neon lighting, which only seemed to induce headaches. I tried a few times, but it was not for me, except for the discovery of the *sound of silence* – absolutely enthralling. I never thought much more about it, other than an awareness that silence under the right circumstance, like when meditating, was audible.

This illusion was shattered way into my adult life – it was tinnitus all along. Disappointment abounded, not because of the affliction, for I was quite adept at filtering out the swishing noises, but rather my sense of loss. The *ability to hear silence* was no longer special.

~

The legal driving age was eighteen – I was impatient. Shirley, my mom's friend, encouraged me and became my instructor, not that her white Mercedes-Benz enjoyed shuddering all over the neighbourhood, while I tried to figure the clutch and accelerator bit. Time alone with her was sheer bliss – treated like a young adult, and slightly infatuated; perhaps she knew.

A week after my birthday, I took my test in neighbouring Bedfordview where it was said to be easier than in Johannesburg. Awkwardly, I pointed to the Mercedes in response to the inspector's enquiry and quizzical look – *spoilt brat*.

"It's not mine, it's my mother's friend's car," I hastily blurted.

"Pull out and park in the same spot," said disinterestedly.

It was unexpected, I was nervous and knew I had to get it right the first time. I remained attentive to the speed limit, indicated appropriately and clutching the steering wheel, anticipated his earlier instruction: *when I thump the dashboard, you must perform an emergency stop as if a child has run in front of the car* – I braked exceptionally hard. We walked back to his office in silence.

Seated, he officiously declared, "You've passed, well done."

Scarcely believable, but there should be a health warning – know your limitations – my *fire energy* was rampant and a sense of invincibility pervaded.

The next time Shirley visited, I nonchalantly asked whether I may take her car for a quick spin. Upon turning the ignition, something else happened – my original thought evaporated as the engine sprang to life with the nose of the Mercedes scenting the freedom of our training route to the airport.

In no time at all we were on the highway – the accelerator floored, and the speedometer ever rising. I had scant knowledge of the evasive action needed in a real emergency. Eight minutes later – destination. A quick U-turn and back, equally recklessly. Fortunately, only the smell and sound of a creaking engine, desperately trying to cool, bore witness. The car recovered its resting heartbeat as did I, notwithstanding feeling foolish and unsure as to whether I had caused any damage. Appropriately, this breach of trust embarrassed me.

A licence in hand, but no prospect to use George's Citroën, his treasure. It was strictly out of bounds, and judging by my initial recklessness – not that he knew – was entirely justified.

~

Upon returning from my military training, I was amazed that I had not lost more form and was quickly able to place well in the league meetings again. Meanwhile, our club had been voted the most improved club in Southern

Transvaal and our province remained dominant in the interprovincial. There was mischief afoot to oust the old guard, Mr Cyril Geoghegan, President of South African Cycling Federation. Although voted in for the twelfth consecutive year, it became his last. Andre van der Zwan, an excellent investigative journalist, headlined, *Cycling split imminent as Coup fails*, talking about a *Rebel League* being formed under the auspices of Jimmy Swift, then chairman of Southern Transvaal, who insisted on a unanimous vote by the province's clubs to endorse this move.

It never happened, but it did send an unequivocal message. Adding further fuel to the fire, Jimmy was quoted: *I realise that the sport is greater than the individual, but there are so many personality clashes that I'm sick and tired of being associated with it. The anti-Southern Transvaal feeling is hampering progress. Whatever we do is criticised yet we are financially better off than the Federation and draw much bigger crowds than any other province* – the next year Jimmy became President.

Andre, with the support of the riders, left no quarter unturned and attacked Geoghan's Federation using a new ruling which *limited the number of riders per race*. Speculating further on what was now needed to keep cycling stimulating for the spectators, he suggested more use of floodlight meetings for top riders only, shorter league meetings and not trying to please all cyclists – it smacked of the *Rebel League*. With a hint of mischievousness, he continued, *there is no doubt that the seniors and top-class juniors like Walter Thornhill and Alan van Heerden attract spectators and the sooner this is realised, the better it will be for cycling in this province*. The latter was a complete non sequitur, but amusing. I had a shrewd idea of what was needed, but no further interest in the politics – there was enough on my plate between cycling, university studies and home life.

It was my last junior championship year. A win in the 400 metre Provincial Championship and a second for our club team in the 4000 metre team pursuit was mine. The pressure of expectation that we would win this event at the South African Championships in Kimberley, simply jinxed us. Instead, both senior and junior teams placed second, but remarkably our time was a mere five seconds slower than the seniors, which was a great accolade and a consolation for our defeat.

The Championship surprise was Joe, *the bullet*, racing on his home turf. He won the sprint and the 1500 metre, while Mike Francis, the burly up and coming Natal rider, placed second and Guy, who was expected to win, third. Overall, we won seven gold medals with the Juniors faring better. The 10 kilometre was mine, while setting a Griqualand record in one of the 1500 metre heats, a mere 1.6 seconds outside the South African record. Rory, from our gang, had his first taste of a silver championship medal in the juveniles.

This only added to our overall elation, and my performance was sufficient to be invited to the Open South African Festival Games in Cape Town three weeks later, all expenses paid. Unexpected, and the real pleasure was the prospect of seeing my father again.

After the Festival Games, Mike Francis, three years my senior, and I somehow ended up in a seedy sailor's bar in the dock area. It was rough; empty cheap glasses were meaninglessly smashed on the floor. Feeling threatened and distinctly uncomfortable, but for unfazed six-foot-three muscular Mike, who sussed the scene and challenged arm-wrestling sailors, effortlessly downing one after the other. Finally, I relaxed upon overhearing a sailor's retort, *they're tough, better not mess with them* – of course referring to Mike, as I trailed nervously in his shadow, relieved.

The evening continued into the early hours. Even the revealing curvaceous Salvation Army female volunteer failed to lure Mike to their soup kitchen, as he was only interested in what he saw.

~

I wish I could say things had settled down at home, but they never did. There were always incidents of one sort or another. One evening, my closed bedroom door could not withstand my mother's frustrated madness in her alcoholic state as she lambasted George with a sexual cocktail of his inadequacies. It culminated in, "Well then, I'm not sleeping in your bed tonight, I'm going to sleep with Walter. He can probably do better than you."

Promptly, my door was opened and closed, and in the dark without a word, she climbed into my single bed against the wall with her back towards me. I instinctively placed my arm around and over her shoulder as if to protect her. And here we found ourselves together in this dark confined space.

What confusion reigned – a feeling of heavy sadness tinged with eroticism. My overwhelming thought, repeated like on a scratched record, *perhaps, if I satisfy her now, then maybe all this family stuff will just go away.* I had never had intercourse.

After a while, Desiree extricated herself from my bed, again without a word, going back to their bedroom. Nothing physically had happened.

In men's gatherings in the '90s, I heard stories of forced incestuous relationships between parent and child, the reasons numerous – a form of punishment often prevalent. In my situation, my story line was different: *nothing had happened, so it could not possibly be a form of sexual abuse.* Or could it?

My poor mother, what was going through her tormented mind that evening? Was she seeking the solace of touch in the same way as my earliest recollection of kindergarten boarding school when I climbed into the bed of other little girls? I will never know, and perhaps she is correct, *let sleeping dogs lie*!

Of course, that was the tip of the iceberg – Desiree was desperately crying for help. I tried in my way, suggesting that she might want to talk to our family doctor, which met with her explosive reaction. Understandable now concerning her circumstances, but not then.

It begs the question of churning memories – whose reality, perception, or truth? Buddhists believe in *mindfulness* and that *our unhelpful thoughts* cause unhappiness. The magnitude of this and its veracity has since become most enlightening.

~

Six months later, after my first military training and being a more robust seventeen-year-old, I was once again on a train back to the Combat School. This time to do an officer's course over an intense three weeks. Now we were treated as gentlemen and future leaders.

We attended fascinating lectures about military tactics, manoeuvres, the latest equipment, and the psychological and mental discipline necessary for warfare. It was like chess; however, strategies were reliant on *intelligence* received. Always prevalent was the universal acceptance of orders, and this ostensible power over other men, merely because of rank was not for me – a more intuitive way of relating was preferred.

Trapped by the system, I went along with it as best I could, while struggling with the thought: *to defend my country but not believe in its ideology was insane.* There were still fourteen years of annual camps, and the guerrilla activity by Swapo (South West Africa People's Organisation) in Okavango, Namibia was intensifying in skirmishes along the border. I took a silent vow, *never to fight in a border conflict and if called upon I would leave South Africa.* How and with what means I was unsure and in a strange way my resolve remained untested.

After my fifth military year, the legislation changed and our intake was not required to do any further training – a blessing in disguise. In all those camps, my sporting privileges allowed a psychological freedom as I cycled away each evening leaving the military confinement behind. If it were not for that, I might not have mentally survived.

There were lighter moments in mistakenly calling a rifle a gun. Our disciplining was to bellow a mantra, while continually having to point our index finger alternately at the rifle and then to our private parts. *This is my rifle, this is my gun, this is for shooting and this is for fun*! The non-commissioned officers' amusement petered out only when they became bored. Yet our slip of the tongue was well remembered; invaluable and imperative for clear and incisive military instruction.

So was the learning to set up an all-round-defence, used to secure an area, like a home, to protect or invade, all done while quietly jumping off a slow-moving Bedford truck. My left knee disliked the full impact, particularly carrying the full weight of combat gear. To be an infantryman was a mug's game: it required exceptional fitness, a durable body that was subjected to enormous wear and tear, and to what end, if not at one with the country's politics.

However, some thirty years later, 28th June 2001, I was most grateful when the Bolivian army arrived in the nick of time, and immediately deployed our practised manoeuvre. My relief was palpable, and the sound of a bullet entering the chamber as they cocked their weapons was a welcome comfort. It happened during a snow storm and a disturbing night of journeying by local bus from the border town of Desaguadero to La Paz.

The angry peasant villagers were protesting – emotions escalated at one of their numerous impeding road blocks. Rocks were hurled as they set upon us. The windows shattered – we were frightened. Slowly, the driver reversed to their menacing chants.

Making matters worse, we had to change a punctured wheel that was almost the size of the Bolivians, who struggled in the cold and snow. It was a Mexican standoff – our situation precarious and tense, and the protestors a mere hundred metres away.

Having survived the ordeal, the next day's newspaper headlines said it all: *Sticks and Stones, Tomorrow Bullets.* One of our group exclaimed, "Ah, what it is to find *Inner Peace*" – I smiled, La Paz.

Back in Kimberley, we continued with the field exercises that reinforced aspects of survival, cleverly designed to challenge conventional thinking – one involved a night manoeuvre and a map reading exercise, where assumptions not clarified and validated would probably result in failure. The goal was to reach a rendezvous point before midnight. If successful, a bed back at base camp was the reward, otherwise a cold winter's night in the veld with temperatures frequently below freezing.

Surprisingly, we were allowed unfettered discretion as to the kit we wished to carry to survive the night should we not complete our mission – that should have been the obvious clue. I was glad to have erred taking my sleeping bag and a groundsheet because when the flare was fired, we were a long way off from our destination. We ran, but soon our crestfallen faces heard the disappointing drone of the Bedford engines fading into the distance. We lit a fire and made ourselves as comfortable as we could, climbing into our sleeping bags, pondering how we could have failed such a simple task – the following day, the debrief revealed the folly of our way.

Various patrol groups of eight to ten men were dropped thirty to forty metres apart along a sand road. The light was failing fast. Naturally, we assumed the distant windmill was our first landmark and speedily set off in search of our next bearing. The terrain took on distorted shapes and our perception altered. Nothing made sense any more. Contour lines, dams, rivers and trigonometric beacons on our maps bore no resemblance to our habitat – we were disorientated and lost.

We started guessing, made more incorrect assumptions and human dynamics being what they are, the more dominant forced their *wrong thinking* – we were not alone in our misfortunes.

The troops that made it home first orientated their physical location, realising that the first windmill was a decoy; the correct one a mere two hundred metres further along the road. Such an invaluable lesson much to our chagrin.

Next, we set up an enormous temporary operational field camp for all our troops – I could only but marvel at the insight and organization needed. Second Lieutenant Marshall oversaw these field exercises, a Sandhurst type English South African, impeccably well-spoken, bilingual, in an Afrikaans dominated military. He was charismatic, incisive and conducted himself with aplomb – probably in his mid-twenties, and he appeared worldly.

It was somewhat easier to relate to him. His authority was unquestioned and gained by respect rather than his rank, a hallmark of an extraordinary leader. It seemed incongruous that such a talented man would wish to dedicate his life to the Military.

Unexpectedly, on the second day, he appeared on the horizon that timeless image of horse and rider. Suddenly, it dawned on me – the military was his play arena – vast resources at his ordering, a vocation and a chance to complete his legal studies.

An empathy turned out to be more of a hindrance for he appointed me to lead an infantry field exercise one evening. The warm and soporific afternoon rays had had their effect – I could hardly recall the field lecture given. Fortunately, the attentiveness of my fellow candidate officers saved the day, and good teamwork pulled us through.

Another evening, a few patrols were joined forming a company of approximately thirty men – our objective was to set up an ambush on the far side of a shallow stream. *Intelligence reports* suggested that the route through the bush would be safe and that the enemy would be crossing in the early hours of the morning. It was imperative to be in situ, undetected, with the trip flares set.

We approached stealthily, the three kilometres to the ambush point. Only predetermined visible hand signs were used, like a clenched fist held at shoulder level signalling the enemy. Once in position, brief radio contact was allowed; then absolute silence.

It was physically tiring, traversing the uneven terrain by the faint light of the moon. After a while, we settled into a rhythm interrupted only by other hand signals, man to man. This non-verbal communication forced other senses to be more alert as we listened to nature's nightlife sounds, or the lack thereof, as an early indicator of an unusual presence. Surely, the intense crunching of our boots over loose stones had to be a giveaway?

My imagination ran amok: *life and death situation with a real enemy out there.* Adrenaline surged as I met the fear within, eased only by the comfort of the comradeship of a group of men thrust together by a common task of survival. But fatigue set in – my mind drifted away and my concentration lapsed. Half-awake in the early hours of the morning I realised I was mechanically following the soldier in front of me and no longer attentive to the clues of nature, nor seeing the terrain any more. I shook myself out of this stupor and realised how easy it was to drop one's guard, lulled into a false sense of security and vulnerable to enemy attack.

Finally, we arrived at the demarcated stream and crossed it, setting up a trip-flare in the water a few feet from the edge of the river bank. We lay on our stomachs taking up our positions approximately four metres apart, facing the river and the direction of the supposed enemy. In our silence, the sounds of the night enveloped us. Intertwined were a myriad of thoughts and the thumping of my heart, interrupted only by a different noise – something was moving in the water. My eyes strained in the darkness. Suddenly, the flare was mysteriously knocked tilting it without detonation – the grey shape turned in sheer fright, dashed right past me at lightning speed and disappeared into the undergrowth.

This surprise and fright triggered a spontaneous nervous reaction, and I shouted an obscenity accompanied by a similar response from either side of me. Our cacophony shattered the night. I was shaking like a leaf. Fortunately, not visible to the others. Our absolute silence now ruptured by anxious whisperings; *what was that . . . did you see it . . . where did it come from*? A farming lad responded calmly; *dit was 'n otter* (it was an otter). An otter; the suburban boy in me neither knew about nor had ever been exposed to this riverine creature. Excitement pulsated throughout my body. My wilderness within, ignited!

Sure enough, we had to repeat the exercise – no recriminations and no witch-hunt. Perhaps, our fatigue was recognised. It was not my night. Upon retracing our steps, in one of those concentration lapses, I slipped and fell into a donga – a reflexive yelp pierced the air of the early morning. Sensibility prevailed, the exercise completed without any further mention of this ineptitude, but I could not help but feel that if we had to do it another time, I would certainly have encountered the wrath of the men.

I realised then that warfare was not a simple game: second nature reflexes needed to be checked, to become almost robotic, void of fear and feelings, to survive – a tall task for any seventeen-year-old.

The last five days of the three weeks were spent fending for ourselves in discrete patrols. Clad in our webbing, we carried our field combat gear and an outdated 303 rifle. The outer plastic sheath of our water bottle usefully doubled as a utensil to eat or drink from.

We completed daily tasks and night missions. Each morning, we had to be at predetermined rendezvous points at 7 a.m. – *a fifteen-minute enemy safe window.* Here we obtained our daily rations and further instructions. Window missed – no provisions for the day, and only our emergency rations of *dog-biscuits* to survive on.

Contact with the other groups was sparse. In the main the tasks were not onerous and once completed, we turned our attention to other forms of enjoyment. It was the middle of winter, overnight temperatures often below zero; night fires were forbidden lest the *enemy*, the observing officers, spotted us in this arid, vast scrubland.

Our first night in the open was void of any visible sheltering spots, other than naturally occurring dongas, six to eight feet deep. Two Afrikaans lads effortlessly adopted a leadership role and using their knowledge of bushcraft, which had me in awe, said, "We will camp and sleep down there, that way we are more sheltered and can light an undetectable fire – it will help keep us warm." They were my champions – disobeying orders and ensuring our survival.

Their next orders were issued in unison, "Place three groundsheets next to each other, slightly overlapping – we will all sleep next to each other, adding body heat and cover ourselves with the remaining groundsheets. It will keep the dew and early morning frost off our sleeping bags."

It took me by surprise. Were we not supposed to be tough military men? Now only a sleeping bag prevented bodily contact – my naivety at its best.

Last ablutions and into our sleeping bags. On the end, I noticed that some of the lads climbed in boots and all. I recalled my mother's voice, *it's important to let your toes breathe at night,* so I promptly took off my boots and socks and laid them beside me. Morning came and indeed there was frost and ice on top of the ground sheets. Needing to make haste for our rendezvous point, I hurriedly put on my cold socks and frozen boots. I felt a slight tingling sensation as the warmth of my feet met the frosty reception. We collected our supplies, continued with our day's activities, while at night I still heard my mother's voice.

The third day was one of those wallowing days; not much to do with time on our hands. The natural inventiveness of our two leaders once again came to the fore – enticed by the idea of a barbecued chicken for lunch, they set about acquiring one from the rural locals. They haggled – we handed over our pooled money, and trusted that the locals would reappear with our treat.

There was much excitement about our upcoming feast. The farm boys assured us, "Don't worry, we know how to kill and pluck. We do it all the time." I was curious to watch the preparation, having only ever witnessed the slaughter of a lamb on my uncle's farm in the Karoo.

The handing over of the chicken was almost ceremonious – the Afrikaans lads receiving the Victor Ludorum, while we bathed in the success of their mission. Away collecting firewood, I missed the slaughter and the removal of the entrails, but saw the evidence of the plucked feathers laying all around. Ingeniously, they had already erected the spit. Two Y-shaped pieces of wood were placed into the ground – the chicken skewered and resting across the uprights.

This was better than my Boy Scout days. Survival, coupled with freedom – we never shot for the pot but did the next best thing. Our joy and solidarity was tangible. The delicious juices dripped, igniting the embers below. Our meal cooked slowly, the aromas tantalising. My taste buds were salivating, activating that part of the brain flashing, *ravenous*! Finally, the ritual chef's announcement, "*Nou's dit reg*! (It's ready now!)".

My teeth, instead of sinking into the scrumptious flesh, rebounded as if they had hit a rubber mallet and, attempting to dispel my disbelief, I tried again – same result. Tough as old boots and incapable of being penetrated. I was perplexed, *was the chicken not cooked before our eyes, its aromatic smells confirming it was edible*? Then, a disappointed voice, "*Hulle het ons gevang, dit is 'n ou haan* (they caught us, it is an old rooster)." Determined, I managed to strip away thin strands of flesh with my incisors, but simply could not masticate it. My euphoria sank at the thought of bully beef and *dog-biscuits* again, particularly after our expectations had been spiced with such excitement.

There were other mutters like *daardie bliksems, as ons hulle vang, gaan ons hulle doodmaak* (those cheats, if we catch them, we will kill them), but like many things in life, events overtake themselves, and the incident was soon forgotten. No doubt, the locals chuckled at our expense and deservedly so – for is it not said, *may the buyer beware*?

The next morning disaster struck – my feet were itchy and painful, covered in red welts and swollen. At the early morning meeting point, I casually mentioned my difficulty, and to my surprise was instructed to return with the invigilators to the combat school for a medical examination. I climbed into the back of their jeep, feeling as if I was letting our patrol down. We sped off; my mood changed, now carefree as if the early morning breeze, blowing refreshingly against my face, signalled another freedom – a break from the field exercises.

The doctor took one look, "Chilblains, you won't be going back. You will need to rest in the infirmary for a few days. The rapid change in temperature between your warm feet and the frozen boots would have caused it." While recuperating, I pondered whether I would be penalised for not completing the field tasks or might it be thought I had engineered it – troops do weird things.

There was no need to worry. Instead, I enjoyed the hospital's five-star luxury: clean sheets, cooked meals, regular tea or coffee – almost on demand. This was another side of the Army that I was unaware of. Care and recuperation in a supportive environment. My horizons were again broadened, and I had grown enormously.

We graduated and became candidate-officers, still needing to complete the obligatory security and health check before becoming commissioned officers. In the interim, we wore strips of white material, colloquially referred to as toilet-paper, on our epaulettes. It carried the weight and respect afforded to an officer, and soon, in my newfound role, I was continually returning salutes received from the men.

However, the return train trip home was to prove a bit of a dichotomy. A fellow soldier stole a military radio transmitter, still in its original webbing. I was amazed at his audacity and almost speechless.

"What are you going to do with it?"

"*Ek weet nie* (I don't know), but I will be able to tune into all sorts of things."

I never gave it another thought other than *senseless at best*. Six weeks later, there was a knock on my door. Two military police stood on the porch – my heart raced as the large emblazed MP letters adorning their arms, seemingly admonished, *you are guilty*! They explained that other troops had reported seeing the radio transmitter and that the thief was probably in my compartment.

Rampant thoughts flooded my mind, sealed by the fate of a train journey – *guilty as an accomplice*, *perpetrator takes revenge* or do I admit it and hope to be treated as an innocent bystander.

Pensively I frowned, as if trying to recall the journey. Then, a considered shake of the head, "No, sorry, I can't help you any further."

The MPs thanked me and departed, but I felt uncomfortable with my deceit. Fortunately, there were no further repercussions, but it did force me to question apparent truths, and wonder how many others have behaved similarly.

~

I missed the '71 road national championships due to the coinciding officers' training camp, but the real highlight that year was riding in the third Fagor Grand Prix in Mozambique. The anecdotal stories have been shared, except for my overall classification – I was in fifth place after my notable longest day stage success into João Belo. My abscess the following day was my nemesis, yet surprisingly I lost only a few more places; finishing ninth overall. Incidentally, it was the same position as the previous year's Somorel Tour and, under the circumstances, a monumental victory.

We were starved of any news of the outside cycling world, other than our Mozambique exposure and hearsay from fellow cyclists who had travelled and raced abroad. Cycling magazines and the press were useful adjuncts. The rebirth of local cycling cajoled enthusiastic journalist Peet van Staden into writing a full-page article on the 1971 Tour de France winner. He was compared to sporting greats of the time: Don Bradman the Australian cricketer, Margaret Court the Australian tennis player, Jack Nicklaus the American golfer, and Pele the Brazilian football player. Eddy Merckx was voted world sportsman of the year – his list of victories, endless. Only two other cyclists had previously won the Tour in three successive years, Louison Bobet and Jacques Anquetil – that year it was Eddy's turn.

While out training, with each stroke pedalled, my imagination soared – I was infused with his strength. Sadly, reality reigned as my fatigue kicked in, but it was a great dream.

~

Military, cycling and now a welcome change, the university skiing club's weekend jaunt to the Lesotho Mountains; my first-time skiing.

Not knowing that Lesotho was an independent country of two million people, landlocked by South Africa, nor that the Basuto were such friendly people, forced me to question the complexity of South Africa's politics. Meanwhile we enjoyed the beautiful pristine landscapes and the crisp Drakensberg air, travelling frivolously in a Volkswagen Combi.

This, the only ski slope in Southern Africa limited by any standards, was over before it had even started. The newness of it all, the tumbles, impromptu snowball fights – all thrilling, but the use of different muscles and skills had an adverse effect. By evening time, my aching muscles howled and my jeans – not the most suitable attire – were soaking wet.

That never detracted from the après-ski, enhanced by the light-headedness at such a high altitude. The companionship around the log fire, and the delicious warming broth and student sangria soon revived the last remnants of aching cold muscles and bones – contentedly, I fell asleep.

A one off – a long way to travel and by student standards an expensive weekend.

~

The anchor to my existence was, of course, my commitment and dedication to cycling. Many cyclists drew strength from the support of the crowd, and I was no different – it was customary when winning a race to throw both hands up in a victory salute and, while slowing down circling the track, to acknowledge their applause with a gentle wave. The odd rider paid scant regard, to their detriment; crowds had their favourites and were equally fickle: a boo today and an applause tomorrow – once, I was booed, and it was justified.

Sensational cycling spin articles written with journalistic licence, soon brought the sceptic out in me. Things are not always what they appear to be, and I was soon questioning my reality and my perception of truth, but again.

A new track season, a new beginning – barely a year into the era of club sponsorships, Rory, Albert and I decided to return to our former club, a difficult decision. We swapped our 3-in-1 Oil logo for Simba Chips' golden lion on a distinctive green background, displayed on the newly designed yellow cycling jersey – it stood out, and we cherished wearing them.

Once again, we were back in the saddle with our buddies, Raymond Hogg and Willie Dawson; no longer as club adversaries. We soon had an opportunity to perform in the Italian team pursuit, a new challenging event, specifically introduced for interprovincial meetings – a great crowd pleaser. It was similar to a team pursuit already described, apart from two notable differences – faster, with riders peeling off in succession. The front rider does one lap, the second rider takes over and so on until the pack of four diminishes to the last rider.

Our pecking order that day: the two juniors first, Willie then me, followed by our seniors, Raymond and Guy. Willie's role was paramount: he had to accelerate rapidly but in a controlled fashion, bringing the group to the maximum sustainable racing speed, while taking the full brunt of the atmosphere creating the desired slipstream as we settled into the testing pace of the race. A peripheral glimpse enabled us to judge our progress against the opposition. We coordinated well with an added reward of an exciting newspaper photograph of the four of us in full flight, proudly wearing our sponsor's jersey, on our way to victory. It was a good meeting with a further win in the junior 10 kilometre and a third place to Jack in the open 10 kilometre.

Our province continued to do well, using the depth of talent on hand to hold mock interprovincial floodlight meetings. Two evenly balanced teams, the Blues, captained by Jack, raced the Greens, captained by Guy – it did a lot to sharpen our abilities and further raise our standard of performance.

The first half of this new track season finished with the usual jostling in league positions, the odd spill and the continued press speculation on *who beat, or should have beaten whom*. There was a glimpse of the new *dark horse*, me, referring to the upcoming premier Johannesburg Grand Prix sprint – it was an exciting time for spectators and cyclists alike and life outside of my home was full.

My annual visit to my Dad resumed, coinciding with another opportunity to participate in the Cape cycle meetings. Things did not go my way – two placings only and worse was to follow – a crash with ten other riders during the famous 25 mile Paarl Boxing Day event. Notwithstanding, and despite the emotional turmoil with my father, I always enjoyed the opportunity to be with him – to have and hold on to a father image still remained one of my deepest needs.

FINAL YEAR

In my final year I only had three subjects, rather than the customary five, and plenty of free time between lectures. Of course, this was sheer bliss as the spare time would give me the opportunity to train like a professional while completing my degree. I lived for cycling – it was my family, my anchor, my way of life and allowed me to be part of a community.

Jack suggested that I should consider helping him, part-time, in his carpet business: *Jack Lester Carpeting – the wall to wall carpet and flooring specialists*! Jack, in his shrewd and inimitable way, quickly sketched out my path to riches, making it sound all too easy. His almost Calvinistic fervour advised: *achieve your studies, train for cycling and deploy your spare time wisely in successfully selling carpets with me.* A most appealing proposition for an impoverished student, and to crown it all an instant catapulting into the league of *fancy wheels*. The bait was taken.

The use of his beautiful red dart-shaped Flamingo, an enthusiast's fibreglass production sports car. It was years ahead of its time, designed and built by three Stellenbosch University students. Performance and road holding engineered to world-beating standards: a strutted Ford engine, seriously fast because of its power to weight ratio; compact inside, with just enough room behind the front seats for my dismantled cycle and our carpet swatches.

Confidently, Jack looked me in the eye, while handing me the large red Van Dyck sales manual, saying, "It's so easy, don't worry, I'll teach you – never talk about price, that's the last thing; it's all in there." My natural inclination was to go to the bottom line first, oblivious that there was a more orderly tried and tested way.

"Tomorrow we'll meet a customer at the Van Dyck's showroom – I'll show you how this business works." Jack has a good way with people. Masterfully, he wove his font of knowledge into his considered educational patter: the same carpet colour appeared different, depending on the strength and refraction of light, while extolling the virtues of an expensive Wilton or Axminster to that of a cheaper tufted. The image of a home was enhanced, and I understood why the price was the last consideration. Jack's air of confidence, dressed in his overalls and his black heavily framed spectacles, was more akin to a revolutionary leader than a carpet purveyor and fitter.

The suggested guidelines for our business involvement were relatively straightforward. I had to generate a minimum of four days' work a month, in return for the use of the car. Jack's neatly designed quotation template, a single foolscap page using carbon copy, captured these details – the practicality and exactness appealed, and seemed a natural extension of my accounting and business side of my studies. The magic was the last entry – my commission – and at my discretion; endless pots of money were surely mine? I was soon to learn otherwise.

Word of mouth worked best; cold canvassing my worst. A meaningful opportunity was afforded by a university lecturer, but my unrealistic add-on, my downfall. Despite my disappointment, the importance of the lesson was invaluable.

On another occasion, cycling past a house in its final stages of building in Bedfordview, I stopped, met and introduced myself to the owner, John de Gouveia, explaining my mission. He kindly allowed me to quote on the carpeting they had already chosen. Timing was of the essence, and I quickly steered the conversation away from price, engaging in interior design talk, as best I could – "Zara is a strong intricate pattern, very decorative. It will make your hallway entrance appear far too busy and will detract from the majestic proportions of your home. Perhaps if we used a plain carpet at the entrance, it would be more expansive, and then we could use the Zara that you like in the larger areas." I went on to point out that proper pattern and colour matching needed a carpet from the same loom – it struck a chord; the other salesman had not discussed any of these finer points.

Determined not to make the same *commission mistake*, I reviewed the quote with Jack – a fortune by my standards. John never questioned the price, and awarded us the contract – a whopping eight days' work and my first sale. I could not wait for completion, was inwardly elated and somewhat astounded by this success.

Had John recognised my spirit of endeavour? He was an immigrant from Mozambique and had to start over again. Or was it a familiarity touching on my racing experiences in the Somorel and Fagor Tours? We became friends, and a year later I was purchasing my provisions from his butcher shop in Bezvalley, at a *friend's price*, of course.

The highlight of my short carpeting career was the refurbishment of the Stewards' room; a classic green corded carpet. The opportunity was courtesy of a friend's father, the manager of the Turfontein racecourse, but there was one major challenge – the size. Jack, again with absolute confidence made light of it all. "It's easy, you lay the first bit, then create a new artificial starting point by tapping a wooden plank on top of the carpet. Slowly work your way forward, repeating the process." I was unsure he had ever done this before, but he delivered – sheer brilliance and a healthy commission as well.

~

Marlene, from the Cape, had moved to the Transvaal when she became an air hostess. Her boyfriend effectively leveraged his six foot plus height into a distinctive, effortless, smooth and stylish pedalling action that was quite unique, but his hallmark was as an audacious raconteur weaving stories with superb hyperbole.

I first met Marlene a few years earlier, at a Cape track event. There was an attraction – she exuded a charm, had a sparkle in her eyes and a natural deep warmth from within. My initial impression had not changed; now she was even more mysteriously captivating and exquisite.

The Flamingo loved dashing out to her home in Kempton Park, near the airport, along the familiar roads of our training rides. Initially, it was innocent, having frivolous fun and doing student things, like building floats and parading through the streets of Johannesburg shaking our charity collection boxes.

Marlene made it clear that she was still in a relationship, and like all lovers they tried, albeit long distance. She spent much time chatting from the ubiquitous public red telephone boxes of that time, while I waited patiently in my jealous Flamingo.

Her boastful boyfriend had proclaimed that *his Alfa Romeo was up for grabs to any suitor who could win Marlene's heart.* Jack and I were bemused by this and his many other incredulous tales.

Time moved on – I stayed over – a little kissing was permitted, but no more.

Years prior, before drifting off to sleep, I pondered how moments of passion might come about – would it be like in the movies with words of *I love you.* No, that did not seem appropriate, nor sincere – I was confused. It was George's wise counsel that came to the fore upon saying goodnight one evening. For some unknown reason, I voiced my concerns about whether I would ever find a girlfriend.

He smiled knowingly, "You will have many, and you really don't need to worry about it."

In the same way as a child takes comfort from the answer – *yes, of course* – to the perennial Father Christmas question – so did I, and contentedly fell asleep.

One morning, when I was about to leave Marlene's flat for university, we had one last passionate embrace. Clearly, the woman decides – she calmly sat down and started unlacing her long boots. I watched taken by surprise. Marlene's guidance led me to the taste of the forbidden fruit – my first encounter.

I was somewhat clueless and a bit disappointed. The hype did not do it justice. I drove off thinking that self-pleasuring was infinitely more enjoyable. The river naturally followed its course and resolved my conundrum the very next day with an immediate change to my perception.

The goddess of beauty and keeper of ancient knowledge allowed an exploration of the sheer carnal delights and pleasures of this newfound way. Nature's divine intoxicant knew how to ensure the survival of the species and my world had expanded powerfully.

Sadly, the clumsiness of my youth prevented me from telling Marlene that it was my first time. The allure remained and she continued to dazzle me with fleeting glimpses of her bountiful qualities, making me feel like the only man in her life – could this be true love?

Our relationship ran its course, and Marlene followed her first love – they lived together for a while, but ultimately parted.

Twenty-five years later, while checking in for a flight from Johannesburg to London, I noticed someone resembling Marlene – could it be? I discreetly enquired. The check-in lady confirmed her first name and that she worked in the departure courtesy lounge; only her surname was different – of course, married.

We hastily reminisced as though there were no intervening years – the brief reunion delightful. In her ground hostess role, she was responsible for important commercial and diplomatic passengers. That evening, I was her VIP guest and escorted all the way onto the aircraft. My departure sealed with a kiss before the passengers' prying eye. Meanwhile, I took my seat in amazement at this perchance meeting.

The London cab driver the next morning was the recipient of the tale. Years had passed, and as if righting a wrong, I decided to call to share my undisclosed secret – she could not have been kinder and with dignity, said, "I never noticed – what wonderful times we had together."

~

There was another side to my mother – her supposedly open-minded declarations about the sexual liberation of that time that distinguished our family from the myopic middle-class values of our neighbourhood. It was unconsciously designed to demonstrate her broadmindedness, and to depict what a marvellous parent she was. This was in stark contrast to how my sister and I experienced our mother.

Upon returning home from university one day, my winter jacket, splayed across my bed, greeted me – *Marlene's underwear was protruding from the pocket.* My mother had rifled through my clothes and in a deliberate act, exposed the *evidence.* I was appalled by her act and felt humiliated. My heart felt heavy. What might follow that evening was dependent on her barometer.

Initially, nothing was said – I remained hopeful. Alas, no – the power of the first sip unleashed Desiree's demons. It was like being bowled over by an uncontrollable mindless barrage, fuelled by her fury and other suppressed emotions. The words spewed from her mouth, "That Afrikaans slut of yours that you are obviously fucking . . . I don't want that bitch in my house any more."

On and on it went, until she had exhausted her store of warped and hurtful things to say. I felt sick, unnecessarily dirty and very disappointed. A mantle of great sadness came over me. Barely uttering, "I may be sleeping with her, but everything else you say isn't true."

It could have been handled so differently. Those countless speeches about her openness on sexual matters and tolerance thereof, that were meant to differentiate our family, were a hypocrisy that stunned me into disbelief.

Sadly, that evening became but another weapon of destruction in our family dynamics; again, George remained silent.

~

By contrast, the second half of the '71-72 track season (January to March), the year I turned nineteen, was rewarding. At the Southern Transvaal Championships, Albert and I tried our hand in the open tandem racing. We were an unlikely pair to win, but in the spirit of it all we had a go, and surprised ourselves with a bronze medal. Was this an omen? Third places continued – the 400 metre, 1000 metre sprint, 1000 metre time trial and the 20 kilometre. Seen differently, it was excellent for it was my first year competing as a senior.

The league season ended on a high note, winning the last race, the 10 kilometre. I was in excellent form and the forthcoming South African Track Championships in Port Elizabeth, only a week away. It became a moment of true glory, a culmination of all my endeavours thus far as I proudly stepped onto the podium, donning the coveted 1500 metre Championship silk jersey. I had beaten the incumbent, Joe Billet and surprised my mentor Jack, who placed third. Jack was the favourite and an experienced former winner.

Jack did go on to win the open sprint, the ultimate title of the fastest man on the track. Before he could even dismount, our elation was such that we rushed over and hoisted him, bicycle and all, victoriously parading him around.

Neither Jack nor I had the physique of natural sprinters, but it never deterred us from entering that event following his maxim, *you can achieve anything you set your sights on*. Rather our differentiating ability was the exceptional burst of speed we both had when accelerating out of the bunch. The illustrious sprinting names like Joe, the incumbent, and Mike, the runner-up, were both natural sprinters. It was a three up final – Jack's strategic thinking in allowing them to race each other, simply outwitted them. History was in the making – the rules were changed ensuring finals would only ever be a contest between two riders.

It took a while for the immenseness of my 1500 metre victory to sink in, especially since it was my first Senior championship racing against names that were previously my heroes. The hardest part was the qualifying heat and the semi-final. I only just made the cut due to the unexpected vagaries of the race where wild card tactics often prevail. The final, of seasoned riders of similar abilities testing their strengths and strategies against each other, is infinitely preferable. Yet, the ability to intuitively change any fixed ideas while the race unfolds is the key to mastery. In the legend years, it was Tommy, while in mine, Joe and Jack. Subsequently, other riders came to the fore.

My consistent performance in this event probably helped in being selected for the first official Springbok team, four years later, in defiance of the international sporting ban. The mixed international group of riders we competed against were subsequently suspended.

However, after the semi-final, I needed to escape the tension at the track, returning to my hotel room to gather my thoughts. I looked calmly at my reflection in the bathroom mirror and tried something that Jack had explained way back after a training session one lazy summer's evening, as the last of the stragglers lay on the grass verge, chewing the cud, before setting off for home.

In his inimitable way, he was holding court, reading and sharing secrets from that infamous purple-cloth-covered book, his Holy Grail, while twiddling a stem of grass between his teeth. That evening, he extolled the principles of self-hypnosis and how to use it to benefit our cycling. Acknowledged with a disinterested but tolerant nod, the other cyclists listened to the inane conversation between the two dubbed *intellectuals*, who were at it again.

I looked in the mirror, deciding to try his suggestion. Did I believe it, or my made-up powerful mantra, repeated over and over? Not really, but what did I have to lose. Clearly, I do not have a chameleon's vision but for some strange reason, calmly said, *you will anticipate any move behind you before it even happens – react and accelerate in perfect timing – you will be the fastest reaching the finish line with a clear margin*! That is how it unfolded – I am not sure who was more astonished – Jack the maestro, or me.

In his playful way, before alighting the podium, with the biggest grin imaginable, he held my hand in a vice-like grip. His sheer delight was my embarrassment – "Now there is only one thing left to do, go and ask Marlene's boyfriend for the keys!"

A slight lack of sensitivity, but reflective of Jack's wicked sense of humour. Not quite done as we stepped off the podium, he exclaimed, "If you don't, I will!"

Needless to say, the keys remained safe.

Did I mention that we travelled down in his *Jack Lester Carpeting* sign-painted Volkswagen Combi? It was quite a long journey and to relieve the maestro's tedium while driving, I did something that somehow annoyed him.

"Do that again and I will crack you" – I did. Whack – his left arm belted out in one solid fluid sideways swipe, hitting me firmly on the cheek. Shocked by my friend's reaction, the reverberation of the pain broke my smugness.

"I told you" – I became more attentive, but that was not the reason for my victory in the 1500 metre.

~

There was something very meaningful in possessing the silk championship jersey; its symbolism enhanced the actual title itself. I still have mine . . . two distinct pastel yellow and green horizontal stripes on a white background, now creamy and all faded with the passage of time. Its smooth texture remains soft to the touch and still fits like a glove.

It has always been a talisman of sorts, whenever worn – as if possessing a supernatural power underwritten by the lore, *only the champion could wear it*. Whenever I did, for some strange reason it was as if it bestowed invincibility.

My strong sentimental attachment has lessened over the years, although I must admit, that on the odd occasion while wearing it riding around Richmond Park in Surrey, powerful memories flood back as if it were yesterday.

It seems the lore crosses geographies. About ten years ago, cycling through the English countryside one Sunday morning with a motley peloton of former racing and other enthusiastic cyclists, an unsuspecting rider, wearing a World Championship jersey, latched onto our group. He was no champion: his riding style the giveaway, but he remained ebullient about his find when questioned about it.

My thoughts drifted . . . *who was the champion, what was the race and how did the jersey end up in a charity shop*? Suddenly, the harshness and cruelty of my disapproving fellow cyclists shattered my reverie. The unwitting cyclist bravely rode on for a while, but his humiliation and silent embarrassment was palpable.

Meanwhile, I marvelled at his good fortune in finding it and why should he not enjoy the imagined spirit of that former world champion? I never became a world champion, but if I had, I would have approved.

~

In July, twelve months after my last military training, I was back at Danie Theron *Krygskool* for the third time, to do a three-week weapons and patrol leadership course. Naturally, my trusted steed was with me. The same deception was deployed to obtain a military pass ostensibly for cycling training, but actually to aid my mental freedom.

This course was instructive, enjoyable and a further gateway into understanding how to become a more efficient and effective soldier. We became adept, and blindfolded could dismantle and put our weapons together again, whether an FN Browning automatic or an old-fashioned, trusted 303 rifle. Some soldiers thrived on the time spent and were meticulous in cleaning weapons, while I was more utilitarian. Not surprisingly, the defence instructors supposedly found *olifante*, 'elephants', while holding my barrel to the light for inspection; a chiding witty reference to microscopic pieces of dust – *you're not a gamekeeper*. Of course, I buckled down, dissipating the 'herd' as best I could, but there was always the odd stray.

Practical instruction followed, and although we never threw live hand grenades, we nevertheless extracted safety pins from dummies before throwing them at an imagined target. On the firing range, the recoil and kickback of the weapons, rather than being boyishly exciting as imagined in stereotype movies, was nerve-racking. Once mastered, there was a sense of exhilaration, tinged with the utmost respect for the weapon and the damage it could inflict.

We perfected our silent hand communications, set up various types of ambushes on different terrains, became aware of wind directions and smells, and learnt the art of camouflage.

The heat from the late mornings onwards made it difficult to stay awake in the stuffy lecture rooms in what were otherwise thought-provoking historical military tactic lectures. Sadly, any form of debate, so encouraged in a university environment, was lacking.

The respect shown for the Zulu King Shaka's military tactical ingenuity and its commanding place of honour within the military, seemed incongruous in apartheid South Africa. The *buffalo horns, impondo zenkomo*, as it was known, was an imagined U-shaped formation with only the chest, *isifuba*, visible at the start of the combat. The horns were invisible and only at the point of the *isifuba*'s engagement would the Zulus stand up and swiftly run and entrap the enemy by closing the horns.

The teachings of Warren Boden's history lessons about another facet of the Zulu military supremacy, flooded back.

> *Shaka's invention: a shorter style spear, a foot long with a broader blade mounted on a two-foot shaft, the iklwa, concealed behind a hand-held combative cowhide shield together with a knobkerrie. It replaced the previous long throwing assegai, and was named after the sound it made upon being withdrawn from the enemies wound.*

Then the famous battle of Blood River, where the Zulus under Dingaan, Shaka's successor, were severely defeated against all odds by the ingenuity of the laager protection. The strapping of ox wagons together, allowed the four hundred and sixty Voortrekkers, led by Andries Pretorius, to survive against the overwhelming odds of twenty to thirty thousand marauding Zulus.

The Boers were God fearing people and a week before this Battle, congregated under a clear sky singing psalms and celebrating the Sabbath, they took a vow: *if delivered from the might of the Zulus they would honour that day for posterity.*

So it happened, outnumbered more than sixty to one and delivered from the attack on Sunday 16 December 1838, it became the Day of the Covenant. This national holiday was colloquially known as Dingaan's Day. Now, in the new democratic South Africa, it is still celebrated, although appropriately renamed the Day of Reconciliation.

The advantage man has over another – superior technology. Initially, the Zulus' new strategy and short hand to hand combat spear made them almost invincible, then the Boers deployed their tactical laager defence and superior weaponry – rifles. School history and military tactical lessons combined, created an expansive vista for the ever-growing world that I was trying to fathom.

Sometimes strange plans are hatched – a trooper casually mentioned that immediately after the camp he was going on holiday, and that to hitch in military attire was incredibly easy. The idea to journey to Cape Town to surprise my father before returning to university seemed novel and doable, particularly as Kimberley was already a third of the way there.

There I stood with a cardboard sign, *Cape Town* – military kit, detached wheels and a frame – hitherto my passport to sanity, now my annoying excess baggage. Sporadic lifts, the doldrums . . . the late afternoon became the early evening before the next puff of wind arrived, disguised as an inebriated lonely soul, except I did not know that then.

"Hop in, I'm going all the way."

I quickly threw my paraphernalia onto the back of his open Chevrolet *bakkie*. We chitchatted to while away the eight hundred kilometres – conversation petered out. The mesmeric drone of the engine and the sound of the tyres on that monotonous straight endless road triumphed – he started to nod off again. This time the car drifted dangerously onto the oncoming traffic side of the road – my inane comment shook him out of his stupor as he jerked the steering wheel. Deftly, he removed a half-jack from the side panel of the door, took a slug and murmured, "This will definitely keep me awake!" He passed the bottle – I refused, knowing it was imperative to remain vigilant.

The tension, as an active passenger-driver, took me back to the countless episodes with my father, already mentioned, as well as to George with his thick-rimmed spectacles. I often wondered whether George had seen the red traffic lights. My only clue was the tone of the engine. I would yelp, "George, the lights!"

The *hitched ride* was turning into my worst nightmare. It was far removed from the delightful days with Aunty Ronnie, where I could just relax and be caught up in my reverie as a kid.

I must have dozed off – it was bound to happen – thud. I awoke as we screeched to a halt. In his *deliverance demeanour*, he excitedly exclaimed, "*Dit was 'n ystervark*! *Kom, ons gaan hom haal* (It was a porcupine! Come, let's go and get him). *Kyk hoe lui sy klokkie* (look at how his bell rings)." The reflexive tail quills quivered one last time – the life force extinguished. Perplexed and overcome I did not have a chance to ponder any further – "Pick him up, let's put him on the back of the *bakkie*," he instructed. I felt sad as I could not believe that this beautiful creature had been killed.

The damage to the front bumper was minimal. Back on the road again, now both wide awake and highly attentive. In his element, he took another swig from his half-jack, fuelling his loquaciousness, "This is the most delicious meat, *ek gaan dit voorberei* (I'll prepare it). Tomorrow morning we're going to have a *lekker braai* (nice barbeque). We will travel for a few more hours, then camp alongside the road."

This was no picnic. Was our next stop not meant to be Cape Town? Neither did I wish to participate in his drunken celebratory mood, particularly as I was dismayed by the death of the first porcupine I had ever seen. Apprehension set in; his manner scarier, reminiscent of the postman that beat his son after our school game of marbles. My mind raced, humouring his suggestions while asking questions around our supposed adventure and the preparation of the porcupine – his answers tedious.

When we stopped to refuel, I decided that this was my opportunity to escape. Casually I said, "You know I have been thinking, I simply must get to Cape Town before midday tomorrow to see my dad."

He exploded, "But nobody will come through at this hour and what about our *braai*." The logic of my argument was losing ground as the petrol attendant concurred with him.

Feeling fearful by the drunkard's forceful manner, I remained insistent, "I'll take my chances on the next lift, thank you." Unconvinced, he glared as if I were mad and ungrateful. My bicycle grabbed first, my most precious possession, for fear that he might speedily drive away, then my army kitbag.

Watching his tail lights fade into the distance, my tension abated. I was alive and away from an uncomfortable situation – the outcome less than certain. How quickly the cold biting air became absolutely refreshing and, as it happened, I was soon on my way directly to Cape Town.

Before leaving camp, an officer suggested that upon arrival I go to the military headquarters on the shorefront, located in the historical 17th Century Good Hope Castle, to request a reissue of my unused train ticket back to Johannesburg. Still in my military uniform, kit bag on my back, cycle in tow and unsure of this ploy, I enquired of a quizzical looking clerk, "Down from the Danie Theron *Krygskool* and need to get back to Johannesburg before ..."

He interrupted and handed me a stamped chit. "Go to the railway station to book your seat."

Flabbergasted and grateful – the military was suddenly not such a bad place after all.

I was glad to see my dad again, sharing military, cycling and university anecdotes, while purposefully making light of the hitchhiking trip. I had nonchalantly taken a step into the unknown – fortunately, there were no consequences, other than my awareness of circumstantial risks as life was adventurously embraced.

During the few days together we visited Norden's factory, his moment to proudly expand on his previous short letter, which also addressed his resurgence.

Have taken over "Nordens" and am now the sole Director of the company called Norden Industries (Pty) Ltd at the same address. Mr Norden is still connected with the company.

Bought all the assets of Norden Cookers myself and will resell at a price to the new company. It has taken me a long time to arrive again after the "Air Excursion" and Tropic period.

Norden Cookers went into insolvency. They were well known in the industry: an extruder and manufacturer of aluminium pots, pans and milk warmers – the latter the most popular, fitting snuggly inside a kettle. Mr Norden was mundane, but the manufacturing process was fascinating – workers, magician-like, swayed their hips nudging a wooden probe to shape the pots.

One evening, back at the flat, my dad mentioned the company's cash flow difficulties.

"Caused by the *big boys* squeezing us. Though, they always pay in the end."

Inexperienced, I asked, "Why not insist they stick to the credit terms?"

"If you push them too hard, you might not get another order" – his explanation, plausible.

I wanted to help, and offered to lend from my newfound carpet wealth, a fortune by my standards – R200 to R400 every other month and by way of comparison, university annual fees were R350.

The rub and nub of it all was a painful, poignant moment; my father did not believe me about the amount of money I earned. His incredulous look and lack of comment or acknowledgement made my heart sink. I lost my confidence to engage in any further conversation feeling unheard and unseen, yet again. Neither did I try to clarify my perception of what had just happened. Perhaps, surprised by my initial success or a little intimidated, he was unable to accept my generosity; a pride issue. I returned home to Johannesburg, not knowing that it would be the last time I would see my father alive!

~

The Flamingo and some spare change from my carpet sales certainly allowed my social life to breathe a little. Mobility was a huge help, but the responsibility something else. Seems some lessons are only learned the hard way – had I not witnessed George's folly on numerous occasions? It was a freezing winter morning and, like George, I did not wait for the engine to warm up. Soon, the familiar sizzling sound . . . and the car grinding to a sudden halt.

Jack to the rescue, instructing – *brake to keep the tow rope taut* – this, my first time behind the steering wheel of the lifeless Flamingo, was nerve-racking.

Inimitably unfussed, he replaced the head cylinder gasket. Alas, it inexplicably blew a second time, shortly thereafter – this time in good weather. Somewhere in conversation, we were discussing this peculiarity with Jack's father who casually enquired whether we had used a torque spanner to tighten the bolts – a torque spanner? – another lesson on the hoof.

Not long after, an engine mount broke. The car shuddered back for more home repairs. It was good to learn about the intricate mechanical functions, but best of all was observing the cordial relationship between Jack and his father as they went about resolving issues – there were never any recriminations.

This was so far removed from the atmosphere at our home, where blame or fault was found in my mother's nit-picking way. It took on catastrophic proportions as the doom and gloom suffocated us – becoming *the way*, but deep down it always hurt.

~

It was the winter road championship in East London and my final year at university with just a few months remaining. Raymond Hogg, then in his mid-twenties, had acquired another vehicle, a second-hand Humber jalopy. Rory, Raymond and I light-heartedly travelled the nine hundred and fifty kilometres there, affording us a sense of freedom and independence.

Raymond's physique was better suited to wrestling, but over the years his consistent application to the rigours of training and racing contributed to a leaner set of muscles. He was a good all-rounder, represented our province and rode in many Rapport Tours. Throughout his cycling career his indomitable spirit prevailed. And he too, on his day, was a champion.

Cyclists were generally an impoverished lot. Any spare cash was spent on our expensive bicycles and accessories. We were always on the scrounge for accommodation and on this trip stayed with one of George's relatives. They were trapped in abject poverty – Raymond's jalopy was like a carriage, and indeed we were their royalty. My sense of embarrassment was greater than that which I felt while visiting my grandmother, disrupting my early indoctrination that there were no poor whites.

But Steven, married to George's cousin, had a richness of spirit and soon we were laughing so much that our sides ached. It related to a tale about the time he came to stay with us in Johannesburg. My mother suggested he make himself at home, while she dashed off to work. Days later, his *faux pas* was discovered upon a chance remark my mom made about the anchovies that were in the fridge.

"Maybe I ate them by mistake. You know, frankly, I had never heard of anchovies. I was starving after my long train trip, saw the picture on the tin thinking it was a type of sardine and made a sandwich. Rather salty, I thought, but I was so hungry that I ate them all. That night I awoke, thirsty as anything and drank glass after glass of water. My thirst would not go away – I thought I was going to die." At each turn of phrase, we rolled about laughing. Finally, "I did not say anything, but I did think that the fancy sardines were just that. And inedible." It was the way he told the story, and the intoxicating laughter bonded us.

Maybe that was part of the elixir that assisted Raymond and I to achieve an unprecedented pre-championship success way beyond our abilities the following day. It became our gift back to them, a neighbourhood boost, hosting the winners.

Upon our arrival in East London, we first headed for the local cycle shop. Always a good place to pick up on the latest gossip and the lie of the land. My treat was a cotton red and black banded cycling road jersey, which I still have; tattered from cycling spills, yet full of stories. Its newness and smell then, imbued me with mystical powers.

There was no stopping us in the two-man time trial, our pre-championship warm-up and opportunity to know the terrain – but, something else governed us that day as we extracted the maximum advantage from each other. In itself an art form – a delicate balance while riding upfront to sense if there is more to give, then the pace is too slow, or if unable to sustain it, then too fast; similarly, for the rider behind to judge when it is propitious to leave the respite afforded by the slipstream.

For us it was neither, just our stubbornness – we just kept hurting, never letting on and often coming through even before the other had slackened. It was our sublime moment – *Cycling times good*, the newspaper agreed – the twenty hilly miles covered 26 seconds ahead of the more seasoned riders, but the championship was theirs. We in our naivety had simply expended too much energy – such is life.

Before returning, Rory and I vented our protest to Raymond's toe-jam smelling *tackies* – they had to be thrown into the sea. Having none of it, Raymond dashed headlong into the surf with whooping cries triumphantly retrieving them. The salt water only added injury to our wounds; alchemically magnifying the foul-smelling odour.

We never made it home in the jalopy. Instead, it gave up the ghost, while we stood in the middle of the night on a deserted platform, awaiting the milk-train. Undeterred, Raymond jollied us along – he saw the funnier side, viewing the calamity quite differently.

It is interesting how, as the reigning 1500 metre national champion, my standing was enhanced amongst my peers, while feeding journalists' imagination as they plied their stock in trade – speculation, sensationalism and spin. The start of the '72 - '73 track season in October was no different, *Top cyclists for opener*, adding further, *Southern Transvaal's top track cyclists will be in Pretoria tonight at the opening meeting of the track season. Guy Ferriman, Walter Thornhill and Jackie Lester are all definite starters. Thornhill is in peak condition and will be one of the leading contenders for the national sprint title next year.*

I smiled – my status had changed – no longer *the dark horse* but *one of the leading contenders*. A lot was happening in my final year at university – my training and racing regime helped relieve the stress and tedium of studying for my final examinations which were now a mere two weeks away.

Sadly, just before completing them, my father died unexpectedly of a heart attack and multiple strokes on Sunday, Guy Fawkes Day, in 1972, two weeks into his sixty-fifth year. A gap of a few days allowed me to fly to Cape Town for the funeral and to return to write my last exam.

DANIE THERON-KRYGSKOOL
K250 Seksieleiers

DANIE THERON COMBAT SCHOOL
K250 Section leaders

28-6-1971 – 16-7-1971

Military - June 1971 - The old fashion faithfull 303-rifle

Bottom - (L to R) Capt Oosthuizen,
Second Lieutenant Marshall
Top - in the middle, me

CHAPTER 11
DEATH AND DECISIONS

I stayed with Adrian and Selina, consumed by the *ripe melon smelly flat* that now became my prison. Selina watched me like a hawk, controlling my every move. I felt as though I was suffocating and longed to be in an emotional haven with genuine caring folk, like Joyce, my father's girlfriend, or playfully with my cousin Joan, who I imagined would bring some light relief to Selina's manner, but it was not to be.

Like vultures at a kill, Selina and Lillian, another of my father's sisters, were squabbling over the Thornhill family Bible, an heirloom that signified my place in the Thornhill family. My dad had mentioned it was to remain with me, the eldest male heir. Great significance was attached to *right of possession* with a complete disregard for my wishes. I fought them off like a lion defending a kill, except my roar was not fierce enough – acquiescing, I gave in.

My conditional decision – the Bible was Lillian's for her emotional strength during her lifetime, and upon death it would be returned – was influenced by fond memories of farm life when my father and I visited her family a few times before my teens. Lillian was married to Wallace Truter, who came from a generation of Saxon Merino and Dorper sheep farmers, living in the surrounding farmlands of the semi-desert area of Beaufort West, in the Karoo. I loved the excursions with Uncle Wallace and my cousins, in his dilapidated farm truck to desolate outlying areas of the arid countryside. We bounced along the sand roads contentedly, while he remained vigilant for fences that needed mending or locating the whereabouts of the sheep. I marvelled at how they found sufficient fodder to survive in the harsh terrain where the rule of thumb is four hectares of land per sheep.

There were Biblical times of plenty, triggered by the rains which culminated in flash floods that immediately swelled the tributaries making some roads impassable for days. The barren fruit trees during the drought years would respond with overladen branches bearing the weight of their bountiful crop; sometimes, close to and even snapping. We busied ourselves removing the excess unripe fruit, assisting the trees' plight. This enforced pruning, *also enhances the taste of the remaining fruit*, claimed Uncle Wallace.

The allure of his playful challenge of a half a crown for every crow killed was like leading me to the promised land of untold pocket money. I could not believe my luck, while being entrusted with the responsibility of an air gun and the freedom to pursue my adventures alone. Not having a natural predilection for blood sports and perhaps to appease my conscience, I accepted his story, not knowing whether it was true, that the crows were a general menace and during lambing season they blinded the lambs by pecking at their eyes. My uncle gave me a quick lesson on how to operate the airgun: to line up the sights and to carry the weapon safely. Immediately I felt more grown up and experienced an inner confidence now left to my own devices; the wide-open dry space surrounded me, while the lazy breathless wind brushed my skin.

Treading the dusty tracks to the burgeoning orchards, a congregation of crows, going about *crow business*, displayed their cunning alertness. At the precise moment I lifted the rifle, their sixth sense intervened – off in a flash – and became my rudimentary hunting lesson.

Another day I tried an experiment, pointing a walking stick at them. They called my bluff and merely looked on. What sublime intelligence. So glad I never killed one, rather my enrichment was of another sort – soul stuff – in observing nature and her intricate ways.

Meanwhile, a slaughtered sheep, skinned and gutted, made me squirm – kidneys for breakfast the next morning were only edible by adding a copious amount of apricot jam – the taste disguised and the last bleat hidden – fortunately, the memory faded as the days drifted by.

The travelling library, a good place for local gossip, always had Lillian return joyously with all sorts of stories. My happier memories tipped the scale, but alas, the Bible was never returned.

I was my father's sole heir, and Selina's appointment as executrix made me uncomfortable. This, partly because of her unpleasant busybody controlling nature, but more because of her insensitivity in ensuring that I knew the loan by her to my father, for the reconstruction of Norden Industries, would have to be repaid before any distribution from the estate. My confusion swirled – the aunt that had wanted to adopt me – now, with scant regard for my emotional state.

Being allowed no time for myself, even the smell of old wooden floors at Valentines did not seem as pleasant as in childhood. I hatched a plan and pretended to go to the local cafe. Out of sight, I ran as fast as I could to the Law Courts, arriving breathless. I demanded to see the Master of the Supreme Court – calmly, they enquired as to the nature of my business. Regaining my equilibrium, I explained my concerns. The clerk assured me that the Master would be advised accordingly.

Then sprinting back to my aunt's confronting gaze, "You've been away a long time?"

"Just a few games of pinball" – the sweat dripped from my face, and no doubt, my guilt showed.

That afternoon Selina and I went to meet Mr Baker, the attorney, to hear the reading of the Will. He was a friendly sort, and in a direct manner advised Selina that the Master had upheld my objection.

She looked directly at him, ignored me and blustered, "What – how?"

"Mr Thornhill junior went to see the Master this morning."

The quick turn of events stunned me – my embarrassment, extreme – if only the floorboards would open and swallow me whole, expunging my earlier deception.

Feeling the need to justify myself, I muttered, "You have a conflict in the monies owed to you and might not liquidate the primary asset in my best interest."

Selina's glare penetrated – how might things proceed? Still a day to the funeral, and having to share their rancid flat.

The welcome sunshine and fresh air outside the lawyer's office relieved the tension, and the bustle of Cape Town's city life enveloped us walking back as if nothing untoward had happened.

It is no wonder that my first funeral, preceded by the turmoil and battles of the previous days, was but a blur. Except for my crystal-clear memory of Desmond, the drunk, emotionally supporting me at that poignant moment when I touched my father's cold skin as he lay in the coffin. My guard dropped from Selina's prying eyes – tears welled and fell.

Desmond touched my shoulder with a gentle squeeze, "It's OK Walter, it's OK." Only Joyce, my father's girlfriend's soothing words and heartfelt hug had a similar effect. The others were automatons, duty bound.

I returned to Johannesburg to write my last examination, passed them all with an ironic twist: a distinction for *Accounting of Deceased Estates, Liquidations and Insolvency* – perhaps my understanding encouraged my bold resistance to Selina's testate appointment.

Meanwhile, further information became available about Norden Industries' business affairs: it was viable, albeit suffering from liquidity issues exacerbated by long overdue debts, a tie-in to our last father-son conversation earlier that year.

Sadly, my dad was hopelessly out of touch with reality. A simple call to the accounts department would have clarified the *overdue debt*. My visit to *the big boy's* head office, as my dad put it, solved the erroneous offset against money owed by the previous insolvent company, Norden Cookers – a cheque of R6,000 was handed to me, there and then.

~

Notwithstanding all, my cycling form held and our Kensington training gang represented our provincial side for the first time that November against the Orange Free State, in Bloemfontein. It was no mean feat; Albert and Rory were still juniors.

Victory was ours by a slim margin under Guy's captaincy. Unfortunately, he severely injured his shoulder, took a crack to the back of his head and when interviewed by a journalist, said, "I don't know what happened. I had completed the changeover with Walter and was slowing down when I fell. I woke up in hospital thinking the front wheel had collapsed but the bike was perfect."

It happened while propelling me into the two-man 1000 metre time trial; I heard the crash but was already pedalling for my life, focused, until across the finish line – victory was ours. Perhaps in Guy's eagerness, he pushed the boundaries too far in achieving an efficient change, slipping at that point of his momentous shove and not while slowing down – these things happen.

We raced, following our dreams, while journalists do what they do best. The headlines – *Thornhill off to WP*. Continuing further, *Thornhill leaves for the Western Province in two weeks' time to take over the business he inherited from his father, who died recently. 'I hope that move will not be a permanent one', Thornhill said yesterday. His feelings were echoed by Mr Harry Bloomfield, convener of the Southern Transvaal selection committee.*

A lot happened in the two weeks before leaving that December. I rode in the invitation *Binneman star-studded* meeting, as it was dubbed, in Port Elizabeth, immediately followed by the Johannesburg Grand Prix. Sprint honours belonged to the Natalian, Ralph Smout, who now dominated sprinting at the interprovincial level. It was always a pleasure to watch his riveting performance. The 10 kilometre race allowed me a win, but my attention was already diverted to my time ahead in Cape Town – this time with no father to visit – an uneasy feeling.

While driving the one thousand six hundred kilometres in Jack's Flamingo, many apprehensive thoughts churned – *did I have the wherewithal to run my father's business . . . how might my life unfold?*

Before leaving, Jack reminded me, *use the car for as long as you need and in two weeks' time when I'm in the Cape, we can chat about your father's business.*

I appreciated his unconditional support and spontaneous gesture, so lacking in my family. Looming was the advent of having to face Selina again; instead, I stayed with my cycling buddies.

Driving alone left plenty of time to muse over the words of my dad's last letter: *Will put some shares in your name for you, after the refloat. If all goes right at least now I can let you have what I was unable to do in the past.* What he was offering was misguided for what my heart really longed for was his love, recognition and a chance to hear him sing his favourite songs again.

An astounded Mr Norden banked the cheque I had collected. Although pleased with my effort, he was unconvinced about my attempts to introduce myself to the core customers in endeavouring to obtain further orders. Neither was I, and as a nineteen-year-old I did not blame him. They were polite – *our condolences, your father was a fine person, but we have sufficient stock for the moment. Maybe after the holiday season, in January, dependent on our December sales.* Quite frankly, I did not know what I was doing, other than following my nose.

Then catastrophe struck between the customer visits: the auditors discovered stock had been inadvertently valued at sales price – artificially inflating profitability – consequently, the business was no longer viable.

Selina and Mr Baker already knew; I was the last to be informed and although an adolescent, my understanding of the accounting implication was immediate. Naturally, I was livid.

Notwithstanding, I visited one last customer. My ruminations continued – my competence, the substantial cash flow injection that would be needed, coupled with a turnaround strategy – the prospects were bleak. The business opportunity had vanished.

There were no other meaningful assets in my father's estate – besides the squabbled over family Bible. My dad had indeed died penniless. I tried to keep a brave face and pretended to be mature and definite about resolving matters, but was finally overcome by it all. A cloud of devastation and depression engulfed me – I felt thoroughly defeated. Was it retribution for objecting to Selina's appointment? I trusted not, but just one of those things.

Then, a miracle changed my gloomy mood. The *Tweede Nuwejaarsdag* (Second New Year's Day), a holiday in the Cape, was almost upon us – a time of celebration – the unique Cape Minstrel Carnival of painted faces and elaborate, colourful outfits. The frolicking through the streets beforehand, accompanied by the touching sound of banjos, evoked joyful childhood memories of the visits to my father.

There, under the shade of an old oak tree on a glorious hot summer's afternoon, was a banjo player soulfully strumming and singing Johnny Nash's number one hit of that November, the month my father died.

> *I can see clearly now, the rain is gone,*
> *I can see all obstacles in my way*
> *Gone are the dark clouds that had me blind*
> *It's gonna be a bright (bright), bright*
> *(bright) Sun Shiny day.*
>
> *I think I can make it now, the pain is gone*
> *All of the bad feelings have disappeared*
> *Here is the rainbow I've been praying for . . .*
>
> *Look all around, there's nothing but blue skies*
> *Look straight ahead, nothing but blue skies.*

His utter contentment lifted my despondency as that joyous, carefree melody seeped into my bones and touched my heart. Tears welled, a smile broke and my woes dissolved. He remained oblivious to my presence and, being grateful for this unexpected encounter, I peacefully walked on.

I never had a chance to grieve properly, nor did I have a suitable support structure during this adverse time. My unconscious reaction was to hold on to my cycling, which gave me a sense of belonging. After all, the fraternity had unknowingly been my extended family and competition a way of life. I climbed back into the saddle, put my head down and kept on cycling; fuelled by the journalistic spin and fed by my successes.

The Press were at it again, *the holder of the 1500 metre national title now lives in the Cape and is still undecided on which local club to join.* And a week later, *Thornhill in Cycling Upset,* continuing, *Walter Thornhill, a former Northern Wheelers rider, who has joined the City Cycling Club, was responsible for one of two upsets at the interclub cycling meeting at Paarl last night. With four laps to go in the 5 miles, Thornhill broke away from the bunch and was an easy winner in spite of the strong challenge from Springboks Eddie Kriel and Tin Theart.* I guess I was the novelty factor, for a challenging sprint involving other riders would have made for far better reading. Not taken too seriously, it became entertaining. I understood the power, influence and spin of the press – I was living it.

I stayed on for the remainder of December and in between the cycling events, had ample opportunity to discuss my state of affairs with Jack – it was unlikely that there was a buyer for this newly reconstructed unprofitable business. My dad and Mr Norden were simply unable to make it work.

Jack was keen that I join him in the carpeting business. My quandary, *do that or become a Chartered Accountant*? Jack, in his inimitable way, made it all sound so easy, "I never finished my studies when I decided to start in carpeting. You've had experience, sold successfully – together we can make a fortune!" His argument was compelling, but our previous arrangement while at University was merely a means to an end.

Ian Coutts, a good mutual cycling friend of ours, from Cape Town, advised otherwise, "Complete your studies, don't worry about Jack. His suggestion is in his self-interest. In the long run, qualifications will be more important to you in making a proper life for yourself." What a dilemma – Jack's friendship, my loyalty to him and, promises of riches against an articled clerk's salary?

Ian was two years older than Jack. The three of us had become good friends a few years prior, when as a State Attorney he was seconded to Johannesburg. He automatically qualified for an honorary membership of our *intellectual club*. We often sat, back to back, in a triangle during track meetings chatting about all sorts of inane matters – our silliness was our way of relaxing. Our friendship blossomed and he too at the age of twenty-six, seemed wiser with the world at his fingertips: a qualified lawyer, an eligible bachelor with a delightful green Alfa Romeo 1750.

The intricacies of his work fascinated me – I would listen to his stories for hours, dismayed by the futility of the legal parameters used in deciding *borderline race classification cases*, part of the apartheid regime's toolkit. It seemed ludicrous that a small subtle detail determined a person's fate – classified White gave legislated privileges, irrespective of ability; while the absurdity of same colour relationships had to be endured by all.

Ian subsequently became the Transkei Government's state attorney, responsible for their legal matters when Transkei became a so-called *independent homeland state* that was recognised by the South African Government only – ultimately, the *puppet states* were absorbed undoing the original political farce.

A year before my father died, rather whimsically, Ian and I decided to travel to Cape Town, a three thousand plus kilometre round trip, for an extended four-day weekend. Two other friends accompanied us, all with our own reasons for being there; for me, it was simply to surprise my dad and see him again – not knowing that this would be the second last time. Driving non-stop, we shared the driving of Ian's converted Colt panel van, another of his cars.

Outside the tiny godforsaken dorp of Britstown, close to the witching hour on a cold frosty winter's night, we collided with a buck that was mesmerised by our lights. The front fender, fan wheel and radiator were damaged. The car limped into town and Ian set about his Heath Robinson repairs – the putty for the radiator, cured on the night watchman's wood burning fire.

The circumstance was such that Ian and I decided to cut our thumbs and become blood brothers, influenced by the romantic portrayal of everlasting friendships in films of that era. The clear bright stars, our motley crew and the shivering watchman in his thick grey coat witnessed our act. Our blood mingled and we swore an allegiance of friendship. Then in a fit of elation, we skipped and sang at the top of our voices along the deserted main street, seemingly matching the lines from the poem by William Butler Yeats, *Mad as the mist and snow*

> *Our minds are the best this night,*
> *And I seem to know*
> *That everything outside us is*
> *Mad as the mist and snow.*

We were indeed in that other world, touching that space where all things are possible.

That was then, but after that December returning overnight from Cape Town to Johannesburg, there was much to contemplate: my father's life, his death, and the way forward. The pinnacle must have been his airline charter days – what imagination, courage and endeavour to enter that romantic era after the Second World War, where people dared to dream again.

Alas, back to another reality – the Flamingo broke down on a Western Cape mountain pass – a long way from anywhere. All I could do was wait patiently.

It was pitch black, an African moonless night – a clear void to the brilliant stars above, almost touchable. Nature allowed me to settle into her space – aware – the stillness, interspersed with night sounds, disrupted only by the distant drone of an infrequent night traveller. I would jump up and wave, but to no avail – only the Flamingo's indicator light kept flickering.

Then, in the loneliness of the night, I started to think the worst. I must have drifted off to sleep, for suddenly I was awoken by the sound of a vehicle slowing. The Good Samaritan had arrived – tow rope attached – park lights on – we were off.

It should have been easy – had Jack and I not done this before? The next forty kilometres, through treacherous passes, were quite challenging – the Samaritan's cavalier approach with no real regard for safety, made it a testing journey of hell on earth as the lightweight Flamingo drifted helplessly behind his powerful *bakkie*. Only the gushing adrenaline aided my judgement in manoeuvring at speed around the bends, while continuously breaking softly to ensure the slack in the tow rope was absorbed. At times, it seemed as if he had forgotten I was even there as my bizarre thoughts pervaded – *the Flamingo could easily flip over, and, the consequences?*

We arrived safely, although I was shaken. Stationary, the fresh chill air of the dawn was a sheer delight to breathe again, while waiting at a deserted garage for the sleepy town to awaken. Tail lights disappeared into the distance, while I reflected on his random act of kindness.

It was Ian's advice that became the clincher; I articled that January to a small firm of Chartered Accountants, Greenwood, Poulton and Co. My Bachelor of Commerce degree allowed a remission of a few years of articles. All going well, two further years of part-time study, sit the dreaded Board examination and qualify within my article clerkship.

The irony was, it was through my mother's auspices that I was articled there for she had previously worked for Mr Greenwood. Her intent was always well meaning but so repeatedly became derailed, and looming on the horizon was just such a momentous crash.

Meanwhile, the journalistic storyline continued – *Thornhill makes welcome return. It was a very relieved Harry Bloomfield, manager of the Southern Transvaal cycling team, who heard the news that Walter Thornhill had returned from the Western Cape and was again available for provincial duty. 'I was dreading the Carlton Shield match against Western Province with Thornhill in the 1500 metre, said Mr Bloomfield.'*

The circus was alive; the scene set for the start of the second half of the track season with touches of spice – Raymond, the *piglet* was now the *Australian import* and Dries, *sparky*, the thirty-two-year-old electrician, was now the *iron man*. Apt as he had set a new world endurance record by cycling nonstop for one hundred and eleven hours around our local track, three years prior.

I was always keen to cycle elsewhere in the country – a chance to meet other riders and a welcome change of scenery. Rory and I thought nothing of driving five hundred kilometres to Natal to compete in the annual Pietermaritzburg Grand Prix one weekend in February.

The sporty Flamingo demanded profound respect. It had been raining. Unaware of the lethal danger of surface oil now floating on the residual rain – an S-bend approached too zealously – we swung sideways, out of control; adrenaline pumped. Spontaneously, the steering wheel was spun. It seemed an eternity before the car violently rectified, and with the repeated manoeuvre, we finally came to a complete stop, as did the traffic on either side of the road. Shaken and stirred, I thanked my lucky stars that we never collided with anyone.

My pulsating heart recovered its rhythm to the thoughts of the consequences. A guardian angel definitely saved that day.

Smart Smout pedals home, read the headlines the next day. Ralph beat Mike Francis in the sprint on their home turf, while Joe and I fought for third place, narrowly mine by a width of a tyre. Rory fared well in the junior section.

Along the way, progressing and growing in the cycling world, Jack had advised, *in sprinting you need to toughen up and be able to rough it with the best*! It was not my inherent way of behaving – I embraced it reluctantly, not that I ever let on. It was more a means of survival within my need to test myself against the fastest in the land.

Sprint racing, unlike today, was a contact sport, where riding elbow to elbow and bumping, was permissible but governed by specific rules over the last 200 metres. Violated, it led to a disqualification. Entering the sprinter's lane (a metre wide and at the bottom of the track) – *once in, not allowed to drift out*. Entering above the sprinter's lane and between the midway safety line (dissects the width of the track) – *the front rider may drift upwards impeding the overtaking rider up to the safety line only, not beyond*. Finally, entering above the safety line – *the rules were undefined, so all was permissible* – that was the issue, a free for all similar to the early part of the race, before the 200 metres, where it was necessary to allow tactics to unfold.

Jack, aware of this glaring omission, had always espoused and communicated to other cyclists a gentleman's informal rule. *If drifting a rider during a sprint above the safety line, then at least a rider's body width must remain for the challenging cyclist to be able to overtake safely,* much like having an imaginary sprinter's lane at the top of the track.

My sprinting ability had improved and unbeknown to me, two years on, it was rumoured that Mike Francis and Joe Billet had formed a pact: *whoever drew me in a heat, at the next prestigious encounter, would ride me off the track.* They did, rather Mike did at the De Beers, Kimberley Stadium, where the track safety fence, for some peculiar reason, was disconcertingly set back a metre from the top of the track. When tactically I tried to accelerate over Mike that floodlit evening about 50 metres before the 200 metre mark, he just kept accelerating and drifted across the track taking me ever higher until I ran out of space – crashing and landing on my head. Next stop hospital – concussed. My second time – previously, on Smout and Francis's home track in Pietermaritzburg, a year earlier; that accident unrelated to *the pact*.

Andre Van der Zwan, contacted Jack to ascertain the verity of the rumour – Jack had not heard about it but knew about the accident. Jack cautioned, *track riding had become hopelessly rough, and if there were not some containment, someone would die* – he never knew how prophetic his words were; two weeks later it happened.

Tommy Shardelow was there that evening in the final of the Pietermaritzburg Grand Prix, saying, "It was awful, a massive bloodstain across the track at the point of impact as his skull split open. The meeting was immediately cancelled, and we left, chilled to the bone."

Ralph Smout tactically drifted before the 200 metre, continuing to hold Mike against the safety fence at the top of the track, and Mike in a sway of his body and a peculiar tilt of his head, hit a floodlight lamp post at near full speed. The autopsy revealed that Mike's skull was a third of the thickness of a normal human being – any major blow to the head would have been fatal.

Over the previous few years, everyone had enjoyed watching Ralph's smooth and powerful scintillating way as he excitingly changed the face of sprinting. It was unfortunate on many accounts – Mike's death, which shocked the cycling fraternity, and the difficulty for Ralph, the epitome of a great sportsman and an absolute gentleman.

Going back to the February Pietermaritzburg Grand Prix, a few years before, Ralph was in his purple patch. The following month, he won the gold medal in the historic 1972 South African Games. This was the first time all ethnic groups could compete officially together; the subterfuge, an invitation event, used to move through and around the rules of the apartheid regime.

Van der Zwan reported on the racially integrated Games: *Undisturbed by reputations, Ralph Smout, Natal's powerhouse, hurried to a gold medal in the 1000 metre sprint during the South African Games at Pilditch Stadium on Saturday. And at the same time, Smout proved he is in world class by beating Frenchman Patrick Pecchio in the final. Smout tipped to capture the National Sprint title from the current holder, Jackie Lester, at the South African Championships over the Easter weekend, beat the Black sprint king, Sam Ramabodu en route to the final. True, Pecchio who recently disposed of world champion Daniel Morelon on an indoor track had problems because of the high altitude. After the race, he had nothing but praise for the South African.*

Clearly, we could compete against the best in the world, but the historical significance of these Games was of utmost importance, encapsulated by the phenomenal spirit of the predominantly white crowd at the Pilditch Stadium, the Afrikaner heartland of Pretoria. Black rider Siphiwe Ngwenya was defeated by Tommy Shardelow in the second round of the sprint.

Siphiwe acknowledged the crowd's standing ovation. I had goose bumps and shivers down my spine – the occasion was momentous and his defeat a massive victory. A precursor of racial integration through sport, a unique way in a new South Africa – it felt right and was a wonderful breakthrough.

Van der Zwan added: *The only black cyclist to receive a medal was Phefeni Mtembu, a bronze medal but if honours were awarded for courage and aggressive riding he would have received a gold medal for his performance in the gruelling 40 kilometre race. He attacked all the time.*

Without Mtembu's hard work, Jimmy Swift's South African record set in 1958 could never have been improved by Linus van Onselin that evening. Subsequently Linus, some forty plus years later, became a world mountain bike champion in his age category.

Besides my welcome home headlines and our quick dash to Pietermaritzburg, the rest of the season was difficult; I was adjusting to working in the day and studying at night. Crowning it all was an awkward unforeseen home predicament. Nevertheless, at the Games, I did manage a third place to Jack's win in the 1500 metre with Joe second, while at the Southern Transvaal Championships a win in the 400 metre and a place in another event. All in all, a lacklustre performance compared to the previous year.

Three weeks later, instead of an expected improvement and peaking for the South African Championships, I simply ran out of steam. My poor performance never went unnoticed. The loudspeaker blared, *could Walter Thornhill please report to the first aid room*; the obligatory random drug test. Years later, an official confirmed that my erratic performance made them suspect that I may have been using drugs. I was tested often – the results always negative. Sure I had a cup of black tea or coffee before an event, but they were not banned substances.

At a cycling dinner, some thirty years later, a British cyclist, who had ridden in South Africa, was reminiscing, and remarked, "We all did."

"Not me."

A deathly silence followed – then, the awkwardness overcome, light-hearted conversation continued once again.

Dear Wally,

Have not heard from you for a long time, are things OK?

Have taken over "Nordens" and am now the sole Director of the company called Norden Industries (Pty) Ltd. at the same address Mr. Norden is still connected with the company. Will put some shares in your name for you, after the refloat.

Bought all the assets of Norden Cookers myself and will resell at a price to the new company. It has taken me a long time to arrive again after the "Air Excursion + Tropic period. If all goes right at least now I can let you have what I was unable to do in the past.

My dad's last letter - continues overleaf

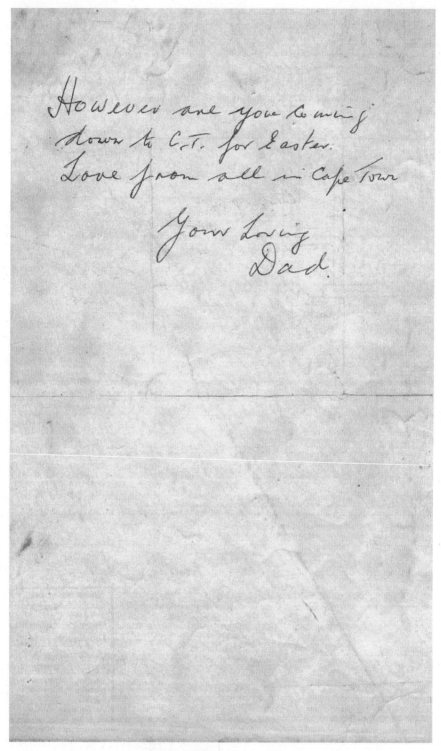

My dad's last letter - overleaf

Sam Ramabadu and Jimmy Swift

Phefeni Mtembu and Basil Cohen

1972 - South African Games at Pilditch Stadium
- Tommy Shardelow and Siphiwe Ngwenya

Blocking Guy Ferriman as we balance
'standing still' during a sprint - Guy (rear)

CHAPTER 12
THE JOURNEY NEVER ENDS

SHOWDOWN

Barely a month into my articles and before the South African championships, Desiree's demons came triumphantly marching to the fore, this time with a sense that victory was complete.

I cannot remember the cause of the incident that precipitated her violent outburst that evening, but the next thing I found myself standing on the lonely black polished veranda looking into the darkness of the night.

Click . . . the key turned. The front door locked, firmly, behind me. I stood, motionless . . . looking desolately into the distance, not knowing what to do – helpless, alone and completely overwhelmed.

Echoing in my thoughts were some of her words, *get out of my fucking house and don't ever come back again*. Beside me was my suitcase stuffed with the clothes she had demonically snatched from the draws in her rampant, out of control way – the case hurled before I was shoved out of the door. Passive George remained just that.

My thoughts were interrupted. Surprisingly, the sound of a car turned into our road and stopped outside the gate; my mind whirled, trying to fathom what had happened, for there stepping out of the car was my girlfriend and her father. I was dumbfounded; hastily trying to make sense of it all.

Calmly, he said, "Don't say anything Walter, just come along and we will try to sort it out later."

I greeted Sharon with a perplexed look, climbed into the car extremely embarrassed, and remained so for the short distance to their home in

Bedfordview – a drive which seemed an eternity. Ben Hanson, a Danish immigrant to South Africa married an Afrikaner and Sharon, their only child, was my second girlfriend.

We sat down to a late-night coffee. Ben lit his pipe, puffing away in a peaceful manner and said, "You can stay here for a few days until you know what you are going to do."

It felt awkward, even though there were no recriminations or questions, just compassion. But not Sharon's mother – her scowling face hid nothing; she chose bed.

A few weeks prior, Sharon and I wished to discuss our rather idealistic view about our sexual involvement. Notwithstanding our anxiety, we bravely requested her parent's audience – tangible thoughts reverberated, *is he asking for her hand in marriage; might she be pregnant*?

It was far simpler – we wished to be together after our intimacy – to wrench ourselves away from each other and return to our respective homes felt hypocritical. Ben, keeping his composure in his inimitable and considered way, slowly puffed on his pipe.

"Under the circumstances that will be fine – let's see how it works."

Meanwhile, Mrs Hanson's cold and expressionless face confirmed her contempt and disapproval. Her glaring eyes shot daggers; she was fuming.

Of course, we tried to be discreet: mostly I left at dawn before the household had awoken. Inevitably, I overslept. Mrs Hanson's smile instantly changed from a warm good morning greeting, as she put Sharon's tea down, to a sullen frozen look of horror.

"You here." Pirouetting without another word, she forcibly closed the door; her message clear, *you are not welcome to stay over, irrespective of what my husband said.*

Being in love, we thought we could overcome these periphery difficulties, until that infamous night when my mother called the Hansons making inappropriate and disparaging remarks about our relationship.

Three days later I found accommodation in a rundown residential high-rise hotel in Hillbrow. My dark, dingy room looked out onto a bare wall that I could almost touch. The half board favoured the old, retired inhabitants with sloppy eating habits – like soup dribbling down their chin. I felt utterly depressed and knew I had to free myself from that prison.

News travelled quickly and within the month, a cycling spectator, who I barely knew, came to my rescue. He was a short, rotund man with a gammy leg like my father's. He laid baize on snooker tables, but more importantly was the caretaker of a five-story-block of flats, a stone's throw from my hotel. There were waiting lists with key money exchanged to achieve preferential treatment.

But his big heart and love of cycling, did the trick – my haven, 503 Orko

Court, Banket Street, a fifth-floor spacious one-bedroom flat. The view of sorts, across a vacant piece of land onto another tall building, was paradise after my previous hell-hole. The reasonable rental left spare change from my articled clerk's salary.

After Pietermaritzburg, I returned Jack's Flamingo and my wheels were my bicycle again. Aunty Ronnie's faithful Chevrolet belonged to the Athol era as if it contained her memories and love of Uncle Jack; the Wolseley arrived thereafter, which she kindly allowed me to borrow.

It was inconvenient having to cycle to her home. Adding insult, it drove like an old fashion tank – solid, but extremely slow and prone to breaking down at the untimeliest moments. The contrast from the days of the sports car, befitting of any young aspiring student, was absolute, and by comparison I was now like a grey old man.

During my move to Hillbrow, my cycling suffered. Unlike a swan's gracious glide in a fast-flowing stream, where their unseen webbed feet work furiously below, I remained in the saddle visibly peddling. Except, I had forgotten to breathe and absorb the enormity of recent events – my father's death, a failed business proposition, decisions about my future and yet another unconscious, careless act by my mother.

That month the wrong type of winds blew – the lonely black veranda that I stood on when my mother turfed me out would regularly be dusted with the fine yellow cyanide sand. Perhaps, it had infected the minds of our parents.

Barely a month later, Piet's open-ended exhausts of his beach buggy, which he had built himself, roared and reverberated between the high-rise apartment buildings announcing his arrival.

"I need a place to stay for a few days. My dad threatened me once too often."

I imagined the altercation – both father and son, obstinate. Piet had been trying to break the shackles of his *verkrampte* upbringing (an Afrikaner Nationalist who opposed any changes toward racial policy during apartheid). *Old laconic grumps* with his steel-like grip on life would probably have said, *if you don't like it you can go!*

Piet stayed much longer, continuing his studies at the Rand Afrikaans University while I worked and attended evening lectures at Wits. Living together was like breaking new ground – it was unusual then for an Englishman and an Afrikaner to be sharing *digs*; something, I never imagined happening. Perhaps we too, like Ramabodu and Mtembu, were contributing in our small way to a changing South Africa as we buried the differences that existed between our cultures.

THE REAR-VIEW MIRROR

In my early twenties, my sympathy violin played with spells of feeling sorry for myself, particularly when I was alone. Self-defeating and winning no lasting favours, it took time to resolve. Had it not been for my childhood and adolescent experiences, I might not have had the wherewithal to cope with life's other challenges. Conversely, at times, these phases were a definite saboteur and an emotional hamper.

The unconsciously learnt behaviours from my parents, more significantly of my mother, had embedded themselves in my psyche, and – coupled with our ancient reptilian *fight, flight or freeze mode* – became an explosive cocktail. Unwittingly, I too could call on this destructive behaviour in my adult life – insidious, and an unexpected guest, not without consequences.

In the work environment, intellect was the mask and the temporary panacea; in intimate relationships, sex had a similar effect – it took a long time to understand this – cleverly disguised and hidden from my consciousness, but not from others.

My journeys of self-exploration, awareness and delving into aspects of spirituality were often synchronistic and timely. After some eleven years of marriage, during a challenging period, I intuitively found myself attending a week-long *Prisoner of Childhood* workshop; hoping to find further clues relating to my learned patterns of behaviour from childhood. Marcia Karp, a renowned psychodrama therapist, who had trained under Moreno, the founder of this therapy, was surprised that I had not read any of her books.

Nevertheless, I enjoyed her facilitation over the five days. My need to succeed at work was an expression for my craving of motherly love – in my misunderstanding, it seemed that a pat on the back, or better still, an acceptable bonus would reflect this love. There were other more painful revelations.

The circuitous route to Marcia was via her husband, Ken Sprague, short and stocky with a huge handlebar moustache that made him look like a mixture between a walrus and a warthog. He practised the same therapy as Marcia, was an artist, a boxer, a communist and had been an aspiring politician. I met him when he was seventy-two and still attending men's gatherings at weekends; I was in my early forties. At some point in the proceedings, Robert Bly would always invite the men over the age of fifty-five to come forward and face the group of over a hundred men.

Our spontaneous, wholehearted round of applause recognised their participation. I remember thinking, *I hope one day I have the courage of a man like Ken to still attend these gatherings* – Ken was older than Robert, and stood out in his distinctiveness. It was not always plain sailing, particularly when men did honest straight talking, adopting a no-nonsense approach.

The surprising thing was, Robert would then turn to the men being applauded and say, "You have a duty to these younger men, sitting before you, to share your secrets as to why you are alive today." The enormity struck me – *life is not the proverbial bed-of-roses.*

Precipitous cliffs pose enormous threats – the treachery of the abyss needs to be respected, cajoled and honoured to avoid that point of no return. My journey traversed many hills, while encountering the barbs along the way – perhaps, my surname is apt.

A month before Aunty Ronnie's death, I returned to South Africa to spend time with her in Cape Town. Intuition? She was a frail eighty-eight, in the care centre of the retirement home for a while longer than she found pleasant and still clutching onto the last remnants of dignity, often overlooked by those institutions. One afternoon, she suggested we visit her more hearty retiree friends for a sundowner – the nursing staff dressed her for the occasion. We set off while I briskly learned to operate the wheelchair with Aunty in it, negotiating the uneven pavements on our way.

Small talk, interspersed with, "The usual, Ronnie?"

"That would be lovely, not too strong," an understatement as a stiff Gin with only a dash of tonic water was poured.

In no time at all an enquiring, "Another?"

Loquacious reminiscing down memory lane followed. We said our farewells, merrily returning, the wheelchair seemingly with a suspension of its own.

Ronnie safely tucked into bed and on my way, I walked into the might of the matron's wrath and rebuke, *we've weaned Ronnie off alcohol – look what you've done. It interferes with her medication, and she becomes aggressive and abusive.* The matron was not amused. I thought back to Aunty's marvellous afternoon reprieve and smiled, thinking, *does it matter?*

A few days later we chuckled about the incident; then her composure changed. Laying serenely in bed she calmly said, "I've had enough and want to go now – can you help me?"

I was taken aback. Holding her left hand in my right, I spoke in placid generalities as she calmly drifted into dreamland, at peace with the world – we stayed like that for hours. Many thoughts flooded my mind, besides the reflections upon our love, affection and caring for one another, and the meaningful parts we had played in each other's lives.

Six years prior, when she was eighty-two, she asked my opinion about continuing to drive long distances, like the twenty kilometres to my sister – we set off, she loved talking, looking at me rather than the road. The journey, a hair-raising adventure, was exacerbated by her difficulty in reading the highway signs as we slowed down to a crawl with motorists dangerously zooming by. We made it, just; my heart in my mouth.

Robust, like a fighter pilot's mission successfully completed, she enquired, "Well?"

Drawing deeply on Dutch courage, not quite sure how to phrase it, nor to offend her, I barely uttered under my breath, "Perhaps it would be better to think about driving in the village only; Gayle's home is just too far!"

Her gracious sigh was audible, "Exactly what I thought!" Triumphantly, she delivered her edict, "Walter agrees – from now on you will all just have to come and visit me!" Our family's relief was palpable, for recently our concerns were heightened when George, then seventy-five, had blacked out while driving; fortunately, no one had been hurt.

Ronnie continued to drive the few hundred metres to the village. Tenaciously, she held on to life – it was as if the need to have the rust spots on the car door repaired was her metaphor. Finally, her frailty took over and she agreed that the car could be sold.

Meanwhile, back in the tranquillity of our unusual last hours together in the solitude of her room, one pervasive thought, all-consuming, swirled – *would it be better to lift the pillow and . . . end what had then become a difficult existence.* I mentally rehearsed it, wondering whether there would be a physical struggle and how to disguise the happening – the urge to help was overwhelming but, I just sat there holding her hand, mesmerised into nothingness until she awoke, saying, "Why don't we call your mother?"

We did. Sadly, I witnessed Aunty's calm composure rapidly turn into sheer anguish as my mother's petty conversation berated her over the money owed for the dry cleaning of her dresses and that Ronnie needed to arrange for them to be collected sooner.

Aunty handed me the phone with tears in her eyes, saying, "I don't know why that woman does this." Her face scrawled in despair and the previous sereneness, now distant. I was in shock and equally distraught – we parted as best we could. A kiss placed on her forehead.

I visited my mother, fuming and demanded to know what the nonsense was all about.

"You don't know a thing. She'll outlive us all, and her clothes have been here for over a month taking up unnecessary space in my home."

I was staggered by her capacity to do and say hurtful, idiotic and illogical things – scary; but dramatizing trivia was her reality.

THE JOURNEY CONTINUES

After Aunty's death, I returned to South Africa to ritually spread her ashes in three places as instructed by a clairvoyant. She added that my mother should bring yellow flowers, as a healing of the unfinished business between the two sisters. Desiree, then suffering with emphysema, spoke further about her childhood disappointment that Ronnie had not done more to remove her from the orphanage; a fact that may well have accounted for and manifested in Desiree's bickering manner and her weird relationship with Ronnie. It took a long time to understand and to digest the unnecessary burden of misunderstanding that my mother had carried, as well as the sheer waste of life force in not resolving this while they were both alive.

Life, Death, and the Beauty of Rituals – the first ceremony on Gayle's marital smallholding, the second on the slopes of Table Mountain and lastly, on Aunty's plot in Athol. The latter my friend Benji, also her executor, reminded me was an explicit request of hers, except I had completely forgotten.

The first ritual's cast of characters: Terry, her godson, his partner Ivor, our sibling families and of course Desiree modestly holding a bunch of yellow flowers. The cousins frolicked and swapped stories, excitedly hanging on to each other's every word. It was a summer's evening; the strong Cape South Easter abated to the light of the rising sliver of a powerful moon. The stars were peeping from behind the scattered clouds.

We instinctively built a rock water shrine with our collective energy and strength. Desiree and Ivor, both keen gardeners, collected shrubs, adorning it. Individual, thoughtful touches, like the magical appearance of Aunty's old pearl bijou used to intertwine and drape through the shrubbery on the shrine – so very, very beautiful. Water trickled, slowly changing the colour of the rocks as it meandered down, captured in our dugout earth basin with floating lit candles reflecting the russet warmth and ambiance.

It was truly so meaningful, Terry's sentiments, calling the next day. My mother equally fulfilled, echoed, *so beautiful, what a wonderful send off for Aunty.* No doubt, finally at one with her sister, whom she loved in her own peculiar way.

We were all spiritually nourished and enriched through ritual space. Its beauty, magic and power; unique and personal. The serenity, the awe-inspiring moments, a place to return to and draw upon its sustenance. We separated from the sanctity of that sacred space, having a renewed sense of vigour, lightness and purpose; Aunty honoured and George remembered – he had died nearly two years prior. My heart was full, and I could not help but think – *in your way*

Aunty, you held on long enough to bring the family together – thank you!

Four years later, my marriage on its brink, Gayle and I took a perchance brother-sister spiritual trip to Peru. During our various musings Gayle felt that the failings of our mother were one thing, but more contentious for her was George's passiveness. "He seldom stood up for me at pertinent moments in my life, leading to my sense of abandonment. It includes you as well, George did nothing that evening I witnessed the *knife-wielding incident*!"

I am not sure which moments were more difficult; they impacted us differently. It was insidious, continual and cumulative. My sense of self-worth was challenged and my self-confidence undermined as I unconsciously turned to the world of cycling to bolster and fulfil those needs.

My self-image improved slowly through conscious awareness, aided by therapeutic self-help techniques. Slippages did, however, happen. Severe emotional stress is still my trigger, oft catching me unawares. Like the tipsy ghosts of the past, they return to haunt me, not as memories but as a second nature learned reflexive reaction.

I searched and still continue searching – whether delving into Shamanism, Buddhism or certain indigenous practices, like those of the Peruvian Quechua or the cultural beliefs of the Balinese, encapsulated in rituals of *Sekala* and *Niskala*. Thank you, the reader, for allowing me to share my indelible moments as part of my healing.

Could it be that my mother was dealing with the repercussions of karma from an earlier ancestral lineage not yet expiated, rather than solely the traumas from her childhood? Could it be the same for Monty, my cousin – the suicide not fully recognised nor being aware of the abusive behaviour of his father. If known, accepted and redressed in whatever way appropriate, might it free him from his morbid state?

Then while sitting quietly ruminating on the peak of Machu Picchu with Gayle, looking towards the tall peak of Huayna Picchu, she remarked, "You know Walter, I think our mother so loved us that she came down in her estranged form so that we could learn the lessons we needed to in this lifetime."

My judgemental mind spewed – anger and fury welled inside – without the slightest hesitation, I retorted, "What absolute nonsense, she could have behaved differently and exercised choice!"

The passage of time and a further exploration into spiritual quests became the doorway into a further healing and an understanding of the different humanistic ways of looking at this. Our life experiences were absolutely necessary to become who we are – equipped for the next part of our journey.

Years later, I called Gayle, "Remember that time on the peak of Machu Picchu? Well, maybe you were right after all!"

The consideration of 'maybe' – very powerful with many possibilities – my way of thinking expanded and my spirit liberated to a newfound freedom.

Indeed, traditional wisdom flows from the elders, and it is befitting that Gayle's sharing was on Machu Picchu while gazing towards Huayna Picchu – old person's and young man's peak, the Quechua translation.

The journey never ends. I laugh more easily about the past, recognising it for what it was, not that I ever enjoyed the traumatic roller coaster rides or the emotional buffeting. They belong to the painful bits of the psychological toolbox of descent and subsequent ascension.

On the way down something else happened, *depression*! I never realised that I suffered from it until I was in the midst of my divorce, with a further ironic twist – it would be another twelve years before I properly confronted it, in a more meaningful way. The immensity of the epiphany, towards the end of those latter therapy sessions, was a realisation that I had also suffered with bouts of depression during my teens – it was only a question of the degree; and cycling, my saviour.

"Your issues may have even started in the womb," postulated Allan Pimentel, my helpful therapist. Had I read *The Secret Life of the Unborn Child*? Not then, but recently I did. It is fascinating how the influence of external factors during pregnancy and specifically the mother's subtle reaction to them, transfer and subsequently affect the predisposition of the infant. They can, however, be subsequently overcome by many other influencing life factors. My mother must have experienced huge emotional difficulties during her pregnancy, so close to the time of my father's airline collapse – it was never shared.

I have had my dark days. While living in Hillbrow, during moments of severe loneliness, thoughts permeated . . . *it would be easy to jump off the opposite building . . . why do people think it is so momentous or that difficult to do*? There were other times, certain things kept me here, and I am grateful.

Stefan's teenage years gave me the opportunity to heal my *inner child*, although that was not realised at the time. Of course, the challenge of single parenting was evident, and creating a place of security and love in our home, paramount – it was my need that Stefan knew that he was loved. Even now I still have irresistible urges to give him a huge hug.

"Stefan, you know, I really love you!"

His warm, endearing, heartfelt response has always been, "I know dad!"

Our communication, since he was a child, was clear, straightforward and honest. A trust developed and besides, he taught me much about myself and about ritual – Aunty Ronnie's last remaining ashes spread on her Athol plot – he was seven, accompanied by Mina his mother, and myself.

"No, not like that, like this dad," uttered playfully in his carefree demeanour.

It came through him in the same way that he wrote about his ideas on creation; not that he recalls either clearly any more. Upon completion of the ritual, we looked up to the sky, flanked by the trees in Aunty's beautiful garden, and observed the cumulus clouds transforming into an angelic newborn child – for us, the honouring and laying to rest of Aunty was complete and there was a sense of elation.

Let there be no misunderstanding, during his formative years of our nearly fourteen years of marriage, Stefan's mother was exceptionally dedicated to his upbringing. He was showered with love, affection and attention, which no doubt created a formidable platform for his growth.

Stefan's maternal grandparents, an Italian grandfather Franco Matania and a Spanish grandmother Carmen Rodriguez lived relatively close by in London. They were embracing and added much to Stefan's sense of family. My mother, unfortunately geographically isolated, had direct contact only when we visited her in South Africa. In many ways, she remained inept: projecting, rather than enjoying and discovering facets of her grandson; but I could be wrong.

Franco was an absolute gentleman and a fine draftsman artist – educated by the Jesuits, and trained by his uncle, Chevalier Fortunino Matania, while besides his uncle's easel. They were both Neapolitans. Franco remained in the shadow of the renowned Fortunino – invited to all Royal events from the coronations of Edward VII in 1902 up to Queen Elizabeth in 1953, and noted for his illustrations of trench warfare and propaganda art during the First World War – Goodbye Old Man is a fine example of his emotive work of a British soldier bidding farewell to his dying horse.

Franco passed on some eleven years ago. Stoic Carmen, still mentally strong yet a frail nonagenarian, was born in Granada and separated, while on a school summer camp in Almunecar, for nine months from her family at the outbreak of the Spanish Civil War in 1936 – she was just eight years old. Only recently did she become tearful for the first time, while speaking of that childhood experience: the harmful stories of the atrocities of the Franco regime, the emotional impact thereof, the period of separation and her bewilderment upon being reunited with her family.

She held her left hand in the air, thumb and forefinger clasped, "Women were held like this by their ankles and sliced through the middle." She used her right forefinger pointing to the vagina of the imaginary upside-down woman, and moved downwards – her action, matter of fact, mine a sense of numbness. At night she would cry, wondering whether it might happen to her mother, and in the daytime, united with the other children, they would play and laugh.

Meeting genial Carmen today, her childhood experiences are difficult to imagine.

Franco and Carmen embraced their life, parenting their two children as best they could. His artist's earnings were meagre, and, in the early days he would hang his art on the railings at Green Park. They had fortitude, and blossomed as grandparents – the arrival of Stefan put a spring into Franco's step. He became the modest patriarch of the family – wise, with a gentle disposition and a twinkle in his eye – my unconscious role model.

Many a delightful weekend was spent at our marital home – sundowner time an absolute delight – Franco never demanding, but always a gracious participant in the evening ritual, knowing when enough was enough. This behaviour as you may imagine was a welcome reprieve from all I had witnessed, and a beacon that it could be otherwise.

The different stimuli and events experienced by Stefan with every extended family member, I trust, were sufficiently rounded, *the rough and the smooth*. Hopefully, he will cherish the anecdotes and the happy times spent together during his childhood and adolescence, equipping him to live a fulfilled life – the gift most parents want for their children – certainly, it is what I wish for him.

After my divorce, there were wayward years for Mina – the almighty reigning bottle a solace for a while. Fortunately, she had more help than my mom in rehabilitation from her suffering attacks of depression and dependency. Her ghosts lingered for a little longer, but with determination she overcame the grip of that malady.

What chance did my mother have? Today we speak with ease about all sorts of different conditions. Not then – I still hear Desiree's helpless, scared voice, *they'll lock me up . . . I'm not mad*! She weaned herself from her drinking habits in her latter years, because of her ardent belief that alcohol and her medication for emphysema should not be mixed – but, her ingrained behaviour remained, sadly, not needing alcohol to trigger it any more.

EXPLORING MY HEART

London – January 2004

Drifting back to my *heart incident* my cardiologist friend, Peter Stubbs, suggested to come over and bring all the various test results. Piet had already returned to South Africa, Gayle remained – I was grateful. The three of us sat on his steps, while he examined the reports. "Based on the mimicking of a heart infarction in the ECG, the x-ray of the echo chamber and the Bruce stress test, I would never have done the angiogram. We wouldn't have known about your abnormality."

While researching further, Peter suggested that I continue exercising, but never more than 70% of my usual heart capacity. So it was – no solution in sight and the operation cancelled. My desperate thinking forced my maniacal trading hand: *if I can double the amount made last year there should be sufficient for Stefan.* Consequently, over the following few months, half of the previous year's gains were lost.

Instead, I should have given myself permission to just be and to attend to my health issues. Surprisingly, no one had the wherewithal to even suggest it – perhaps they were equally shocked into silence.

About three months later, Peter called and suggested we get together. "I've been considering . . . the known cases died in their teens with a few in their late twenties. You're in your fifties – something is different – if we never knew about your condition, you would be living your life fully. Please forget about everything that has been said; I will write a definitive letter to your GP."

It is easier said, *exorcise all.* Well, I started by treating myself to a bespoke racing cycle, a titanium Seven. Rewarding has always been a difficult thing to do, as though I am unworthy.

Anyhow, my trusted steed from university days, with its top tube nearly completely rusted through from the sweat over the years, was exchanged. The only thing salvageable was a pair of Campagnolo pedals, which recently found a new home, serendipitously – by a reciprocated random act of kindness.

Riding alongside a fellow cyclist around Richmond Park, I commented, "Great retro bike."

"Good spot, how do you know?"

"I rode one of them a long time ago. Would you like a pair of 'Campag' pedals?"

"Sure would", was his quick response.

The beautiful *Eye of the Child* book cover was a gift from that exchange.

~

London – November 2004

I embraced Peter's advice and set about a daily cycling routine, culminating in a decision to compete after an absence of some thirty years. Notwithstanding living with uncertainty, an unconscious-conscious vacillation played itself out in endeavouring to satisfy my deep need to prove that I could survive and that my heart was in fine fettle. Peter became aware of my intent.

"Before you race again, I want to stress-test your heart."

Back to the Bruce treadmill stress test – twenty-one minutes of ever increasing speed and gradient.

"It's a crude test, never designed to be completed. Olympic athletes can do it.

See if you can," all said quite blandly, as was Peter's way.

A tall task and, to boot, I do not enjoy jogging. When it came to the final minute, I thought it was an impossibility. Heart pounding, lungs exploding and the final thirty seconds – like death. Adrenaline gushed, each second seemingly an eternity with plenty of time to consider, *quit*!

Peter turned to me, nodded and smiled, "It's the second time that I've seen it completed." Admirably, the technician looked on confirming it was her first, while I, elated, huffed and puffed.

It was not only the absence of competing, but also, I had not touched my road bicycle for some eighteen years. When Stefan was about four years old, it was time to give it its second lease of life – utilitarian – complete with mudguards, child seat, light and dynamo. It became our time together – whizzing off to our local club or attending to errands – yet, Stefan always remembers the unfortunate moment I inadvertently closed his helmet and pinched the skin on his neck.

You may wonder why my bicycle lay dormant for so long – it had to do with my love-hate relationship with the sport – the enjoyment was stifled by a sense that my youth had been robbed. The single mindedness and sheer dedication was oft coupled with the loneliness of training on my own, not mentioned yet. Hours and hours of pedalling in the blazing sun, thoughts travelling just so far, and back again.

Then another synchronistic event happened when Stefan was nine years old. He was riding his own bicycle by then – I had punctured and we were hobbling home, as best we could, when we met a cyclist and started chatting. It was Ron Nixon, who subsequently became a close friend and encouraged me to join him on his weekly rides into the Surrey countryside.

Initially, I could not even find my cycling gear and rode in trainers and an ordinary T-shirt for over a year. Our conversations grew, and Ron always said: "Man and cycle are one, much like horse and rider; and the man that returns is different from the one that went out."

Slowly, it seeped back into my psyche, and my excitement knew no bounds upon discovering my old gear. And, at about the same pace, extraneous items were individually removed, the dynamo, the light, the mud guards; the child seat had long since gone – all needed to casually garner a slight advantage over Ron, who was excellent at *climbing* the Surrey hills. The last touch of eccentricity remained, dangling loose yellow handle bar tape that blew in the wind.

Whenever we would pass the specialist cycle shop at the top of Box Hill, Ron would often remark: "I see you on a new machine, a Colnago, a Pinarello or one like that. Why don't we just stop and have a look-see." I would always resist, but upon the heart incident, unbeknown to Ron, I ordered a titanium Seven from my friend Mick Silles, an English cyclist of my age, who worked at another specialist shop.

Mick, a character – short pants, tattoos that no one dare ask about, and sometimes a single painted toenail that peeped – had initially attended to fitting me for the bespoke cycle. The tri-athlete fraternity nicknamed him 'the undertaker' – referring to his previous occupation.

Knowing of its imminent arrival after a wait of some three months for its manufacture and, after another glorious ride I casually suggested to Ron that we do our 'look-see'. Ron, as you can imagine, was delighted.

We walked in – Mick's face beamed – with a finger to my lips, I quickly signalled from behind Ron. Mick fell into roll, while Ron led with his chin. "Walter", pointing to me, "would like to consider a state of the art cycle."

Mick casually nodded, looked and pointed towards a Seven, almost to the point of indifference. This offhanded customer treatment agitated Ron no-end, probably because of having plied me for so long to make the pit-stop. Angrily, he blurted out, "Aren't you going to at least measure him?" Mick smiled, remained relaxed and with a considered grimace said, "No, not necessary, I can just look at him, and tell his size." We continued to chew the cud, finally leaving – Ron exasperated by this most peculiar happening.

Two weeks later, the Seven ready for collection, I called and confessed all – Ron smiled, and the three of us, Stefan, Ron and I, ceremoniously descended upon the unsuspecting shop and customers. Armed with a picnic basket of goodies: a flask of freshly brewed coffee, almond and chocolate croissants and no less, a bottle of champagne, we celebrated life. The smiles continued, and in the frolicking Mick suggested it was custom to at least sleep with your bike on the first night, and in the spirit of it all, I did.

Whenever Ron and I are together, and have cause to celebrate, we instinctively say, "Cheers – to punctures".

~

Back in the saddle – my training was upped. Then to South Africa in March 2005 for the annual Cape Town Cycle Tour, attracting some thirty-five thousand riders of all calibres. Unable to ride the inaugural event of 1978 as it overlapped with track championships, my sights were now ambitiously set on achieving *a sub-three* (108 km in under 3 hours) – a respectable achievement.

It was not to be – blustery winds of 40 km per hour impeded race times and instead, I was eleven minutes slower. Interestingly, in 2017 the race was cancelled for the first time in its history – the 100 km per hour wind prevented even the professional cyclists from starting.

Then an eventful three-day London to Paris charity ride in June, equipped me for the Calgary road racing World Master's Games that July in Edmonton, Canada – Stefan joined me. Upon registration, I overheard that they were still allowing entrants for the track events, my forte.

Sheepishly, I enquired and soon rented a bike from a local club with enough time during the ten days to ride both the road and track – not something a serious competitive cyclist would do, but why not?

It had been twenty-six years since I last raced on a track. Two fifth places later: the 500 metre time trial and the sprint. The latter, a sudden death between those eliminated in the quarter-finals, became my *Chariots of Fire* finish – an exciting win. Simultaneously in thrusting my bike across the finish line the front tubular rolled off and burst. The grinding sound, rim to concrete, deafening as I entered the steeped bank of the track. The cyclist behind scattered to avoid the danger of a possible collapsed rim and its consequences. Somehow, I managed to control the bike, stopping a half a lap later.

Stefan recorded it all on video with a picture jolt and an excited hollow in the middle of the sprint, "Go Dad, go!"

And the following year, I raced in Manchester, England, in the 2006 World Masters' Championship – that is when Beth revealed her secret.

~

A year later, on the 24th October I heard the news – Peter Stubbs had passed away from a massive coronary while working at the hospital – he was just fifty-two.

Initially, he called for an Orthopod complaining of severe backache. Then amidst it all, while being examined he realised what was happening. He diagnosed his own condition, instructing the team to operate immediately. In a cruel twist, sadly, the operation did not save him and he died later that same day – his family were devastated.

So was I – Peter's calming influence and counsel had given me hope. Those subtle encouragements, like, "When you win a World Master's Championship I'll write the definitive article for The Lancet." Now, I felt naked, destitute and unsure – who might I turn to?

At Peter's memorial service, a celebration of his life, Amrani spoke about how Peter had inquisitively pushed him and that together they had forged pioneering frontiers. It became clear to me they were professional medical brothers.

Immediately after the service, I went straight to Amrani and introduced myself, disconcertedly, "Hi Mohamed, I'm Walter."

He interrupted, "I know." I was surprised, and explained my sense of isolation.

He smiled, "Come and see me."

I did, Mohamed could not have been kinder. "If you ever need surgery, I will do it. Meanwhile, I would like you to see my colleague, Dr. Charles Ilsley, who specialises in these quirky cases." His letter to Ilsley was equally humane, "Essentially, he is now a friend of mine and was originally referred to me by the late Peter Stubbs."

Thereafter, I saw Ilsley annually for various check-ups and additional tests – this was my new comfort blanket.

Years went by and in one consultation Ilsley said, "You know, I believe the medical profession have had it all wrong. Those reported deaths . . . some other ischemic issue was probably going on simultaneously. I've been thinking about it – the coronary artery pressure is different from the aorta and pulmonary – annoying, much like a kid pushing an adult continually, but not life-threatening. Do you like my theory?"

You bet I did!

MEMORY, TRUTH AND PERCEPTION

I have lived with many fears, erroneously. *Scarcity mentality*, a prevalent one, regardless of my prior successes in the business world of Commodity Trading and International Banking. Now it rests better, things do after all evolve and resolve. Many lessons were learned from other adversities and an awareness that often the poorest are richer in spirit as they embrace life in its simplest form.

Once, I had more than sufficient financially, yet, circumstantially, I was not wise enough to quit. The volatility of subsequent stock market trading and a few fundamental errors of judgement ensured a substantial depletion. I could not help but think, *was I emotionally re-enacting my father's plight*?

One such evening, years after my divorce, I experienced a catastrophic loss. Devastated and forlorn I turned to Stefan sharing my concerns. His reserved response became the most powerful gift imaginable – survival – as he calmly said, "But dad, at least you're alive!"

It did take a while for the sagacity of those few words to sink in and find a place of resonance. The implications were vast and coupled with my concerned parenting of Stefan, it kept me sane and present.

Stefan went to university, staying in residence, while I immersed myself back into the corporate world, consulting. They were good years. Later, the congruence of near simultaneous events – nefarious corporate shenanigans, duped by a duplicitous individual and, personal relationship difficulties – tipped me over the edge into severe depression. Out of my depth, a guardian angel ensured that I was well out of the reprehensible business dealings, while on the relationship front we became perfect mirrors for each other to re-examine our lives, albeit our timing was not aligned.

This perfect storm, with hindsight, as horrific as it was, turned out to be a great hidden gift – at the time, I did not see it. Rather, I was gripped by the morass of depression and at a very low ebb. If you know that space, you will recognise how difficult it is. Tasks take on enormous proportions – somehow, I managed to make an appointment to see both my local doctor and Allan, the therapist that I had consulted during my divorce. The dull reception room of the surgery signalled – a dreary pamphlet stuck on the wall, *Depression and Low Mood Disorders – help to hand*!

It became Shaka's perfect pincer movement. The National Health Service's Cognitive Behaviour Therapy and traditional therapy; equally invaluable but different. Traditional, is time honoured in consciously assisting the process of awareness of the root cause, while Cognitive, the quick fix in interrupting unhelpful thoughts. Over the ensuing period, it was clear that I had masked depression most of my life.

Time passed, and I arrived at a comfortable place of understanding, feeling healed and ready to embrace life fully again. In parting ways with Allan, then a wise seventy-four-year-old, I said, "Our time is done!"

Kindly, he responded, "It probably is, but why don't you use me for a while longer, a sounding board, to discuss and probe other cultural belief systems and modalities you are interested in."

I did, for another six months, after which I joined my sister on a spiritual tour – we listened to the teachings of the Dalai Lama, in Dharamsala and met Tenzin Palmo at her monastery. Both beautiful, humble people in search of their truth. After that, I sat contemplatively in Bali and started writing *Eye of the Child*.

Memory and truth – all relative. Mine, yours, the Dalai Lama's or Monty's. He still puts his father on a pedestal, unaware of *Beth's secret*. Deep down, I suspect he has an inkling, particularly after the response to a question.

"When last, did you speak to Beth?"

"Well, we had a fallout. Beth and my sister, when she was alive, were always going on about how horrible my father was. I often said, 'If you don't tell me what you are on about, then I can't respond'. Anyhow, I even wrote to Beth apologising for whatever it was that my father was supposed to have done, and do you know, she didn't even have the courtesy to reply."

Beth adamantly instructed me never to tell him, which left me vacillating and in a quandary. I believe she does owe him an explanation of her truth, adult to adult, except that will probably never happen, she is ninety-two now. I was drawn into her saga as a type of confidant, yet upon reflection, duplicitously – I was never told about Monty's letter.

While completing my writing in South Africa, I did the relative rounds garnering snippets separately from Monty and the two Vals. I spent a delightful Sunday afternoon-evening with Jimmy's wife, eighty-two and widowed two years prior. It was an eight-hour marathon. She, mostly held court in frank conversation, sharing other family anecdotes that I was unaware of, perhaps aided by the ever-present Grim Reaper.

One such related to her marriage. "Jimmy was a tyrant during our marriage but changed, especially during his last two years while suffering from a very rare cancer, Merkel's. Seventeen head grafts later, a facial deformity and suppurating wounds. He never complained – just so grateful for everything I did for him. You know Walter, I always wanted to be a nurse."

My previous image of Jimmy was shattered, while her wish was fulfilled. Her nervous affliction, an eye-twitch-wink as if letting you into a secret, slowly dissipated the more the hours passed with her unburdening. A serene atmosphere enveloped as she reclaimed her persona – a joy to behold.

Some twenty-five years earlier, Sarah Fisher, an acquaintance, suggested I attend an Adult Children of Alcoholics meeting – that advice was ignored. Our birthdays were on the same day, she a year younger. Sadly, she passed away a few days after her sixty-first birthday. During her latter years, she did an enormous amount of excellent work and founded SMART (Substance Misuse, Advocacy Research and Training). She also helped in the policy development, guidelines and drafting of legislation in and around substance use in South Africa, which essentially gave users a second chance.

Only recently, I finally read a book on Adult Children of Alcoholics. It would have been beneficial had it happened sooner. Considerable confusion would have been removed in understanding my earlier and present behaviour, and may have allowed a shorter road to redemption. I still have not attended a meeting. Perhaps I will, while keeping an open mind to see what comes of it.

About two years ago, I was encouraged to attend a Co-Dependents Anonymous meeting – disappointment was the understatement. I felt displaced, their stuff not mine and in any case, I was beyond it. But I questioned whether my reaction was analogous to the time when I first attended *men's movement*, thinking how interesting and fascinating the men's stories were, but that they had nothing to do with me. It took a while before I dropped from my projections and judgements into my feeling heart; a realisation that all our stories are intertwined.

Perhaps, as Melody Beattie said in her book, *Codependent No More,* "If you don't like the first group you attend, find another meeting and go there. Each group has its personality. Continue going to different groups until you find the one that feels comfortable." Maybe I will attend another, before closing that door.

This extraordinary ride of dreams and aspirations pursued, and the humility experienced along the way, has equipped my kitbag with many different tools. Hopefully, while respectful of those dark other places – a time honoured process that is never done – I will stay out of the woods. My early cycling participation was my first beneficial coping mechanism, besides a strong will to survive and embrace all life offers.

Nowadays, my varied interests help, although my friends' perception of my Alice in Wonderland croquet matches, amuses them no end. I try to defend myself – *it's a zen place; concentration on the very blade of grass the ball needs to alight upon. And, chasing the balls through the hoops – physically and mentally demanding – an absolute charming meditation of sorts where all extraneous thoughts disappear.* They still merely smile.

Am I over the worst? I hope and trust so!

Upon reflection, something shifted over the four years of writing this book. The true gold of healing rests deep within, encrusted with a delicate coat of compassion for all living things and a softness of forgiveness.

My wish – *to live the opportunities within the paradoxes of life, and may our journeys be meaningful and fulfilled*!

~

Desert Thoughts was written before my heart incident, some fifteen years ago, during two separate walking trips in the Mauritanian Sahara Desert.

When was it last
That you felt the comfort of a stone,
Or the heavy weight of your heart.
When a man crossed your path, on a donkey,
Content in his world
Yet you must walk on.

Many years pass,
How many is unimportant,
Yet you still carry that deceptive bag
With all its goodies,
At times with delicious reprieves.
It fools us all, doesn't it?

And you return to the desert.
This time the wind greets you
With more than you bargained for;
Searing, singing sand obliterates your sight,
Cutting into your very essence.

Day after day
It seems as though it will never end,
You did not wish for this conjuring of old demons,
Those that walk beside you
That you refuse to honour,
Let alone see.

Ah Ha,
And when was it last
That you wore the brittle bark
Of an ancient palm tree
On your lifeless skin?

It's not easy
And it matters not,
For soon the one becomes the other
As you return to your roots of creation,
Seeing your very being,
Perhaps, for the first time.

But Don't Wait That Long!

*Peru, Machu Picchu - Gayle and I looking
towards Huayna Picchu*

The old rusted steed, Stefan and me

*Mick the 'undertaker' on the right, holding the
new Seven, with Ron between Stefan and me*

*Manchester Masters 2006 - wearing my SA
Championship 1500 metre jersey from 1972*

My penchant, and Franco Matania's playfulness

EPILOGUE

CYCLING FRATERNITY

Tommy Shardelow and his wife Margaret live life to the full; in their early eighties – six grandchildren and three great-grandchildren keep them more than fully occupied. Tommy is regularly honoured by the Legends of the Pedals – the fund-raising dinners – a platform to share anecdotes. Tommy's one alcohol experience happened after the 1954 British Empire Games' farewell party in Vancouver. "I don't remember checking in or boarding the plane, and awoke to an announcement that we would shortly be touching down at Shannon airport. Anyhow, after that Vancouver incident, I vowed, there and then, never to touch another drop as it certainly did not agree with me. While growing up, my father ordered brandy by the case and drank a bottle a day. I always said my mother never knew he was drinking until he came home sober one evening. I think my father did me a favour and scared me off drink!"

Jack Lester, seventy, still active and at the helm of his company. He has seven children, four from his first marriage and three from his new partner, one of which is adopted, twelve grandchildren and one great-grandchild.

Jack said, "In the Jewish religion, you come into life to do two things: Mitzvahs, and to accomplish what was not achieved in a previous life."

More importantly, he reminded me once that I had said, *I would disown my mother*, and his immediate retort was, "You can never disown your flesh and blood." How right he was!

Albert Styger – How enjoyable to reconnect after some forty odd years. Recently, we did a few mountain bike rides together, sharing many man-to-man stories.

He remains competitive, runs his own family IT software business and as a grandfather is happily remarried.

His accident put paid to his earlier competitive cycling days. Who knows what his further cycling successes may have been?   Now philosophically, he comments, "I need to cycle nearly every day – it keeps me sane and helps my back enormously!"

Allan de Roche – a family man, two sons, four grandchildren, and remains as humble as ever – "My son was a far better cyclist than me; his Schoolboy Southern Transvaal records still stand."

Raymond Hogg – Happily married to Lesley, and remains a larger than life character.

Cliffie Steward became a commercial pilot, and while out cycling in Dubai, one morning, was fatally struck by a motor car.

Joe Billet, *the bullet*, a family man, sadly succumbed to an inflammatory illness in his early sixties, dying shortly thereafter.

Ralph Smout – at a recent historical cycling reunion, we had a moment to discuss the unfortunate mishap – "There is not a February the tenth that I do not think about that day." Ralph remains the epitome of a true gentleman.

Chris Harvey, one of eight adopted children from a wealthy family, subsequently fell on hard times. He worked for Jack on occasions, and while living on Jack's smallholding, he was murdered during a petty robbery on the 19th June 1999, at the age of fifty-two.

Tin (Theuniss) Theart was financially assisted in his rehabilitation from alcoholism by the *Legends of the Pedal Trust Fund* – does he still talk to bees?

Ian Coutts – reminded me, "Cycling is not just cycling – it's a way of life!"

Willie (Willliam Charles) Dawson – continued to celebrate life.
Ian and Willie's cycling lives were in tandem, both belonging to the Cape City Cycling Club then onwards to Johannesburg – they remained good friends.

Willie, a successful businessman, sadly died recently, aged sixty-two, from an unfortunate work-related accident.

Basil Cohen, survived by his loving wife, Adele, their two children and ten grandchildren. The fraternity has only good things to say about him, *a friend, a mentor, a fair business man and a heart of gold, he did a huge amount to encourage black participation in cycling during the apartheid days.*

Raoul de Villiers did an enormous amount for the sport: The Rapport Tour, Vice-President, then President of the South African Cycling Federation in 1975 and again in the 80's.

I was saddened to hear, many years after it had happened, of his premature death from a heart attack in his early fifties. It was too close to home and reminded me of my father's death.

Raoul had spoken well of him at the time, and I held on to those sentiments. They knew each other through the Commercial Travellers' Association.

Gotty Hansen (Pehr Gotthard Bernhard) survived Bonnie after fifty-seven delightful years of marriage (five daughters and seven grandchildren later).

He won, like Mike Payne, the most coveted trophy in the land, the Paarl Boxing Day 25 mile in 1959.

"There were eight to ten thousand people around the stadium. You couldn't hear yourself think and the atmosphere was like winning the World Title," said Gotty – six years later – he won it again.

At the age of eighty-one, in 2015, the world governing body, UCI, recognised him for his tremendous contribution to the development of cycling in South Africa and abroad.

FRIENDS AND RELATIVES

Piet continues his search, and has been reading *A Course in Miracles*, daily, for the past thirty years. Incidentally, he shares a birthday with Jack Lester.

Beth remains chirpy, is in her nineties, and vows to live to at least a hundred.

The two Vals are both in their eighties, and in their different ways are keen to share all sorts of candid anecdotes.

Monty still keeps his father on a pedestal.

Desiree (4 July 1926 - 23 July 2010). Her emphysema continued to deteriorate after George's death. In her latter years, she lived on a continual supply of oxygen, dying fourteen years later, aged eighty-four.

Ten days before a sense prevailed, calling just before departing on vacation. For some strange reason, not knowing it was me, she angrily blurted, "I'm not dead yet." A most peculiar comment.

Taken aback, I recalled an earlier time questioning why she held on tenaciously.

"I love to hear the birdsong and see the flowers and the spring buds opening."

I have thought about that a lot.

Gayle's marriage ended through divorce after thirty-five years, having nurtured two delightful children into adulthood. Since then, her educational interests have expanded from Montessori to Steiner ideology.

While discussing *Eye of the Child*, Gayle divulged that throughout her life she felt *unloved and unwanted* by Desiree – that was another shock. Was her *inner child* rather than the *adult* talking?

Gayle's care, compassion and unflinching support of Desiree throughout our mothers remaining years was absolute. "After she had stopped drinking, she became the mother I always wanted, and in the last few years, we could have meaningful conversations as against the problematic drama filled past. That last week of her life was a gift of precious closeness – it was beautiful. My best time together, not wanting her to be on her own. I placed photos all around. The nursing staff commented on the peace and serenity in her room – I was so grateful!"

"There were spiritual moments, Desiree saying, 'You must let me go now.' I had never heard her speak like that before, and in the next breath, she talked about George, Ronnie and you. Suddenly, I realised that maybe you were still holding her back – that's when we called you, on holiday.

Remember, you spontaneously sang to her, *que sera, sera*. She smiled, at peace, and our tears flowed, joyfully!"

Yes, I recall, and also that Desiree sang it to me as a little boy. The chorus became my beacon of future possibilities; that, even after her demons surfaced. The wheels of time had turned. In that moment, I sung to her, as overwhelming emotions pulsated through me. Everything had to be done to hold the notes and not choke. It became our closure.

. . . as for Gayle, she said, "Throughout that last week I realised that Desiree completely and unconditionally loved me and that her love was always there. Maybe, my fears and interpretation of things may not have been true, but it was my truth!"

Gayle's recognition and love from our mother finally happened – our mother held on long enough, allowing our healing!

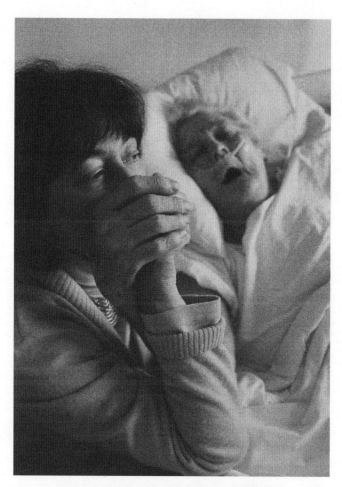

Gayle and Desiree - last days, holding on,
and letting go; the beauty of 'life and death'
(photo courtesy of Shari Thompson,
Gayle's daughter)

And me? Well, while in Bali I met, perchance, Wayan Nariashy, the Balian healer featured in Elizabeth Gilbert's, *Eat Pray Love*. Nonchalantly, I responded to a question of hers . . . , "Hoping to write." She paused, then smiled, and kindly said, "You must first remove all confusion from your mind, then you will be able to write."

And, after the writing was all done, in selecting the early family photographs, my overwhelming sense was one of a longing, and a love. They did their best, within their wherewithal – perhaps, it is like that for all of us.

Incidentally, also nestled amongst the illustrious list on the Paarl Boxing Day 25 mile trophy is my engraved name, the year '75.

But mostly, I remain inquisitive about life . . .

1975 - Paarl Boxing Day 25 mile Minaar Throphy –
(L to R) Bobby Nefdt, me, and Hennie (Wiele) Wentzel

AUTHOR'S NOTES

Certain names of relatives have been changed to avoid unnecessary anguish.

Only pertinent information, as relates to Eye of the Child, has been included in the *abridged family tree* and the *epilogue*.

Countries

South Africa became a Republic in 1961, and changed from imperial to the metric system ten years later.

Mozambique obtained independence in 1975.

Rhodesia became the Republic of Zimbabwe in 1980.

Regions and provinces, measurements and currencies, are reflective of the respective periods.

Abbreviations

ANC - African National Congress
UCI - *Union Cycliste Internationale*

PATERNAL GRANDPARENTS

Walter Thornhill
(British) b 1878 Liverpool d 1943
m
Rachel Elizabeth Everson
(Dutch) b 1881 d 1960

7 children b between
1902 and 1914

THORNHILL ABRIDGED FAMILY TREE

Certain names changed to avoid unnecessary
anguish. Only specific information
shown as pertinent to the book.

Nationalities shown, other than South African.
Uncles and Aunts from eldest to youngest.
Bloodline in bold.
Born 'b', died 'd' and married 'm'.

MATERNAL GRANDPARENTS

Frank Ridewood
(British) b 1877 Liverpool d 1934
m
Aletta van Haagen
(Dutch) b 1881 d 1972

3 children

UNCLES & AUNTS	COUSINS
Grace m Clifford Shephard	Val & Jimmy
Pam m Damien	Monty & Sarah
Selena 2nd m Adrian van Bergen	No children
Walter Albert* b 1908 d 1972 3rd m **Desiree Thurle Ridewood****	**Walter John Thornhill (me)***** b 1953
Johnny m Doreen	Marilyn, Joan & Charmaine
Lillian m Wallace Truter	2 cousins
Beth m Vernon	Julia

Walter John (me)***

m Mina Matania

1 child - **Stefan** b 1989

UNCLES & AUNTS	COUSINS
Aletta Rownetta (Ronnie) b 1909 d 1997 m Jack Prentice b 1901 d 1966	No children
William John b 1907 d 1953	No children
Desiree Thurle** b 1926 d 2010 2nd m **Walter Albert Thornhill*** 3rd m George Lostrom b 1913 d 1995	**Walter John Thornhill (me)***** & **Gayle Lostrom******, my sister b 1961

Gayle****

m Stephen Thompson

2 children

OFFICIALS, CYCLISTS AND SCRAPBOOK

Officials (previously cyclists)
    Basil Cohen   (Maccabi)
    Raoul de Villiers   (Provincial)
    Gotty Hansen   (UCI)

Provinces

Cape
    Tin (Theuniss) Theart   (Springbok)
    Ian Coutts   (Provincial)
    Willie Marx   (Springbok)
    Linus van Onselin   (Provincial)

Natal
    Mike Francis   (Provincial)
    Ralph Smout   (Springbok)

Orange Free State
    Joe Billet   (Springbok)

Southern Transvaal

Bez Valley Gang
Allan de Roche   (Provincial)
Gavin Beetge

Kensington Gang
Albert Styger   (Provincial)
Rory Budler   (Provincial)
Willie Dawson   (Provincial)

Junior Cadre
Alan van Heerden   (Springbok)
Cliffie Steward   (Springbok)
Rodney Emmenes   (Springbok)
Neil Emmenes   (Springbok)

Seniors
Jack Lester   (Springbok)
Tommy Shardelow   (Olympian)
Raymond Hogg   (Springbok)
Chris Harvey   (Springbok)
Mike Payne   (Springbok)
Dries Oberholzer   (Springbok)
Stephen Lipa   (Maccabi)
Jimmy Swift   (Olympian)
Guy Ferriman   (Springbok)

SCRAPBOOK EXTRACTS
MY ANCHOR

"THERE ARE SO MANY KINDS OF RACING
THE STRAIGHT SPRINTS RACED IN HEATS; OR IN
MATCH RACES: WHERE THE TWO RIDERS WILL
BALANCE FOR LONG SECONDS ON THEIR MACHINES
FOR THE ADVANTAGE OF MAKING THE OTHER RIDER
TAKE THE LEAD — AND THEN THE SLOW CIRCLING
— AND THE FINAL PLUNGE INTO THE DRIVING PURITY
OF SPEED ..
THERE ARE THE PROGRAMMES OF THE TEAM RACES OF
TWO HOURS; WITH A SERIES OF PURE SPRINTS
IN THEIR HEATS TO FILL THE AFTERNOON; THE
LONELY ABSOLUTE SPEED EVENTS OF ONE MAN
RACING AN HOUR AGAINST THE CLOCK; THE
TERRIBLY DANGEROUS AND BEAUTIFUL RACES OF
100 KILOMETRES ON THE BIG BANKED BOWL;
THE STRANGE WORLD OF 6-DAY RACES; AND
THE MARVELS OF ROAD RACING IN THE MOUNTAINS .."

WHEELS OF GLORY

"THE SMOKY LIGHT OF THE AFTERNOON ...
THE HIGH BANKED WOODEN TRACK —
THE WHIRRING SOUND THE TYRES MADE ON THE
WOODS AS THE RIDERS PASSED —
THE EFFORT AND THE TACTICS AS THE RIDERS
CLIMBED AND PLUNGED; EACH ONE A PART
OF HIS MACHINE ...
THE RIDERS IN THEIR LIGHTER CRASH HELMETS
BENT LOW OVER THEIR HANDLEBARS; THEIR
LEGS TURNING THE HUGE GEAR SPROCKETS —
THE DUELS THAT ARE MORE EXCITING THAN
ANYTHING —
THE RIDERS ELBOW TO ELBOW AND WHEEL TO
WHEEL; UP AND DOWN AND ROUND
AT DEADLY SPEED; UNTIL ONE MAN
COULD NOT HOLD THE PACE AND BROKE
AWAY AND THE SOLID WALL OF AIR
THAT HE HAD BEEN SHELTERED AGAINST
HIT HIM .."

Thornhill's day

WALTER THORNHILL was in great form at Hector

Nic with his characteristic cigarette

THORNHILL SNATCHES VICTORY

SOUTHERN TRANSVAAL cyclist Walter Thornhill ended the season on a high note at Hector Norris Park yesterday.

Thornhill, who will represent

the ride-off for third place. The sprint was also won by Thornhill, who beat Steward in the final.

final, his hardest race came   in the second rou

CYCLING

Thornhill and Lester shine

SPRINGBOK Jackie Lester and Walter Thornhill were promoted to the B class after good rides at the rain interrupted cycling meeting at Hector Norris Park yesterday. Rain twice stopped racing.

There was little to choose between Lester and Thornhill in the 1 500 metre A class race. The winner was Lester in 2 min 0,41 seconds, with Thornhill second and Alan Dipple third.

These three riders showed their worth in the 20 km race, which was cut by four laps when a thunderstorm threatened racing.

Thornhill beat Lester by half a wheel in 11 min 57,8 sec with Dipple third.

The Rand Prix will be held at Hector Norris Park from 10 a.m. to 10 p.m. on Saturday.

Thornhill; 2, B. Webber; 3, M. Heneke. Time: 2:0.8.
B class 1 500 metres — 1, W. James; 2, G. Taylor; 3, A. Rex. Time: 1:52.8.
A class point to point — 1, O. Barnard; 2, S. Nefdt; 3, M. Beacke. Time: 3:50.2.
B Class Devil take the hindmost — 1, G. Kemp; 2, D. Hosmer; 3, S. Nefdt(a). Time: 4:38.
Juvenile 1 500 metres — 1, L. Thomspon; 2, G. Thompson; 3, G. Eh. Time: 4:54.
A class 1 500 metres handicap final — 1, A. van Heerden; 2, H. Impey; 3, C. Steward. Time: 1:51.1.
C class 10 kilometres — 1, O. de Bree; 2, Impey; 3, G. Heswell. Time: 13:56.1.
Juvenile 6 lap handicap — 1, O. Cooke; 2, S. Thompson; 3, J. Eh. Time: 4:36.8.

DEAN BARNARD . . . looked every inch a champion in the making in his first competitive outing at Hector Norris Park yesterday. Here he matches his pedalling power with Walter Thornhill

Nóú moet Thornhill kom help

THORNHILL IN ELECTRIC FINISH

By Peter Thomson

WALTER THORNHILL, the 17-year-old Wits University student who captains the Johannesburg Cycle Racing Club, showed off the rejuvenating benefits of a week's holiday when he flashed home first in a blanket sprint finish in the gruelling 50km event at Hector Norris Park yesterday.

Thornhill, who is essentially a sprinter, was fortunate to get away in a decisive, field-buttering break made by Dean Barnard, Raymond Hogg, Dries Obermeister and Chris Harvey and although he did not have as much mileage behind him as the other riders, he found sufficient reserve to get up in the sprint to win from Barnard and Hogg.

Thornhill's time for the

event — 26min. 11.5sec. — was only 28.5sec outside the South African record, held by the Troyeville Springbok, Jackie Lester.

The strongmen of the breakaway bunch were without doubt Barnard and Hogg, who both looked remarkably fit considering they had ridden in a 50km event at Bloemfontein late on Saturday night.

Barnard, the 18-year-old hard-heads prodigy, constantly stretched the bunch out as he went through to take the pace, and one could not help but feel that if he had decided to go it alone about two or three laps out from the finish he would

almost certainly have taken the honours.

Such was the tremendous pace set out front by these five riders that only one other in the field of over 30 — young Jeff Lincoln — managed to stay the distance after a truly plucky ride.

THE RESULTS

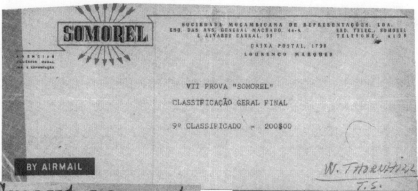

Smout races to a gold medal

By ANDRE VAN DER ZWAN

UNDISTURBED by reputation, Ralph Smout, Natal's powerhouse, hurried to a gold medal in the 1 000 metres sprint during the South African Games cycling meeting at Pilditch Stadium on Saturday.

PHEFENI MTEMBU . . . courageous and aggressive

WALTER THORNHILL (left voltooi) en ALAN DIPPLE het glutereend op Hector Nop...
Japark in Johannesburg in die Suid-Transvaalse fietsryproewe 'n tyd van wêreldgehalte...
in die tweeman-tydtoets oor 1 000-meter opgestel. Hil tyd van 1 min 06 s is dieselfde...

Hulle jaag vinniger as wê

JOHANN PIETERSE WALTER THORNHILL en Alan Dipple het gisteraand op Hector Norrispark in Johannesburg in die Suid-Transvaalse fietsryproewe 'n vertoning' van wêreldgehalte gelewer. Hulle het die tweeman-tydtoets oor 1 000 meter in 1 min. 06 s afgelê en 'n onoorwinlike kombinasie vir dié wedren gevorm.

Patric Sercu van België en Xavier Kurman van Switserland (albei beroepsfietsryers) het in die onlangse wêreldkampioenskappe 'n tyd van 1 min. 07 s opgestel. Dit is 0,01 s. stadiger as die twee Suid-Afrikaners se tyd.

Die twee jaers het daar het male sonder tal die kilometer, penkoppe

CYCLING

Bok team announced

CALEDON. — A Springbok cycling track team, the first since 1969 when South Africa opposed Australia, was announced yesterday by Raoul de Villiers, president of the South African Cycling Federation.

The team, featuring five new caps, meets a combination made up of the overseas stars competing in the KWV Tour of the Winelands, in Port Elizabeth on Wednesday night.

The team is: Jack Lester (S. Transvaal — captain), Ralph Smout (Natal), Andy Theron (Western Province), Tony Impey (Southern Transvaal), Alan Dipple (Southern Transvaal), Walter Thornhill (Southern Transvaal), Robbie McIntosh (Natal) and Joe Billett (Griqualand

Walter steals Paarl show

27·12·75

Norman Crews

PAARL — You didn't need astrology yesterday to work out who will be four of the stars of 1976. The Boxing Day meeting here told you that.

Three are not new faces but, if anything, next year could be bigger than ever. The other is a Paarl schoolboy with a promising future.

Cyclist Walter Thornhill and athletes Adam Barnard and Ewald Bonzet led the way yesterday, while newcomer Johan Dreyer set a South African under-19 record in the 2 000 m with a time of 5 min 34,2 sec.

This chopped over three seconds off the old mark —and that on a slow gravel track.

The three stars of yesterday's meeting all have ambitions this season. Tohrnhill is chasing a couple of national titles; Barnard hopes to break 75 m in the hammer; Bonzet is desperately trying to raise another R400 to join Danie Malan on the American Indoor Circuit.

Although yesterday Barnard heaved the hammer a mighty 71,54 m — the second best ever in Africa

— and Bonzet clocked 14 min 28,5 sec for the 5 000 m they were both upstaged by Thornhill.

Paarl is cycling country and Thornhill's 25-mile victory had the enthusiastic crowd streaming home contented.

Thornhill's victory happened like this. After 75 laps of the 87-lap race his partner in arms, Lester, punctured.

The field slowed to give the popular Springbok a chance to fight his way back. But Scot John Curran was not going to be so sporting and in a trice he had caught Lester. Now the race was on as the field tried to catch them.

Five laps from the finish they did and Kobie Strumpfer and Chris Willemse were the next to take a flyer. Their all out effort was stopped with only a lap to go and then it was all Thornhill. He hurtled out of the 35-rider bunch to win almost on his own.

Afterwards he said: "What did you think of that?" and one could only say: "Brilliant."

Thornhill angry over ruling

Norman Crews

A South African Cycling Federation ruling could force Walter Thornhill out of the sport.

Spectacular sprinting but rain is winner

Durban Grand Prix.

"The sport is h... t having ... ng pass... you can can't," g...

Norman Crews

The rain and cold were the only winners at Hector Norris Park yesterday. Even some spectacular sprinting by Walter Thornhill and Jackie Lester could not erase that.

Junior rider topples aces

15/4/78

By ARCHIE HENDERSON

FOUR of Southern Transvaal's leading cyclists suffered defeat in the 20 kilometre race at yesterday's Southern Transvaal league meeting, when junior Walter Thornhill emerged with top honours.

Thornhill snatched the narrowest of victories in this gruelling track event at Hector Norris Park when he beat Dean Barnard, Raymond Hogg, Chris Harvey and Ince Oberholzer.

The 20-kilometre — the last event on the programme — has always proved an exciting race, and yesterday was no exception.

RIGHT:

● A tense moment in the tandem event as Mike Francis (light helmet) and Joe Billet — a formidable pair by any standards — watch for Willie Dawson and Piet Deleray to make an attack. Francis and Billet won.

JACKIE LESTER . . . is sprint duel.

Thornhill takes the crown

BLOEMFONTEIN, Saturday. — Springbok Walter Thornhill flung his arms high after winning the 1 500 m final at the South African cycling championships at the Free State Stadium here.

It was a triumph for Thornhill and a reply to the selectors who dropped him for the second Test against the international team last month.

First Alla nDipple tore past him with Thornhill in close attendance, and in the back straight Thornhill hurtled past with D... Southern Tr... Kemp maki...

Thornhill ... 31.5 sec.

RAND DAILY MAIL, Monday, October 18, 1971. 19

CYCLING

LESTER ON THE WAY BACK

FERRIMAN

HOW...

THORN...

DAWSON

WOLFER

THORNHILL

WALTER TO RIDE AGAIN

WALTER THORNHILL, who has recovered from his accident in Kimberley two weeks ago, will be back in the saddle at the open cycling meeting at Hector Norris Park tomorrow night.

Thornhill, one of the top cyclists in Southern Transvaal over the short distances, will be going all out in a bid to gain a place in the provincial squad.

Southern Transvaal take on Natal at Hector Norris in two weeks, in what could well be the decider of the Carlton Cup interprovincial competition.

If Thornhill's form merits selection it should take a lot of the pressure off Johan Strydom in the sprints, where he will have to face Ralph Smout, the Natal flyer.

Smout beat Joe Billett in two straight rides in Durban on Saturday, and Strydom will be hard-pressed to out-ride the tough Natalian.

Thornhill in cycling upset

Walter Thornhill, a former Northern Wheelers rider, who has joined the City Cycling Club, was responsible for one of two upsets at the inter-club cycling meeting at Paarl last night.

With four laps to go in the five miles Thornhill broke away from the bunch and was an easy winner in spite of a strong challenge from Springboks Eddie Kriel and Tin Theart.

The second upset came in the final ride in the match sprint event when Springbok Steve Viljoen was eliminated. Chris Scheffer of Paarl won the first and third rides, but lost the second by the width of a tyre.

Bellville won the Paarl Valley Cup with 19 points followed by Typo with 12 points, Paarl with eight and City Cycling with six.

Inter-club results were:

1,000 metres time trial: J. Strydom (Typo), 1; T. du Toit (Bellville), 2; D. Penwarden (Bellville), 3 — 1min. 15.7sec.

One mile: T. Kriel (Bellville), 1; S. Viljoen (Bellville), 2; T. Theart (Bellville), 3 — 2min. 32.7sec.

Match sprint: C. Scheffer (Paarl), 1; S. Viljoen (Bellville), 2; T. Strydom (Typo), 3 — 13.6sec.

4,000 metres team pursuit: Bellville ...

● A burst tyre, one of the gravest hazards a cyclist faces in a track race . . . and it happened at Hector Norris Park yesterday. Here (left to right) is the sequence of events which ultimately led to a rider, E. Rouillaird, being taken to hospital.

THORNHILL TO DEFEND TITLE

Walter blasts the best

Jon Swift

AMONG the Southern Transvaal's top cyclists, there is a well-known dictum: "Watch Walter Thornhill."

The mercurial Thornhill showed the reason for this caution on the part of the other riders during the provincial championships at Hector Norris Park yesterday.

Mr Raoul de Villiers

Thornhill is rarin' to go

By ANDRE VAN DER ZWAN

WALTER THORNHILL, the Northern Wheelers "express," is an angry man. First he was made the scapegoat for Southern Transvaal's defeat against Western Province and last Sunday he suffered the humiliation of being disqualified for the afternoon.

Now Thornhill, one of the finest riders in Southern Transvaal, wants to restore his image — starting with the floodlit meeting at Hector Norris Park tonight.

26   The Star   Monday April 4 1977

Officials and riders in clash

Larry Lombaard

Basil Cohen, an executive on the Southern Transvaal Cycling Union, is fuming at the men whose rights he has always fought for — the cyclists.

"I am disgusted at the behaviour of certain cyclists at the Facoln Club's league

WALTER THORNHILL... refused to pay again.

Walter bursts into contention

8-4-75

Jon Swift

THERE was just no stopping Walter Thornhill at yesterday's league cycling meeting at Hector Norris Park. But the wily Walter used more than just his wit yesterday.

When Herald photographer Tony Crookall took this picture yesterday the three Springboks Martin Nefdt, Ralph Smout and Jackie Lester and Walter Thornhill were idling around the track prior to some sharp training. Tonight it will be all out racing when they take part in the tandem invitation contest. It will be a best of three races series. Nefdt and Smout are on the inside and Lester and Thornhill on top.

● Proudly holding up the trophy he won in the Pepsi 10km race is cycling ace, Walter Thornhill.

CYCLING

Thornhill pipped in brave fight-back

By MYMIE SMYTHS

NEIL Emmerens and Cliffie Stewart fought out a gruelling marathon to take the madison in the final 35-min 43.6 sec at Hector Norris Park, Johannesburg yesterday.

Alan Dipple and Tao Jinner were the pacemakers and they kept the pace with Jackie Lester and Steve Jarman, Walter Thornhill and John Russ in hot pursuit.

Thornhill created the lead in the race but came back to take the lead. It was only at the final lap in a thrilling last dash that Thornhill lost his position to Emmerens and Dippie, the breakthrough.

● E. Rouillard, bleeding from cuts and abrasions, is placed on a stretcher. He was taken to the South Rand Hospital. After treatment and x-ray examinations, Rouillard was allowed to go home.

Springbok Walter Thornhill bursting through in the final lap of the 40-lap Madison at Hector Norris Park. But he petered out to let in Cliffie Stewart, left, and Neil Emmerens, right, who won the race.
Picture: ALAN VAN ROOYEN

Guy Ferriman about to over[take] to clinch the Southern Tran[svaal] Hector Norris Park

CYCLING

Wily Walter

THE Grand prix final at the Krugersdorp Wanderers cycling track on Saturday proved a triumph for the wily Walter Thornhill.

He beat Springbok Jackie Lester, the South African champion, and Alan Dipple.

Lester, considered one of South[...] dest riders, could only manage third with Dippie taking second place.

Peter Kemp, of Pretoria, won the 1 500 metres. Once again Lester was on the losing side, this time by a hair's breadth. Kemp won in 1 min 35.06 sec.

July 2nd 1975

Top SA cyclist killed on road

HUGO LANDSBERG ... training ride

Back in the game: former Springbok cyclist Walter Thornhill with dog Tao before a training ride.

Back in the saddle – after 25 years

ACKNOWLEDGEMENTS

Where to start, or how to quantify the heartfelt support and collaboration over these past four years? Not surprisingly, synchronicity seems to have played its part, starting with an incorrectly addressed email to one of our group, attending the Dalai Lama's teachings in September 2013.

It had the response you might expect, "Wrong person, but don't forget I was an editor and would be delighted to help you with your book." Shelley Epstein, an educational writer and editor, for that initial hand holding and encouragement to get down to write the difficult and possibly more interesting stuff. Then, thinking it was all done, your push, "You've ended Eye of the Child on a minor key. What you really need is a punchy concluding chapter, in dealing with the adult consequences" – how right you were.

So was Cynthia Kemp, another editor and writer, albeit quite different . . . "Coincidentally I'm reading quite an old book at the moment (Nobel Prize for Literature, 1982: *One Hundred Years of Solitude* by Gabriel Garcia Márquez) and the first sentence reads: 'Many years later, as he faced the firing squad, Colonel Aureliano Buenda was to remember that distant afternoon when his father took him to discover ice.' This opener immediately grabs the reader's attention, and all subsequent reminiscences are viewed with the firing squad in mind, keeping one riveted" – hope I achieved what you had in mind.

Help came in various forms. A delightful inspiring *residency* in the Cradle of Humankind on the magnificent *farm* of my good friend Benji Liebmann. Varying degrees of editing, suggestions, and appraisals by many – Isabelle Boyd, Felicity Bingham, Gill Brooksmith, George Bryant, Chet Burchett, Alan Chance, Golda Deeks, Bia van Deventer, Annelie Janse van Rensburg, Natalie Kadas, Eva Marie Klopper, Mina Matania, Hazel Pennington, Allan Pimentel,

Tao, Shari Lee Thompson, Deidre Wallace, and Wendy Feess.

Dr. Caterina A. Zaiontz, Senior Lecturer of Psychopathology and Transcultural Psychology – Università Cattolica del Sacro Cuore, Milan, Italy, was the first person to give a serious, academic review, which forced me to think about and articulate the content better – it became my turning point of belief in this book.

Once I had completed the writing and well into editing, I decided to do a Hay House online writer's study workshop – a bit upside down, I admit. But there were gems, Deepak Chopra's and Caroline Myss', that ensured my greater awareness of redaction. Deepak stressed that anecdotes must add to the main arcs of the book, while Caroline was clear that the uniqueness of the voice matters, and not the supposed life changing happenings.

The men from men's gatherings and the elders facilitating (Robert Bly, leader of mythopoetic men's movement, Malidoma Somé, a teacher of West African spirituality, and Martín Prechtel, shaman and initiate of the Guatemala Maya culture), must be honoured – their brutal frankness and open communication made me aware of their stories, rich in essence, and different from and often more challenging than mine – thank you for your sharing and teachings.

In a similar vein, my ancestors, my parents and stepfather, relatives, friends, and the odd enemy, and the marvellous cycling fraternity that each in your ways have made this life so interesting. Those forgotten . . . forgive me, such is amnesia.

Richard Olivier, for encouraging me in my *head-spaced* banking days to attend the annual Wild Dance weekend men's retreats. Slowly, over the years, I dropped from my head to my heart. At these gatherings, I met William Ayot, a most generous spirited man – thank you for a meaningful, heartfelt foreword.

That first trip with Gayle, my sister, to Peru, was a time of meeting Freddy Quispe Singona, then only nineteen and affectionately known as Puma, and Don Maximo, his eighty-one-year-old grandfather – keepers of Andean spirituality, which were shared in ritual and ceremony. A film crew playfully dubbed him, *one take Puma*. Puma always said, "Grandfather says, 'If you don't hear it first time, then you were not ready'". I thank them for sharing their rich cultural heritage, and the villagers of Chincero for allowing me to partake and dance with them as an *Ukukus*, half-bear and half man, on the Andes mountains during the festival of Señor Quoritti, a three-day sacred annual pilgrimage.

I've always dubbed my sister, particularly in our adult lives, the *gate keeper* to many spiritual and enlightening doors – she opens them, while I continue the journey. In our childhood, she bore witness, best captured in her precis of *Eye of the Child*.

"The Eye of the Child is a book that manages to balance the darker sides of life that many of us have lived through with hope, humour and humility. The reader is effortlessly transported through a time of upheaval on many levels, not only through the wonderful imagery but because it is written from the author's heart.

As I read some of the darker scenes, I knew what was about to happen, while others were remembered only as I read. Somehow, I had managed to file the memories away, where they lay undisturbed, till now.

The difference for me was that while most readers can imagine a scene where a door is broken down, I did not need to. I see the exact kitchen door, my father having broken it down, in an attempt to stop my mother from taking her life. I see myself standing there as a child witness to this scene, while at the same time reading it through the eyes of an adult now, and wonder how we made it through into adulthood after having endured such pain?

My experience while reading this book is different than most, in that it was also my journey. As such, I feel the pain perhaps a little more intensely, but I also celebrate the growth and learning that takes place along the way. I find myself with more questions than before and wonder at the resilience of mankind and our ability to change. Mostly I salute my brother for having the courage to write this poignant masterpiece."

I too, salute you my sister for making this our journey.

And my son, Stefan James Thornhill, like all our children are such great teachers, and besides showing me ritual, for specifically allowing me to nurture him, and through that, heal my *inner child*.

Like any odyssey, there are trials and tribulations. At times, I felt like a mendicant monk, and with the best intent those that helped, proceeded with their lives, as they should. Yet throughout there was always a gently enquiry, a prod of encouragement, editing suggestions, and a vision that this book would birth. That support was generously given by a very special and dear friend, Jennifer Schormann – thank you!

~

Thank you for reading Eye of the Child

A review, sharing, comments, or suggestions are most welcome.
This can be done via my website www.walter-thornhill.com
or my email address, walter@walter-thornhill.com

Travel well . . . and may your life be fulfilled